P9-DMZ-638

Hiking Michigan's Upper Peninsula

Eric Hansen

FALCONGUIDES ®

GUILFORD, CONNECTICUT
HELENA, MONTANA
AN IMPRINT OF THE GLOBE PEQUOT PRESS

FALCON GUIDES®

Copyright © Morris Book Publishing, LLC

All rights reserved. No part of this book may be repro-
duced or transmitted in any form by any means, electronic
or mechanical, including photocopying and recording, or by
any information storage and retrieval system, except as
may be expressly permitted by the 1976 Copyright Act or
by the publisher. Requests for permission should be made in
writing to The Globe Pequot Press, P.O. Box 480, Guilford,
Connecticut 06437.

Falcon and FalconGuides are registered trademarks of Morris
Book Publishing, LLC.

Photos by Eric Hansen
Maps by XNR Productions Inc. © Morris Book Publishing, LLC
Spine photo © Michael DeYoung

Hansen, Eric, 1948-
 Hiking Michigan's Upper Peninsula / Eric Hansen. — 1st ed.
   p. cm — (A Falcon guide)
 ISBN 978-0-7627-2588-5
   1. Hiking—Michigan—Upper Peninsula—Guidebooks. 2.
 Upper Peninsula (Mich.)—Guidebooks. I. Title. II. Series

 GV199.42.M5U664 2005
 796.51'09774'9—dc22

                                          2005046058

Manufactured in the United States of America
First Edition/Second Printing

To buy books in quantity for corporate use
or incentives, call **(800) 962–0973**
or e-mail **premiums@GlobePequot.com**.

The author and The Globe Pequot Press assume no liability for accidents happening to, or
injuries sustained by, readers who engage in the activities described in this book.

To my parents, Homer Richard Hansen and Dorothy Shaffer Hansen, who taught me to navigate the wilds of the backwoods at a very young age.

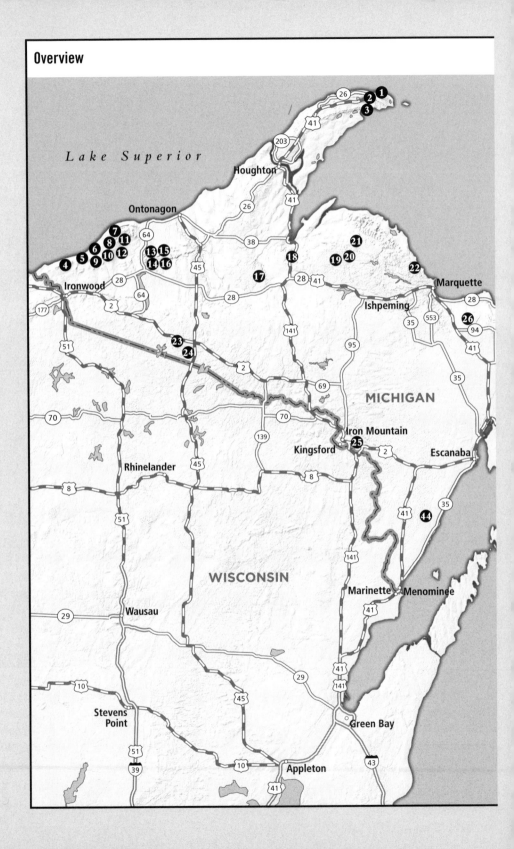

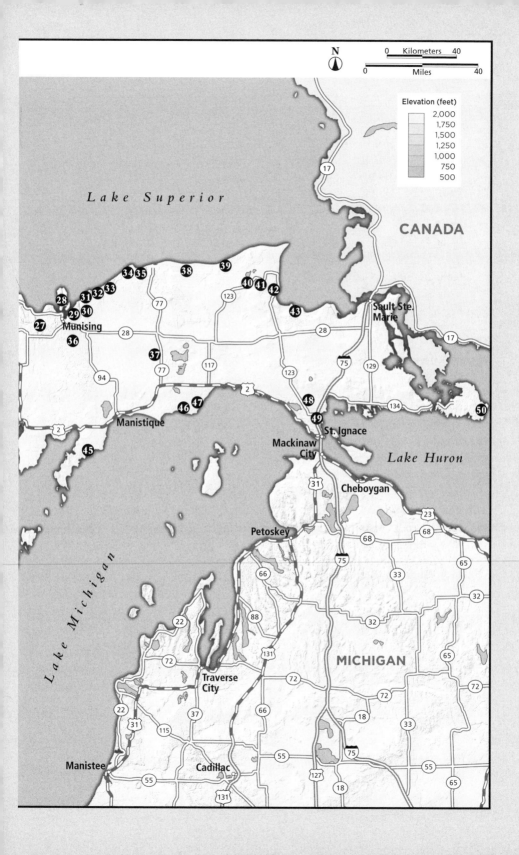

Contents

Acknowledgments

This book would not have been possible without the help of many people. I would like to thank the numerous hikers who found time to return my questionnaires and inform me of their favorite routes. Many of those folks are active in the Michigan Nature Association, the Milwaukee Nordic Ski Club, the North Country Trail Association, Northwoods Wilderness Recovery, the Sierra Club, The Nature Conservancy, the Upper Peninsula Environmental Coalition, or the Wisconsin Let's Go Hiking Club.

Doug Welker and Marjory Johnston generously shared their immense knowledge of trails and routes in the Upper Peninsula. Charlie Eshbach and Jeff Knoop tutored me on the Tip of the Keweenaw. Denise Herron steered me to the Little Garlic River and other gems. Mikel Classen tipped me on the picturesque coast near the Blind Sucker River. Jessie Hadley, of Woods and Waters Ecotours, offered keen insight into the quiet corners of the eastern U.P.

Bob Sprague, park interpreter at Porcupine Mountains Wilderness State Park, was a vital sounding board for my hike selections there. Bob Wild, park interpreter at Tahquamenon State Park, passed on his considerable knowledge of that notable ecosystem.

Jon Dorn, managing editor of *Backpacker* magazine, assigned a Trap Hills article that sparked this book project. Kristin Hostetter, of that same publication, sharpened my writing skills during her tenure as equipment editor. Thanks also to other editors there—Annette McGivney, Dennis Lewon, Gina DeMillo, and Kris Wagner for savvy advice, and a string of assignments that dovetailed well with this book project. Jim Gorman, during his time at *Backpacker,* drilled me on the fundamentals of landscape writing.

Dave Foreman and Howie Wolke provided inspiration with their visionary volume, *The Big Outside,* an inventory of North American wilderness. John Hart, author of the practical and poetic guidebook, *Hiking the Great Basin,* set a standard I will always aspire to.

Thanks to all the tireless activists of the Trap Hills Conservation Alliance. Dave and Judy Allen, Doug Cornett, Jon Saari, and Scott Bouma offered valuable advice and timely support.

I'm grateful to poet Harvey Taylor for spiritual sustenance over the years. My aunt, Marjorie Swann Edwin, a fearless campaigner for human rights and the planet, supplied a steady stream of encouragement.

I also owe thanks to copy editor Katie Sharp, project editor Jan Cronan, and the rest of the staff at Globe Pequot Press for their knowledgeable assistance.

Special thanks to my spouse, Anne Steinberg, for frontline editing that kept me on track and a faith in this project that smoothed the rough spots.

Any errors are mine, not theirs.

Introduction

Hiking the Upper Peninsula

The Upper Peninsula is a mighty land. Wild and off-the-beaten track, it has a long history as the backwoods retreat of the Upper Midwest—a 300-mile long swath of quiet forests; sparkling, pristine water; remote shorelines; and eye-catching vistas. Better yet is the sheer mystery of the place. The U.P. has a well-deserved reputation for rewarding explorers who invest the time to explore its nooks and crannies.

Ask me that most pointed of questions, "Where would you go if you had two weeks to take in the best of the U.P.?" and the decisions would not be easy.

I would start at Marble Head, a remote headland on Drummond Island's east end, where the rising sun first touches the U.P. I'd savor the sweeping views across Lake Huron's North Channel, then begin a zigzag course west. My first stop would be the Tahquamenon River, but not just to see the waterfalls. I couldn't leave without touring the notable virgin forest between the thunderous Lower Falls and the almost 50-foot-tall, and 200-foot-wide, Upper Falls.

Then I'd jump southwest to walk one of Lake Michigan's quietest mainland shorelines, the wave-washed beach and bedrock coast leading to Birch Point. Swinging north I'd stop by Seney National Wildlife Refuge for a sojourn with Trumpeter Swans and other notables.

Visiting Lake Superior, possessor of more than a tenth of our planet's freshwater, is always high on my list, and two commanding heights west of Grand Marais offer striking viewpoints. A classic 12-mile long promenade along the rim of the craggy Pictured Rocks shoreline unfolds between Miners Beach and Beaver Lake. The Grand Sable Banks are an immense sandy headland, nearly 300 feet high and 5 miles long.

Time might be tight, but as I motored past Munising, I'd take a break to contemplate the delicate veil known as Olson Falls, as well as the sparkling cascade of Laughing Whitefish Falls.

With a sturdy vehicle I'd brave the dusty roads beyond Big Bay and find my way to the Yellow Dog Falls. Some of the most pristine water in the Upper Midwest pours off a wilderness plateau here, and the tumbling white water and old growth forest are hauntingly picturesque.

Next I'd take a big swing north to the rugged land's end known as Tip of the Keweenaw Peninsula. Almost an island in the middle of Lake Superior, this wild cape features rock-ribbed shoreline at Horseshoe Harbor and white pine elders at the Estivant Pines. Hikers who find their way to Bare Bluff will find rich rewards: sweeping views stretching to the far off Huron Mountains and soul-satisfying solitude.

Leaving the Keweenaw, I'd head south to the 16,000 acres of virgin forest and forty spring-fed lakes of the Sylvania Wilderness. A stop to explore the quiet forest and stunning views of the Trap Hills would be in order, before arriving at one of the

stellar wilderness tracts of the Upper Midwest—Porcupine Mountains Wilderness State Park. There a broad chunk of 35,000 acres of virgin forest nestle clear-running streams and thumping waterfalls leading to Lake Superior. I'd linger in the hemlock cathedrals on the Pinkerton Trail and follow the dancing cascades of the Little Carp River to its headwaters.

Two magnificent and compact sets of waterfalls would provide a grand finale. On the west side of the Porcupine Mountains, the Presque Isle River races to Lake Superior in a thunderous series of drops. A little farther west the Black River rivals the Presque Isle, dropping through a picturesque gorge featuring five named waterfalls.

North Country Trail

In the 1960s a 60-mile long footpath was built in the Chequamegon National Forest in Northwest Wisconsin and named the North Country Trail (NCT). At the time there were no great ambitions for it to be more than a trail through Wisconsin's Northwoods. The name, however, caused a stir. In the years that followed, the idea of a trail stretching across a wide tier of northern states spread, and a movement to build the NCT was born.

Today the North Country National Scenic Trail features more than 1,700 certified, off-road miles of trail. Those trail segments are along a route that stretches from northern New York to North Dakota.

Some of the most scenic stretches of that long national pathway are in the U.P. The list of notable NCT segments that made the cut for this book is extensive and includes the thunderous white water of the Black River Waterfalls and sweeping vistas of the Trap Hills in the west. In the central U.P., NCT hikes along the quiet shores of Craig Lake and the charming Little Garlic River are well worth a visit. Farther east the NCT offers spectacular views of Lake Superior in the Pictured Rocks and Mouth of the Blind Sucker River trail segments. The stretch along the Tahquamenon River, including the famous waterfalls, is a "can't miss." A little north of the Straits of Mackinac, the Maple Hill stretch is a subtle forest beauty.

Trail maps and up-to-date reports on new trail additions are on the North Country Trail Association's (NCTA) Web site (see Appendix). Hikers can also find information there on local chapters and insight on how they can help build the trail.

Saving This Place We Call the U.P.

For the strength of the pack is the wolf, and the strength of the wolf is the pack.
                                                    —Rudyard Kipling, "The Law of the Jungle"

◀ *One of a long string of tumbling cascades along the Little Carp River.*

You, and others like you, can make the critical difference in whether the places we enjoy today are worth visiting in the years to come. Your knowledge of savvy methods to respond to threats to the U.P.'s wild lands is a key part of the strategy to protect them. Citizen watchdogs are the eyes and ears that blow the whistle on polluters and other illegal activity.

You are not alone. You can plug into a broad network of like-minded folks. A good place to start is with the following organizations: Northwoods Wilderness Recovery, the Sierra Club, and the Upper Peninsula Environmental Coalition (see Appendix for contact information). You can also do a great service for yourself, other hikers, and the community at large by keeping abreast of conservation issues that impact the U.P. Information is power. Typically, forest management, water, and development issues are prominent. Recently, widespread mining exploration in the western U.P. has moved to the top of the list of concerns. At least two proposals for sulfide mines (a type of mining associated with notable pollution) seem to be imminent. One of those mines would be on the Yellow Dog Plains in western Marquette County. The other would be near the Menominee River.

Weather

Weather in the U.P., is a source of local pride, often seen as a test of character. At its fiercest it will challenge you with ninety-degree heat and below-zero windchills. Fortunately there is a lot of fine hiking weather between those extremes. In addition to the obvious seasonal variation, there is sometimes a wide difference between the weather on the north and south shores of the U.P. At times, strong onshore winds create these differences. The Great Lakes often have a moderating effect on temperatures along their shores, resisting heat and cold that may be dominant just a few miles inland.

For hikers more than a casual distance from their vehicle, it pays to know the forecast and be prepared for worst-case scenarios, such as cold rain showers accompanied by strong winds. Several hikes in this book follow Great Lakes shorelines. Be aware that coastal routes are glorious in good conditions but merciless in their exposure to high winds when the weather gets rowdy.

Seasons

Spring hiking, with its woodland wildflowers, colorful birds, and open sight lines through the leafless forest, can be the best of the year. It is a time when marsh walks along dike routes, such as the Seney National Wildlife Refuge, can lead to extravagant bird migration scenes. Bug presence is minimal, and weather is often temperate and ideal for walking. The weather can be volatile, however; keep track of forecasts and bring appropriate clothing. Right after snowmelt, trails are frequently wet or muddy. A walk along a sandy beach may be appealing then. Also remember that there may be fine hiking along Lake Michigan beaches while the Lake Superior snowbelt is still thick with snow.

Norwich Bluff offers some of the best views in the Trap Hills.

Summer, with its long hours of daylight, lends itself to lengthy hikes, with time to linger at distant destinations. Hot temperatures are a comfort factor directly related to how much of a hike is in the deep shade of the forest canopy. Shady forest trails tend to be reasonably comfortable throughout the summer. One way to escape summer heat is to walk near the Great Lakes shorelines and enjoy cooler lake-effect temperatures. Bugs are numerous in early summer and slowly decline as the season progresses. Thunderstorms can soak hikers and expose them to dangerous lightning.

Fall is the favorite season for many hikers. It is hard to disagree with the merits of a forest ablaze with color. Shorter daylight hours dictate an earlier return from hikes. Full rain gear is a good idea for the cooler temperatures and lingering rain showers of fall. Bug season ends, and hikes that would be miserable in June are prime in late September. Hunters are out and about, however, so wearing some blaze orange is prudent.

Winter snow cover on hiking trails is a sure thing in the U.P. That deep snow may halt the hiking season, but for snowshoe and ski enthusiasts it is a pleasant opportunity to travel the trails in another manner.

Grand Portal Point looms on the horizon beyond Spray Falls. This is just one scene from a peerless 12-mile promenade along the craggy Pictured Rocks coast.

Clothing

Two truths are the basis of a savvy clothing strategy. First, layer your clothing and you will have options. Temperature, wind, shade, and precipitation can change during a hike. If you have clothing choices, you will be able to add or subtract a layer and be more comfortable when those changes occur. You will be able to walk without becoming overheated, cold, or wet. Second, synthetic thread does not absorb water as cotton thread does. Essentially this means that any moisture in the fabric dries quicker because it is between the threads, not within them. This fundamental advantage of synthetic clothing keeps the hiker drier, with less chance of becoming chilled. In cool temperatures or high winds, that advantage can become a critical safety factor.

The season and length of your hike determine what clothing is essential. A cap and sunblock could be the bottom line for a short warm-weather hike, but consider a long-sleeved shirt and pants for protection from the sun, bugs, and briars.

Rain gear quality should reflect the relative threat of becoming chilled and hypothermic. On a short, warm-weather hike, that threat may be low, but in cooler temperatures, and on longer outings, take along full rain gear as well as a sweater and warm hat.

Hiking boots are a basic part of your clothing system. Boots that feature a water-proof/breathable liner will keep your feet toasty in a chilly autumn rain and ease the going when trails are wet.

Being Prepared

Being prepared has its equipment aspects, but in the end it is mental. We set out on hikes with a set of assumptions in place. We are confident that our physical capabilities and gear can deal with the conditions and terrain we expect to find. In a way we are using a mathematical formula that goes like this: confidence + conditioning + gear + conditions that are reasonable and as expected = successful outing. Trouble arises when one of the factors in this formula changes and the formula no longer computes. That change could be a severe heel blister, twisted ankle, sudden lightning storm, or cold rain squall. At that point conditions may exceed our capacity to deal with them. There is no warning light on a dashboard, but savvy hikers recognize that moment's approach and trim their sails appropriately.

Even a small fanny pack has room for a small amount of gear that can make a big difference when problems arise. At a minimum take a compass, energy bar, water, knife, aspirin, bandages, antibacterial ointment, matches, and space blanket emergency bag. Tightly folded garbage bags take up less room than your wallet and can pinch-hit as an emergency shelter or rain gear.

Treading Lightly on the Land

Zero impact is to hiking and camping what catch-and-release is to fishing. It all boils down to one concept: With a little forethought, we will still be able to enjoy the outing we are taking today in five years—or fifty.

If you pack it in, pack it out. Leave nothing but footprints. Human sanitation is especially important in the backwoods, away from toilets. Dig a six-inch deep hole, well away from any stream or water, relieve yourself, and cover the hole with dirt. Pack out your used toilet paper in a plastic storage bag.

How to Use This Guide

One goal framed the research for this book: to find and catalog the best natural ambience, accessible by foot, in Michigan's U.P. Two questions cut to the essence of that quest: Which hikes offer a strong connection with the natural world? Where are the routes that offer outstanding samples of what is unique in the U.P. ecosystem? I sought out hikes that were quiet and a pleasure to the eye and offered treats such as waterfalls, wildlife, vistas, old growth forests, and remote shorelines.

Deciding not to just take trails at face value, I looked for new wrinkles. For example I examined linear trails for their optimum "gem" segments. I also gave serious consideration to which combinations of trails offered the best experience. At times I recommend off-trail routes along Great Lakes shorelines.

Field research came from almost 900 miles of hiking. I hiked every foot of trail described in this guide. The purpose of this book is to organize that pool of knowledge in a way that allows you to locate outings suitable to your tastes and abilities. You can make an initial screening of the hike chapters by checking the Hike Finder in Appendix A. The hike locator map offers a quick scan of which hikes are in a given area. Hike chapters begin with a summary of the facts a reader would need to evaluate that hike. The **Type of hike** section puts each hike into one of four categories:

Loop hike. A loop hike begins and ends at the same point without walking the same stretch of trail more than once. At times finishing the loop may require a small amount of road walking to return to the starting point.

Lollipop hike. A lollipop hike is a loop with a stem, or occasionally two stems. If the loop segment of the lollipop is very small in proportion to the stem, it falls into the category of out-and-back hikes.

Point-to-point hike. A point-to-point hike involves walking from one point to another, typically using a second vehicle or a bicycle for the return trip.

Out-and-back hike. An out-and-back hike is one where you hike to a location and retrace your steps to return to your point of origin.

The total mileage for each hike appears under the heading **Distance.** Keep in mind that precise measurement of trail miles is time consuming and rarely done. Most mileage figures, whether from official sources or my notes, are usually an estimate.

Each hike has an overall **Difficulty** rating:

Easy. These are well-marked trails, and the length is less than 6 miles. There is reasonably good footing and no obstacles worth mentioning.

Moderate. These hikes are on marked or obvious trails, old woods roads, or lanes. They are less than 10 miles long, and footing may be rougher in places than easy hikes.

Difficult. This rating reflects either a hike length of more than 10 miles or conditions or navigation that requires considerable skills and/or perseverance. Difficult hikes may be on unmarked trails or old woods roads or involve considerable off-trail travel. The footing may be rough and there may be steep climbs.

An asterisk after the overall difficulty rating indicates a route or trail that requires some attention to follow. Some scanning may be necessary to spot the next blaze and the trail itself may be faint or show no wear marks at all on the ground.

Best months lists the time during which the hike is normally free of snow and reasonable to walk. Early or late season snowstorms can change that.

Any map listed from a land agency or trail organization shows the featured hike or a large portion of it. These maps are often basic but perfectly adequate for easy hikes and some moderate ones. USGS topographical maps are useful for some moderate and difficult hikes. Unfortunately it is not unusual for these maps to predate the existence of the hiking trail in question. Topographical maps that show the area, but not all of the trail mentioned have *(inc.)*, for incomplete, after them. Having both the land agency map and the topographical map is a good idea. The North Country Trail Association also has worthwhile maps. Michigan's U.P. has many outstanding attributes, but significant elevation change is not one of them. Therefore elevation profiles are not included in this book.

A **Fees and permits** section lists necessary items such as state park vehicle stickers or backpacking permits.

Each hike summary also includes a brief description, **Finding the trailhead,** that describes how to locate the start of the hike from a nearby town. Finally there are headings that list nearby **Camping,** as well as a **Trail contact** if you need more information.

If there are other aspects of a hike that are important for you to know before your outing, you will find them under the **Special considerations** heading.

How to Use the Maps

The maps in this book use elevation tints, called hypsometry, to portray relief. Each gray tone represents a range of equal elevations, as shown in the scale key with the map. These maps will give you a good idea of elevation gain and loss. The darker tones are lower elevations and the lighter grays are higher elevations. The lighter the tone, the higher the elevation. Narrow bands of different gray tones spaced closely together indicate steep terrain; whereas wider bands indicate areas of more gradual slope.

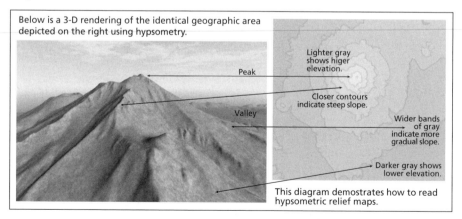

Below is a 3-D rendering of the identical geographic area depicted on the right using hypsometry.

Peak

Valley

Lighter gray shows higer elevation.

Closer contours indicate steep slope.

Wider bands of gray indicate more gradual slope.

Darker gray shows lower elevation.

This diagram demostrates how to read hypsometric relief maps.

Map Legend

Transportation

===〈75〉=== Interstate

===〈8〉=== U.S. highway

───〈107〉─── State highway

───〈519〉─── Other road

= = = = = Unimproved road

▬ ▬ ▬ ▬ ▬ Featured Trail / Route

- - - - - - - Non-featured trail (verified)

- - - - - - - Non-featured (unverified)

••••••••••• Featured cross-country route

Physiography / Hydrology

⊔⊔⊔⊔⊔⊔⊔ Bluff / Cliff

///////// Boundaries
Park / Forest

 Lake

☀ ☀ ☀ Marsh / Swamp

〰 Stream

〰 Intermittent stream

Symbols

⋈ Bridge

⚲ Building / Shelter

◬ Campground

† Cemetery

○ City

🔳 Entrance station

⇒ Falls

•—• Gate

☀ Lighthouse

🅿 Parking

▲ Peak / Elevation

🀫 Picnic area

▪ Point of interest

⬥❼ Trail junction

⑲ Trail locator

🚶 Trailhead

❓ Visitor information

👁 Viewpoint

Western Region of the Upper Penninsula

Many of the western Upper Peninsula's most notable viewpoints, in the Trap Hills and elsewhere, are above the sharp south faces of tall ridges where the north slopes are more moderate. That highland pattern reflects the resilience of the ancient rock to gouging glaciers and the strata's tilt toward Lake Superior.

Those ridges are the high points of a broad, elevated upland where streams tend to be short and steep and the visual delights of tumbling white water are a regular treat. At the Porcupine Mountains, a vast virgin forest complements waterfalls racing to Lake Superior. Pristine water takes a more placid form at the Sylvania Wilderness, where spring-fed lakes of legendary clarity alternate with a remarkable chunk of ancient forest.

Hikers can immerse themselves in the serenity of old growth forests, opt to explore a wild shoreline, or tour splendid sets of waterfalls. Quiet wilderness lakes dot the backcountry, where loons call and solitude is there for the asking. Lofty vistas, offering sweeping views stretching forty miles and more, are at the Keweenaw Peninsula's Bare Bluff, as well as the Trap Hills and Porcupine Mountains (the Porkies).

1 Horseshoe Harbor

Highlights: A spectacular bedrock shoreline on the north shore of the Keweenaw Peninsula.

Location: 5 miles east of Copper Harbor.

Type of hike: Out-and-back.

Distance: 1.6 miles.

Difficulty: Moderate*.

Fees and permits: None, but consider a contribution to The Nature Conservancy.

Best months: May through October.

Camping: Fort Wilkins State Park, 3 miles west of the trailhead, has 159 campsites.

Map: USGS Fort Wilkins quad (inc.).

Trail contact: The Nature Conservancy, (906) 225-0399, www.tnc.org.

Finding the trailhead: From Copper Harbor drive east 2.3 miles on U.S. Highway 41 to the end of the pavement. Continue east for 0.8 mile on a graded dirt road known as the Mandan Loop Road. Then turn left (north) on a narrow, dirt two-track road known as the Horseshoe Harbor Road. Drive that road 1.2 miles north and east to the trailhead. Parking pullouts are on the south side of the road.

Special considerations: This hike travels through the Mary Macdonald Preserve at Horseshoe Harbor, a property of The Nature Conservancy. This is a special place—treat it well. Read the guidelines on the signboard at the trailhead.

The Hike

A certain aura, a whiff of raw fury, hangs on the shoreline here. Even on a benign summer day, the stark reefs of eroded conglomerate rock seem to speak of the epic storms of November; wind and waves sending spray sky high, and a timeless clash between the lake and ancient bedrock.

The U.P. and the Keweenaw have other notable wave-washed shores. This one though, with its exposed location and striking rock architecture, is a worthy contender for ranking as an icon.

Begin your visit by walking north on a broad and rocky trail that starts opposite the trailhead's parking pullouts. After a woodsy 0.3 mile, the trail emerges onto a rock cobble beach, the Lake Superior shore.

Before you a string of bedrock islands shelters a cove, a rough rectangle in shape, and a quarter-mile wide. A passing bald eagle swooped down to claim one of these rocks during my August visit. At the northwest end of the inlet, the reef of bedrock that forms the islands rises into a rock ridge 15 feet high.

Walk north along the cobble beach to that bedrock wall at Mile 0.4, and then west along its base. A gravelly flat beneath, and just south of the rock, offers passage west.

From time to time low-angle ramps in the rock wall offer the nimble a viable way to the top of the rock. There, orange and green lichens, able to thrive on the most wind-exposed spots, accent the rock. Nooks and crannies shelter miniature

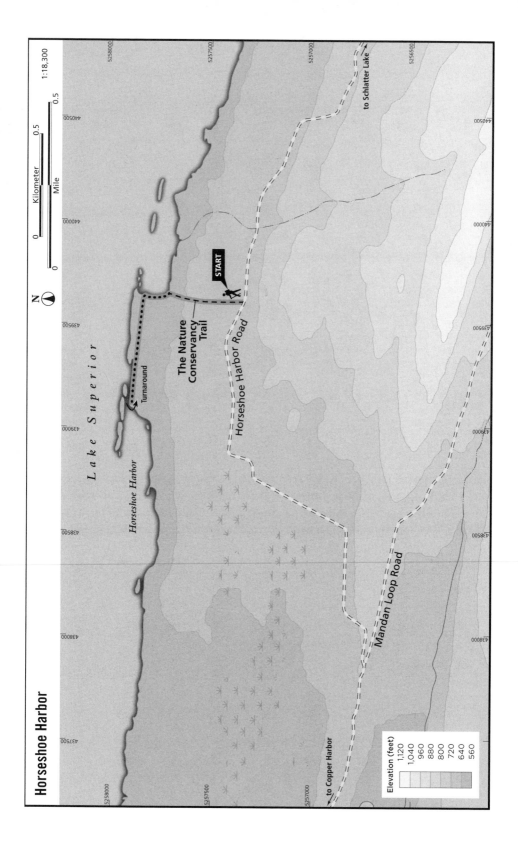

Horseshoe Harbor

1:18,300

Lake Superior

Horseshoe Harbor

Turnaround

The Nature Conservancy Trail

START

Horseshoe Harbor Road

Mandan Loop Road

to Schlatter Lake

to Copper Harbor

Elevation (feet)
1,120
1,040
960
880
800
720
640
560

Hardy plants and ancient bedrock along the rugged Horseshoe Harbor coast.

flower gardens, reminiscent of the last tiny patches of greenery on a high mountain.

Continue hiking west to Mile 0.8, where the rock reef once again becomes a string of islands, and the shoreline curls south, forming another bay. This makes a good turnaround spot for the hike.

Key Points

  0.0 Trailhead.

  0.3 Beach.

  0.4 Bedrock rib.

  0.8 West end of bedrock rib; turnaround point.

  1.6 Trailhead.

2 Estivant Pines Loop

Highlights: A notable stand of virgin white pines.

Location: 2 miles south of Copper Harbor.

Type of hike: Lollipop.

Distance: 2 miles.

Difficulty: Moderate.

Fees and permits: None, but consider a donation to the Michigan Nature Association.

Best months: May through October.

Camping: Fort Wilkins Park at Copper Harbor has 159 campsites.

Maps: USGS Lake Medora, Fort Wilkins quads (inc.); "Estivant Pines Sanctuary Guide" (available at Copper Harbor visitor center).

Trail contact: Michigan Nature Association, (517) 655-5655, www.michigannature.org.

Finding the trailhead: From Copper Harbor, drive south 1 mile, on paved Lake Manganese Road. At that point turn left (east) onto a graded gravel road (now following signs to Estivant Pines), also known as Lake Manganese Road. After driving 0.9 mile on the gravel road, turn right (south) on an unnamed dirt road, part of an intersection triangle of roads. After less than 0.1 mile, turn right (west) on another dirt road, Burma Road, and drive 0.4 mile west to the trailhead parking area, on the left (south) side of the road.

Special considerations: This hike travels through the Estivant Pines Wilderness Sanctuary, a property of the Michigan Nature Association. This is a special place—treat it well. Read the guidelines on the signboard at the trailhead.

The Hike

Some of the finest specimens of virgin white pines in Michigan are here, a haunting remnant of the vast swaths that once stretched across northern Michigan. These ancient trees, a few elders reaching the age of 400 years, stand in groves scattered across the sanctuary's 377 acres.

Begin your hike from the south end of the trailhead parking area. Walk south on the broad trail 0.2 mile to a signed trail junction (designated Junction A for identification purposes on the map). Disregard the Memorial Loop Trail to your left (east) and continue walking straight (south), reaching another junction at Mile 0.4 (designated Junction B on the map). There turn right (west) on a narrower footpath, the Cathedral Loop Trail.

Hike west—rocks and roots sometimes challenging—on the Cathedral Loop Trail. The trail loops around to the south, passes a hollowed out white pine snag, and reaches its namesake, the Cathedral Grove, at Mile 0.8. Giant white pines line the trail here, loaning their aura to what may well be the most contemplative locale of the hike.

When you are ready, continue hiking on the Cathedral Loop Trail, now heading north and reaching the junction with the Memorial Grove Trail at Mile 1.0 (designated Junction C on the map). Turn right (east) here and hike eastward on the Memorial Grove Trail, reaching that grove at Mile 1.4.

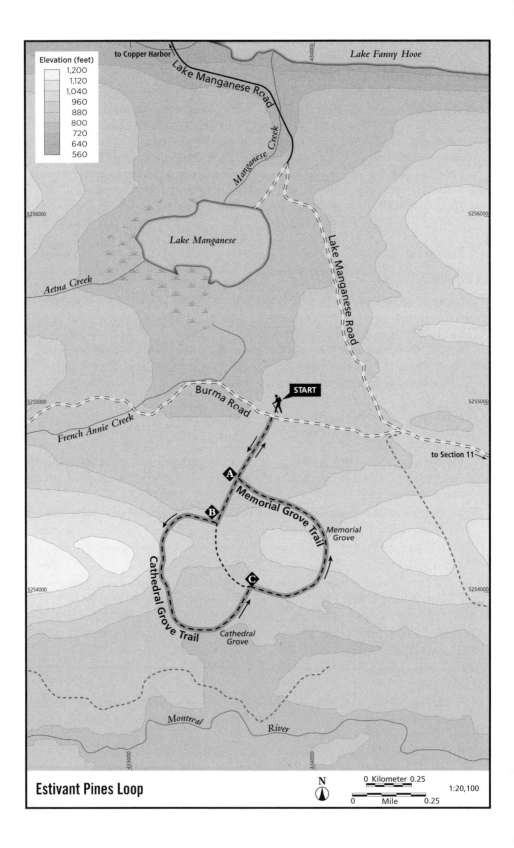

Elevation (feet)
1,200
1,120
1,040
960
880
800
720
640
560

to Copper Harbor

Lake Manganese Road

Lake Fanny Hooe

Manganese Creek

5256000

Lake Manganese

Lake Manganese Road

Aetna Creek

5255000

Burma Road

START

French Annie Creek

to Section 11

A

Memorial Grove Trail

B

Memorial Grove

Cathedral Grove Trail

C

Cathedral Grove

5254000

Montreal

River

Estivant Pines Loop

N

0   Kilometer   0.25

0   Mile   0.25

1:20,100

Follow the Memorial Grove Trail, from its namesake stand, as it loops north then west and meets Junction A at Mile 1.8. There turn right (north), returning to the trailhead and the end of the hike at Mile 2.0

Key Points

0.0 Trailhead.

0.2 Memorial Trail junction (north), Junction A.

0.4 Cathedral Loop Trail junction, Junction B.

0.8 Cathedral Grove.

1.0 Memorial Trail junction (south), Junction C.

1.4 Memorial Grove.

1.8 Junction A.

2.0 Trailhead.

3 Bare Bluff

Highlights: Spacious views of the Keweenaw Peninsula and Lake Superior from a notable viewpoint. Solitude. On a good day the views stretch to the Huron Mountains, 40 miles south.

Location: Keweenaw Peninsula, 5 miles south of Copper Harbor.

Type of hike: Out-and-back.

Distance: 2.6 miles.

Difficulty: Moderate*.

Fees and permits: None, but consider a donation to the Michigan Nature Association.

Best months: May through October.

Camping: Fort Wilkins State Park, 5 miles north of the trailhead, has 159 campsites.

Map: USGS Lake Medora quad (inc.).

Trail contact: Michigan Nature Association, (517) 655-5655, www.michigannature.org.

Finding the trailhead: From Lac La Belle, drive 1.9 miles east on Bete Grise Road. Then, turn left (northeast) onto Smith Fisheries Road. Drive east 2.5 miles on that road to a logging pullout on the road's east side and park there.

Special considerations: Bare Bluff is part of the Russell and Miriam Grinnell Memorial Nature Sanctuary, a private nature preserve, which is the property of the Michigan Nature Association (MNA). Treat it well; read the MNA guidelines on the blue sign. Hikers visiting during the late spring/early summer nesting season should be aware that Merlins (a falcon species) could be nesting nearby, perhaps on a ledge below the cliff top. Proceed in a cautious, respectful manner—both for the birds' sake and your own. Merlins can be very aggressive. Be aware that the viewpoint is the top of a high cliff.

The Hike

East of Bete Grise the pavement ends, the shoreline turns forbiddingly rocky, and one of the truly great U.P. landscapes—a back of beyond known to locals as the Tip

Bare Bluff's remarkable view of the tip of the Keweenaw Peninsula.

of the Keweenaw—begins. Here woodlands stretch shore to shore, accented by rock-topped ridges, lakes, and cascading streams flowing to the big lake. It's a swath of wild country penetrated by only a few seasonal roads, and reminiscent of Isle Royale. Fortunately recent efforts by The Nature Conservancy translate into ongoing protection for large chunks of the tip. Earlier the MNA purchased a few key tracts.

Bare Bluff, a memorable viewpoint, is one of those MNA properties. An airy cliff top on its south summit, some 500 feet above Lake Superior's waters, offers sweeping vistas that are among the finest in the U.P.

Hikers familiar with Sugar Loaf, the well-known lookout just west of Marquette, may find a comparison useful. Picture a similar vantage point, but on a wild Keweenaw shoreline, a narrow footpath leading to the heights, and not a soul around.

Begin your hike by walking east on the unnamed logging road. During my visit I found an active logging operation here, and the contrast with the idyllic spot beyond could not have been greater. Persevere: Bare Bluff is well worth it.

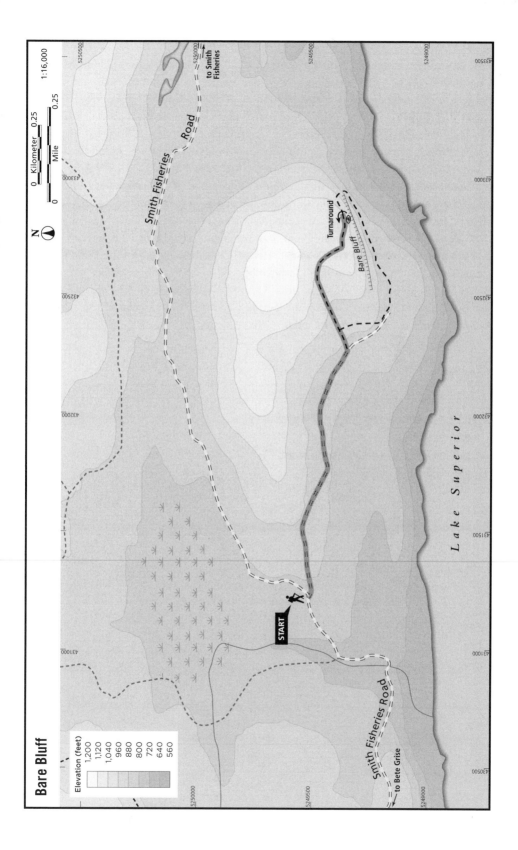

Bare Bluff

1:16,000

N

Elevation (feet)
1,200
1,120
1,040
960
880
800
720
640
560

0 Kilometer 0.25

0 Mile 0.25

Smith Fisheries Road

to Smith Fisheries

Turnaround

Bare Bluff

START

Smith Fisheries Road

to Bete Grise

Lake Superior

Continue walking east on the logging road to Mile 0.7, where a blue MNA signboard on the left (east) side of the road marks a trail running east into the woods, as the logging road swings downhill to the right (south). Take a moment to read the guidelines on the MNA signboard. Then walk east on that trail for 150 paces; there a MNA map board marks a trail junction at Mile 0.8. Turn left (north) and follow that path, marked by both blue and yellow diamonds, uphill. Steadily ascending, the trail swings east, becoming a tad faint but marked by yellow and orange flagging, just before it emerges onto the bedrock of the lookout at Mile 1.3.

There a stunted maple and oak forest ends at a high ledge, offering magnificent views. To the east the scalloped shoreline stretches past the tumbling white water of the Montreal River to Keystone Point, and then Keweenaw Point, land's end, the tip of the tip. Look west and Bete Grise's beaches bracket the mouth of the Little Gratiot River, Lac La Belle, and Point Isabelle beyond.

I was there on a day of some humidity and could easily see Keweenaw Point some 6 miles off, but haze obscured Manitou Island a few miles beyond. On a good day the Huron Mountains, 40 miles south across Keweenaw Bay, appear on the southern horizon.

Key Points

- **0.0** Trailhead at logging landing.
- **0.7** Trail begins at Michigan Nature Association sign.
- **0.8** Trail junction.
- **1.3** Bare Bluff Overlook; turnaround point.
- **2.6** Trailhead at logging landing.

4 Black River Waterfalls

Highlights: A spectacular parade of five waterfalls.
Location: 15 miles north of Bessemer.
Type of hike: Out-and-back, in two stems.
Distance: 8.3 miles.
Difficulty: Difficult.
Fees and permits: None.

Best months: May through October.
Camping: Ottawa National Forest's Black River Harbor Campground, a quarter-mile west of the trailhead, has forty campsites.
Map: USGS Black River Harbor (inc.) quad.
Trail contact: Ottawa National Forest, (906) 932-1330, www.fs.fed.us/r9/ottawa.

Finding the trailhead: From Bessemer drive 15 miles north on Black River Road (Gogebic County Road 513) and turn right (east) into the trailhead, which is also a picnic parking area.
Special considerations: Parts of these trails are eroded and rough and have an abundance of exposed roots. Use caution on wet rocks near the river and waterfalls.

The Hike

Waterfall fans (and who isn't one?) have two incredible choices in the western U.P. The Presque Isle and the Black Rivers make thunderous, booming descents to Lake Superior. Like a peerless set of twins, both rivers sport a parade of waterfalls that stand tall in any short list of U.P. white-water shows. Better yet, both of these sets of cascades are compact, creating outstanding hikes.

This hike tours the westernmost of those two streams—the Black River—as it tumbles through a delightful gorge to Lake Superior. First the route skirts the river's mouth, Black River Harbor, and ascends its east side to the perfect vantage point for Rainbow Falls. After offering that memorable view, it returns to the river's west side, passing four waterfalls before arriving at Conglomerate Falls. From that cascade the route returns to the river mouth.

Begin your tour by walking northeast from the trailhead's information board, following an asphalt path to the Black River Bridge (Mile 0.1). Cross the sturdy suspension bridge to the river's east bank and follow the North Country Trail (NCT) up steps to the top of the bluff, where the broad dirt trail curves south. Consider a short side-trip here. In the middle of that curve on the NCT, a narrow footpath runs north 120 paces to a bench—a pleasant spot to soak in views of Lake Superior and the Porcupine Mountains to the east.

To resume this hike, walk south, following the NCT through fine hemlock groves and descending to a perfect vantage point to view Rainbow Falls at Mile 0.9. Rainbow Falls, a spectacular 40-foot drop, begins with a water slide down a rock ramp and accelerates into two thumping ledge drops.

Then retrace your steps north to the Black River Bridge (Mile 1.7), cross and walk south past the trailhead. An NCT sign marks the spot where the trail ascends

into the woods, leading south to the west side of Rainbow Falls, where nearly 200 steps descend to a viewpoint overlooking the top of the falls (Mile 2.2).

Reverse your path, ascend the stairs, and follow the broad trail southwest to the Rainbow Falls Trailhead parking area. There, go straight, walking west 110 paces, following NCT blazes to CR 513 (Mile 2.5). Turn left (south) and hike 0.8 mile south, on the shoulder of CR 513, to a forest service sign marking the trailhead for Sandstone Falls (Mile 3.3).

There, turn left (east), walk sixty paces east on pavement, then northeast on a broad dirt trail, the Sandstone Falls Trail. Descend almost 140 steps to a viewpoint at Sandstone Falls' two-step plunge (Mile 3.6). First the flow drops 5 feet off a broad sandstone ledge, pauses, and then tumbles an additional 20 feet.

From Sandstone Falls return to the Sandstone Falls Trailhead (Mile 3.9) and walk to the southwest corner of the parking area. There the NCT runs south, first near CR 513, then turning southeast. Soon it approaches the rim of the river gorge, and steps descend to a viewpoint for Gorge Falls (Mile 4.5). Upstream from Gorge Falls a dark, forbidding chute of bedrock and conglomerate leads to a pinch point. The current narrows to an 8-foot wide flume and tumbles 20 feet to the gorge below.

After viewing Gorge Falls, return to the rim and walk south along the broad dirt path there. In short order the rim path passes two more sets of stairs descending to viewpoints, then arrives at stairs descending to Potawatomi Falls (Mile 4.6). Potawatomi Falls is a knockout, a sparkling and complex bridal veil cascading 40 feet.

Return to the rim and follow the NCT south along the top of the bluff. At times a tad rough and eroded, roots exposed, the trail arrives at Conglomerate Falls (Mile 5.3). Here the river splits around a rock dome, taking a stepped plunge into the gorge, a 30-foot-high descent. During my visit, large trees littered the center dome, mute testimony to the river's power.

Conglomerate Falls marks the southern turnaround point for the hike. To return to the trailhead, follow the NCT north, downhill to the Black River Harbor parking area.

Key Points

0.0 Trailhead.

0.1 Black River Bridge.

0.9 Rainbow Falls (east side); first turnaround point.

1.7 Black River Bridge.

2.2 Rainbow Falls (west side).

2.5 Trail joins CR 513 (walk on shoulder).

3.3 Sandstone Falls Trailhead.

Gorge Falls. The Black River races to Lake Superior in a set of five thumping waterfalls.

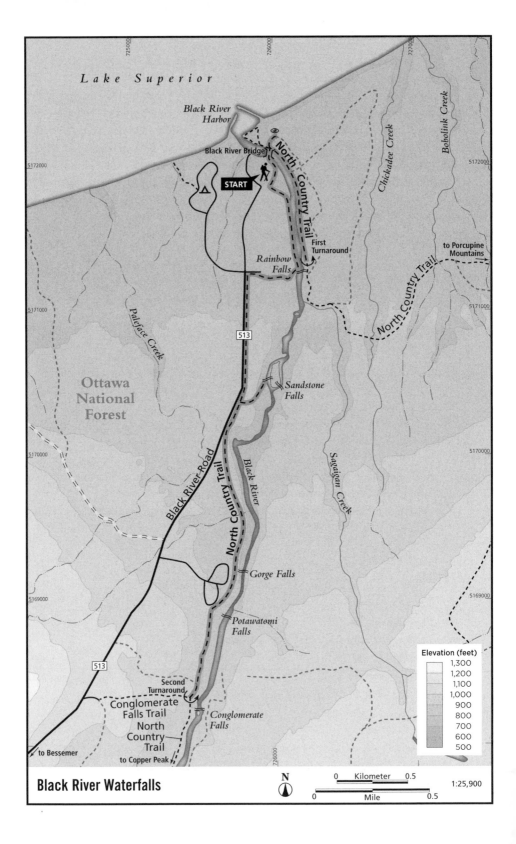

Lake Superior

Black River
Harbor

Black River Bridge

START

North Country Trail

First
Turnaround

to Porcupine
Mountains

Chickadee Creek

Bobolink Creek

North Country Trail

Rainbow
Falls

Paleface Creek

Ottawa
National
Forest

513

Sandstone
Falls

Black River Road

North Country Trail

Black River

Sagaigan Creek

Gorge Falls

Potawatomi
Falls

513

Second
Turnaround

Conglomerate
Falls Trail

North
Country
Trail

Conglomerate
Falls

to Bessemer

to Copper Peak

Elevation (feet)	
	1,300
	1,200
	1,100
	1,000
	900
	800
	700
	600
	500

Black River Waterfalls

N

0	Kilometer	0.5

| 0 | Mile | 0.5 |

1:25,900

3.6 Sandstone Falls.

3.9 Sandstone Falls Trailhead.

4.5 Gorge Falls.

4.6 Potawatomi Falls.

5.3 Conglomerate Falls; second turnaround point.

6.0 Potawatomi Falls.

6.1 Gorge Falls.

6.7 Sandstone Falls Trailhead.

7.5 Trail leaves CR 513.

7.8 Rainbow Falls (west side).

8.3 Trailhead.

5 Presque Isle River Waterfalls Loop

Highlights: A splendid and famous collection of waterfalls.
Location: Porcupine Mountains Wilderness State Park (PMWSP).
Type of hike: Loop.
Distance: 2.3 miles.
Difficulty: Moderate.
Fees and permits: Michigan Department of Natural Resources vehicle sticker.

Best months: May through October.
Camping: Presque Isle Campground, just west of the trailhead has fifty campsites.
Maps: USGS Tiebel Creek quad; PMWSP map by Nequaket Natural History Associates (available at the visitor center).
Trail contact: Porcupine Mountains Wilderness State Park, (906) 885-5275.

Finding the trailhead: From the intersection of M–107 and South Boundary Road, in PMWSP, drive south and west 24.1 miles on South Boundary Road. Turn right (north) on Gogebic County Road 519 and drive 0.9 mile to the trailhead at the Falls picnic area. Alternatively, from the junction of M–28 and Ontonagon County Route 519, just east of Wakefield, drive north 16.5 miles on CR 519 to the trailhead.

Special considerations: During high water the river channel at Mile 0.3 of the hike is impassable and not the dry bedrock described here. Parts of these trails are eroded and rough and have an abundance of exposed roots. Use caution on wet rocks near the river and water-falls. The waterfalls and river currents are dangerous. Boardwalk sections of the trail are there to protect wet areas. Stay on the boardwalk to prevent erosion scars in this picturesque area.

The Hike

Three thundering waterfalls, tucked into a stretch of river just over a half mile long, put on a memorable show here. A parade of cascades and swirling rapids adds to the setting, while striking old-growth trees, virgin white pine, hemlock, and white cedar line the riverbank.

Manido Falls, one of several thunderous drops on the Presque Isle River near Lake Superior.

Begin your tour from the east end of the picnic area parking lot, following a broad trail east fifty paces to a fork in the trail. There turn left (northeast), follow the sign that says FOOT BRIDGE TO ISLAND and walk 170 paces north to the top of a set of wooden stairs.

Descend the stairs to the suspension bridge. Continue descending, going straight (east) as the West River Trail enters on a raised boardwalk from the right (south), halfway down the stairs.

Walk eastward across the bridge (Mile 0.1), pausing to enjoy the unfolding river scene below. Upstream a roaring cascade feeds the swift water below the bridge; downstream, tan river water meets blue lake water. A series of striking potholes mark the bedrock beside the current, half-circles scoured by river gravel churning in powerful eddies.

Once on the island the official East River Trail swings right (south). I'd suggest a short side-trip to explore the island. Walk straight east, less than 100 yards through open forest, and you'll come to a lagoon—the east channel of the river when flows are high. Turn left (north) and follow the lagoon's shore north a short distance to the Lake Superior shoreline (Mile 0.2), a contemplative spot.

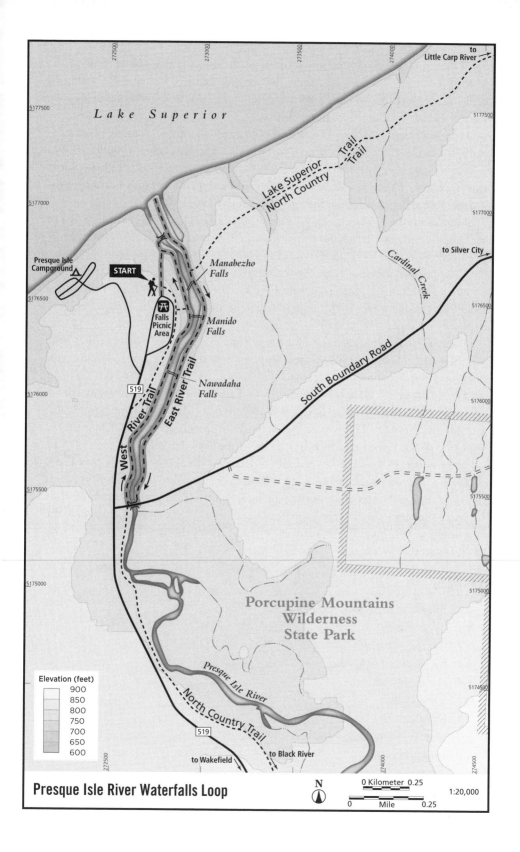

Lake Superior

272500 273000 273500 274000

to
Little Carp River

5177500

Lake Superior
North Country
Trail
Trail

5177000

to Silver City

Presque Isle
Campground

START

Manabezho
Falls

Cardinal Creek

5176500

Falls
Picnic
Area

Manido
Falls

South Boundary Road

5176000

519

West River Trail

East River Trail

Nawadaha
Falls

5175500

5175000

Porcupine Mountains
Wilderness
State Park

Presque Isle River

North Country Trail

Elevation (feet)
900
850
800
750
700
650
600

519

to Wakefield

to Black River

5177500

5177000

5176500

5176000

5175500

5175000

5174500

Presque Isle River Waterfalls Loop

N

0 Kilometer 0.25

0   Mile   0.25

1:20,000

When you are ready, retrace your steps, picking up the official trail at the bridge's east end and walk south. At the southern end of the island is scalloped bedrock, the overflow channel's dry waterfall. Just to the west is the rowdy cascade viewed earlier from the suspension bridge.

Hike southeast, crossing the bedrock channel. Continue walking southeastward, following a marked path into the woods, then steeply up a bluff to a trail junction (Mile 0.4). Turn right (south) on the East River Trail, as the Lake Superior Trail goes left (east). Walk south on the wide path, through beautiful old-growth forest, descending the bluff to Manabezho Falls (Mile 0.6).

Manabezho Falls, a booming 22-foot drop, is a knockout. Its name, like that of the other two named falls here, comes from fabled spirit warriors of Native American legends.

Continue hiking south on the East River Trail (also blazed for the North Country Trail here), reaching Manido Falls at Mile 0.7. Manido Falls, a thumping ledge drop about 8 feet high, spills into a deep pool flanked by broad aprons of bedrock.

Resume hiking south on the East River Trail, reaching Nawadaha Falls at Mile 0.9. Nawadaha Falls, another 8-foot drop, funnels the river's flow into the near bank, creating a sparkling white-water show.

From Nawadaha Falls, hike south on the East River Trail, past a steady stream of cascades and swift water to South Boundary Road (Mile 1.3). Turn right (west), crossing the Presque Isle River on the South Boundary Road bridge. Once on the west side of the river, turn right (north) onto the West River Trail.

Hike north on the West River Trail (also marked for the North Country Trail), viewing a mirror image of the sights seen from the West River Trail. A series of steps and walkways lead north past viewpoints at the three waterfalls, then intersect the steps that descend to the suspension bridge that you crossed at the beginning of the hike. There, turn left (west), ascend the steps, and retrace your earlier steps to the trailhead at the Falls picnic area.

Key Points

0.0   Trailhead at picnic area.

0.1   Suspension bridge.

0.2   Lake Superior shore.

0.4   Lake Superior Trail junction.

0.6   Manabezho Falls.

0.7   Manido Falls.

0.9   Nawadaha Falls.

1.3   South Boundary Road bridge.

1.8   Nawadaha Falls.

2.0 Manido Falls.

2.1 Manabezho Falls.

2.3 Trailhead at picnic area.

6 Shining Cloud Falls

Highlights: Shining Cloud Falls—often mentioned as the best waterfall in the park's interior—plus countless cascades of the Big Carp River, the Lake Superior shore, and virgin forest throughout the hike.

Location: Porcupine Mountains Wilderness State Park (PMWSP).

Type of hike: Out-and-back.

Distance: 11.2 miles.

Difficulty: Difficult.

Fees and permits: Michigan Department of Natural Resources vehicle sticker.

Best months: May through October.

Camping: Backcountry camping is available along the trail, within PMWSP regulations. The park's Presque Isle Campground has fifty campsites, and is 5 miles west of the Pinkerton Trailhead.

Maps: USGS Tiebel Creek, Carp River quads; PMWSP map by Nequaket Natural History Associates (available at the visitor center).

Trail contact: Porcupine Mountains Wilderness State Park, (906) 885-5275.

Finding the trailhead: From the intersection of M-107 and South Boundary Road, in PMWSP, drive south and west 19.7 miles to the Pinkerton Trailhead.

Special considerations: Use reasonable caution on wet rocks near the river and waterfall.

The Hike

Shining Cloud Falls is a bit of a backcountry icon, and rightly so. Some of its mystique might derive from the romance of its name or its reputation as a backcountry landmark.

This waterfall is remote, about as far from a road as you can get in the Porkies, or even for that matter, in the whole U.P. It is not a gimme. It is not one of those waterfalls you can drive up to, or walk a quarter-mile-long manicured path to reach. That said, I think there is much more than sweat equity that elevates the Shining Cloud experience. The waterfall itself is striking, but it is only one part of a remarkable outing, a sojourn with the essence of the Porkies, its wild core.

What follows is a description of one way to hike to Shining Cloud Falls. Besides being the easiest and shortest route, it is arguably the most beautiful. This hike skirts the Lake Superior shore, ascends beside the cascades of the Big Carp River, and wanders through virgin forest throughout the outing.

Begin your hike to Shining Cloud Falls by walking north on the broad, shady Pinkerton Trail. Narrow boardwalks bridge a few damp spots. A bridged crossing over the gentle riffles of Pinkerton Creek marks Mile 1.0. A bench overlooks the stream.

About 1 mile later, after threading through memorable hemlock groves, the path reaches another bench, this time on a bluff high above the swirling cascades of the Little Carp River. Swinging northward, the trail reaches a junction with the Lake Superior Trail at Mile 2.9. Turn right (east), following the Lake Superior Trail across the bridge over the Little Carp River, reaching the junction with the Little Carp River Trail at Mile 3.0.

Turn left (northwest) on the Lake Superior Trail, as the Little Carp River Trail goes right (south). Follow the Lake Superior Trail northwest 0.2 mile to the mouth of the Little Carp River. Here the trail swings right and begins a run to the northeast. It travels through open woods, typically 100 feet or so inland from Lake Superior, to the mouth of the Big Carp River. An appealing alternative route is a stone's throw north of the trail—the shoreline of our planet's largest freshwater lake.

Whether you walk the trail or opt to hike the shoreline, you will reach the mouth of the Big Carp River at Mile 4.2. Just before the bridge a junction marks the departure of the Cross Trail to the right (south). Ignore the Cross Trail and walk northeast across the bridge over the Big Carp River. The trail then swings to the right (east), switchbacks up a bluff, and reaches a junction. Turn right (east) on the Big Carp River Trail as the Lake Superior Trail goes left (north).

About a quarter of a mile later, the trail descends to river level. Robert Sprague and Michael Rafferty, authors of *Porcupine Mountains Companion,* describe a dozen notable cascades and waterfalls in the river's next mile. This stretch of river is pure liquid poetry, and you should consider budgeting some time to spend here.

One and one-quarter miles from the river's mouth, the path ascends another bluff, and the sound of a large waterfall drifts through the woods. At Mile 5.6 the trail reaches a viewpoint, beside a huge standing snag overlooking Shining Cloud Falls and its gorge.

Shining Cloud is a bi-level falls. First the flow drops 10 feet to a ledge, then splits evenly and tumbles another 12 feet to a pool below. In its second drop, the left side cascades down a rock ramp, while the right side is more of a vertical fall.

It is possible to descend to the falls' base safely, but it requires some judgment and balance. First continue east on the trail until you are above the top of the falls. The first routes that appear below you are dangerous. A little farther on you will notice steep switchbacks, dirt paths descending to the top of the falls. When the river is at moderate flow levels, a rock ramp there is dry and leads to the bottom of the falls. Whether that rock ramp is a safe move on any given day is a judgment you will have to make when you are there.

Option: A 6.5-mile round-trip hike to the mouth of the Little Carp River, from the Pinkerton Trailhead, has considerable appeal. That shorter outing features the forest scenes along the Pinkerton Trail, the charming cascades of the Little Carp River, and the Lake Superior shore.

◀ *Shining Cloud Falls. Twin torrents deep in the Porcupine Mountains backcountry.*

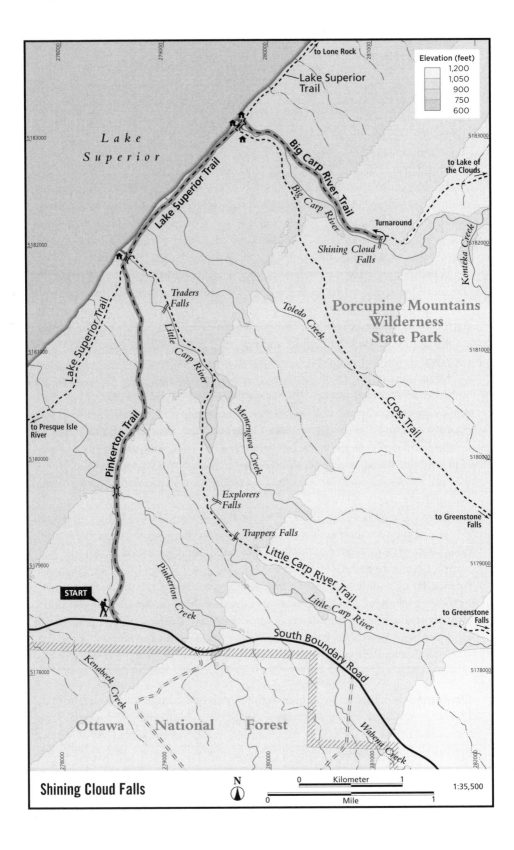

Shining Cloud Falls

Key Points

1.0 Pinkerton Creek.

2.9 Lake Superior Trail junction.

3.0 Little Carp River Trail junction.

4.2 Big Carp River Trail junction.

5.6 Shining Cloud Falls; turnaround point.

11.2 Pinkerton Trailhead.

7 Lake Superior Shoreline

Highlights: A wild Lake Superior shoreline chock-full of soul-satisfying solitude; broad views; and intricate, tilted bedrock strata.
Location: Porcupine Mountains Wilderness State Park (PMWSP).
Type of hike: Point-to-point.
Distance: 9 miles.
Difficulty: Difficult*.
Fees and permits: Michigan Department of Natural Resources vehicle sticker.
Best months: May through October.

Camping: Backcountry camping is permitted along the hike within the PMWSP regulations. Union Bay Campground, with one hundred campsites, is 5.5 miles east of the trailhead.
Maps: USGS quads Carp River; Government Peak quads; PMWSP map by Nequaket Natural History Associates (available at the visitor center).
Trail contact: Porcupine Mountains Wilderness State Park, (906) 885-5275.

Finding the trailhead: From the intersection of M–107 and South Boundary Road in PMWSP, drive west 6.4 miles to the Lake Superior Trailhead.

Special considerations: The start and finish of the hike are 3 miles apart along M–107. Six miles of this hike are off-trail. Although the navigation is relatively simple, this hike requires some competence and confidence. If you think that the quality of this outing would justify some precise footwork on the rocky shoreline, I would encourage you to sample it. Alternatively, if you have an intense dislike of rough trails, it is doubtful you would enjoy the shoreline portion of this hike. For some the tilted bedrock strata of the shoreline may be reminiscent of routes in the canyons of the Southwest—a delight. Also consider that this is a shoreline route. It can be glorious in fine weather and dreadfully exposed when high winds and squalls hit.

Remote shorelines are important wildlife habitat. As you are hiking be sure to give wildlife lots of elbowroom, especially during the spring and early summer nesting season.

Biting flies may be a factor along the shoreline in late June or early July. Check conditions at the PMWSP visitor center.

The pristine and picturesque Lake Superior coast east of Buckshot Landing.

The Hike

Having a vast stretch of Lake Superior shoreline to yourself has a way of growing on you. The appeal deepens when you realize that much of that shoreline features a tilted bedrock stratum, a playful obstacle course for nimble hikers, and a haven for miniature wildflower gardens tucked in rocky nooks and crannies.

Better yet, the hike begins with 3 downhill trail miles that offer several high views of Lake Superior and finishes with a memorable off-trail walk through cathedral groves of hemlock elders.

Begin your hike at the Lake Superior Trailhead on M–107, walking north. Initially the trail is broad, and a virgin hemlock forest marks the first few minutes of walking. The trail soon enters an area where the trees are stunted because a fire seared the soil and killed the nutrients.

The trail descends and now and then rises slightly on shallow ridges that mark ancient shorelines. Exploring the rock glades that dot these rises can yield rich rewards: secluded ledges with Lake Superior views. At Mile 1.3 a conglomerate spine of rock, a "whaleback," parallels the trail for 150 paces, offering more views and an alternative route for agile hikers.

At Mile 3.0 the trail reaches the spur for the Buckshot Cabin. Backtrack past the long boardwalk you just crossed to a small boardwalk bridge over a minor drainage. Follow the east side of that drainage north, off-trail, about 200 yards to the Lake Superior shore, which is marked by reefs of slanted bedrock.

This is a good time for a reality and weather check. With good conditions hike east, the beginning of the 5-mile shoreline segment of this hike. The bedrock quickly ends and another reality check begins. For about 1 mile the shore consists of hamburger-shaped cobble, footing that is tolerable but a bit of a tedious plod.

Persevere through the cobble stretch and the shoreline begins a bedrock rhythm I found most enjoyable. This is hiking similar to moderate white-water paddling—minor route-finding challenges are almost constant but hardly threatening. It's a world full of small wonders—lakeside rock featuring smooth wave-washed radiuses, springs, and seeps nourishing green patches; frogs in "tide pools"; mossy crevices; and tiny colonies of wildflowers. These are tough wildflowers, able to withstand the full force of Lake Superior gales.

Beyond the intricate shoreline scene, the big wonder—the largest freshwater lake on Earth—seems to stretch forever. Bald eagles patrolled the coast, veering offshore as they spotted me.

After 4 miles of shoreline hiking, a wide bay begins. A mile later, at the middle of that broad indentation in the coast, Cuyahoga Creek enters the lake. A mere dribble in late summer, it crosses the bedrock in a series of pools. Just east of the creek's flowing water, take a slightly worn path that leads off the rocks into the forest. The path and a forested flat quickly end at a steep, but short slope. The route is simple. Ascend and stay just east of Cuyahoga Creek, as close to the rim of its ravine as practical and hike 1 mile south, off-trail through the open forest to where the creek crosses M–107, just east of the Government Peak Trailhead. There are a few minor brushy areas, but in general the forest is open, old, and elegant and the travel pleasant. Here and there traces of a deer path line the rim of the ravine, easing your way. However, much of the way features impressive hemlock elders and it was tempting to stay with them rather than walk out to the road and the end of the hike.

Options: Combine this hike with the Escarpment Trail and you have an outstanding 13.6-mile loop, which ends with a 1-mile road walk. From the Government Peak Trailhead follow that trail south 0.1 mile then turn right (west) onto the Escarpment Trail. Follow that trail west 3.6 miles, past sweeping views, to the Lake of the Clouds Trailhead. From there hike the broad grassy shoulder of M–107 east and north 1 mile to the Lake Superior Trailhead.

Alternatively consider a shorter hike to Lake Superior. The 6-mile round-trip hike to the shoreline east of Buckshot Cabin features both high views of Lake Superior from rock ledges and a perfect break spot on the shore. Depart from the Lake Superior Trailhead on M–107.

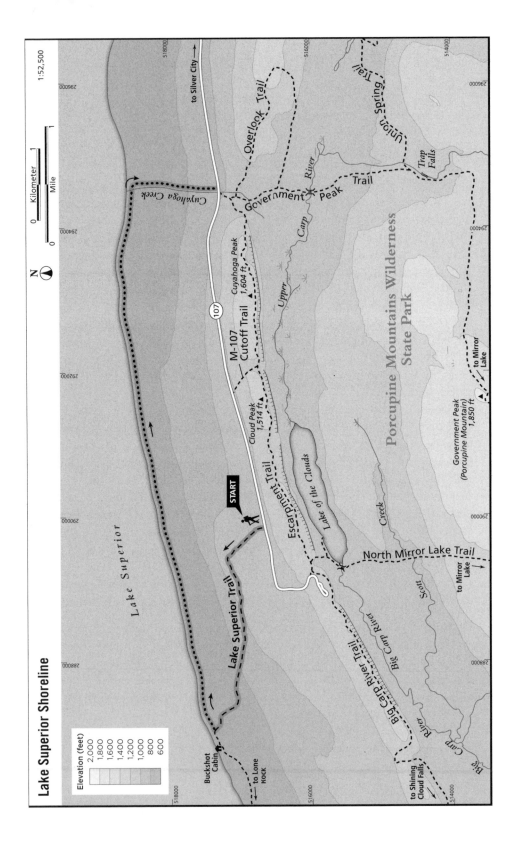

Lake Superior Shoreline

1:52,500

Key Points

0.0 Lake Superior Trailhead on M-107.

1.3 "Whaleback" conglomerate rock parallels trail.

3.0 Buckshot Cabin spur.

3.1 Lake Superior shoreline.

8.0 Mouth of Cuyahoga Creek.

9.0 M-107 at Cuyahoga Creek (Government Peak Trailhead).

8 Lake Superior/Big Carp River Loop

Highlights: A classic loop featuring the Lake Superior shore, cascades of the Big Carp River, Shining Cloud Falls, old-growth forest, and broad views from the escarpment.
Location: Porcupine Mountains Wilderness State Park (PMWSP).
Type of hike: Loop.
Distance: 20.5 miles.
Difficulty: Difficult.
Fees and permits: Michigan Department of Natural Resources vehicle sticker.
Best months: May through October.

Camping: Backcountry camping along the trail is available within PMWSP guidelines. Four of the park's backcountry cabins—Buckshot, Big Carp 6, Lake Superior 4, and Big Carp 4—line the hike's route. Union Bay Campground, with one hundred campsites, is 5.5 miles east of the trailhead.
Maps: USGS Carp River (inc.) quad; PMWSP map by Nequaket Natural History Associates (available at the visitor center).
Trail contact: Porcupine Mountains Wilderness State Park, (906) 885-5275.

Finding the trailhead: From the intersection of M-107 and South Boundary Road in PMWSP, drive west 6.4 miles to the Lake Superior Trailhead.

Special considerations: Parts of the Lake Superior Trail can be muddy in wet periods. Waterproof boots and trekking poles are handy for puddle hopping. Between Shining Cloud Falls and the junction with the Correction Line Trail, the Big Carp River Trail fords its namesake stream. The last mile of the hike follows the grassy shoulder of M-107.

Biting flies may be a factor along the shoreline in late June or early July. Check conditions at the PMWSP visitor center.

The Hike

This hike has it all. Every scenic attraction that draws hikers to the Porkies is here. Rock balconies in the first few miles offer broad Lake Superior views, before the trail descends to parallel the lake's wave-washed shore. After a 6-mile-long sojourn near the big lake, the route turns inland, ascending alongside the cascading Big Carp River to Shining Cloud Falls. After the 10-mile mark, old-growth forest brackets the rest of the hike's path as the trail winds its way up the Big Carp River Valley, passing below the cliffs of Miscowawbic Peak. For a grand finale the hike switchbacks

Grand finale on the Big Carp River Trail—sweeping views along the Escarpment.

up to the Escarpment and offers a parade of far-reaching views from that ridge's heights.

Begin your hike by walking north, on the broad Lake Superior Trail, from the trailhead on M–107. For a few minutes the trail passes through a forest of old-growth hemlock, but that soon changes to a much younger stunted growth, an area where fire seared the soil after logging occurred one hundred years ago.

Every now and then the trail interrupts its descent, pausing on rises that mark ancient shorelines. Typically these shallow ridges feature rock glades; a little poking around on these slabs often yields your own private viewpoint. A conglomerate spine of rock parallels the trail for 150 paces at Mile 1.3, offering more views and an alternative route for nimble hikers.

At Mile 3.0 the trail reaches the spur for the Buckshot Cabin. Respect the privacy of the cabin folks, but consider visiting a memorable break spot nearby on the slanted reefs of bedrock along the Lake Superior shore. To reach it backtrack past the long boardwalk you just crossed to a small boardwalk bridge over a minor drainage. Follow the east side of that drainage north, off-trail, about 200 yards to the shoreline. Then retrace your steps to the Lake Superior Trail and continue hiking westward. For the next several miles, the path skirts the lakeshore, typically a little inland. You will hear waves but not always see them.

Periodically, short spur trails run to the shore, often at campsites. Aptly named Lone Rock rises a quarter mile offshore, near one of these spur paths, at Mile 5.5. About a mile later the trail begins 1-mile-long segment that is actually on the shore, or just barely inland. A rise to a low ridge, a dip to the shore, and another rise brings the trail to the bluff above the mouth of the Big Carp River.

Bear left (south) on the Big Carp River Trail at Mile 9.0 as the Lake Superior Trail continues right (west). The Big Carp River trail runs south and east, first on a bluff above the river's dancing cascades, then at river level.

About a mile from the lake, the trail ascends another bluff and soon arrives at a cliff-top view of Shining Cloud Falls, 50 feet below, at Mile 10.4. Shining Cloud is a bi-level falls. First the flow drops 10 feet to a ledge, then it splits evenly and tumbles another 12 feet to a pool below. In its second drop the left side cascades down a rock ramp, while the right side is more of a vertical free fall.

Safely descending to the bottom of the falls safely takes some judgment and balance. First continue east on the trail until you are above the top of the falls. The first routes that appear below you are dangerous. A little farther on you will notice steep, switchbacking dirt paths descending to the top of the falls. When the river is at moderate flow levels, a rock ramp there is dry and leads to the bottom of the falls. Whether that rock ramp is a safe move on any given day is a judgment you will have to make when you are there.

Continue hiking eastward on the Big Carp River Trail, arriving at a ford of its namesake stream at mile 13.0. At typical summertime river levels, this is an easy wade, not even knee deep. Bear left (north) on the Big Carp River Trail at Mile 14.0 as the Correction Line Trail goes right (east).

About a quarter mile north of that junction, the Big Carp River Trail crosses its namesake stream again, this time on a sturdy bridge. The trail soon begins a nearly 2-mile-long run beneath the slopes of Lafayette and Miscowawbic Peaks. After traveling through memorable hemlock cathedrals, the trail passes beneath Miscowawbic Peak's cliffs, ascends to a saddle, and continues to the top of the Escarpment. There notable views stretch to the east, past Lake of the Clouds to Cuyahoga Peak, while a blue swath of Lake Superior shows to the west, past Lafayette Peak's rounded summit. Copper Peak's ski jump, 20-some miles off, pierces the southwest horizon. Beginning at Mile 17.7, and for the next half-mile or so, the views are near constant. This is an open stretch of trail locals call "The Meadows."

Viewpoints continue but become more intermittent as you hike east and arrive at the trailhead, the parking lot for the Lake of the Clouds Overlook at mile 19.5. Walk east through the large parking lot and continue east and north on M–107. The shoulder is wide and grassy, allowing safe passage to the hike's end, the Lake Superior Trailhead at Mile 20.5.

Lake Superior/Big Carp River Loop

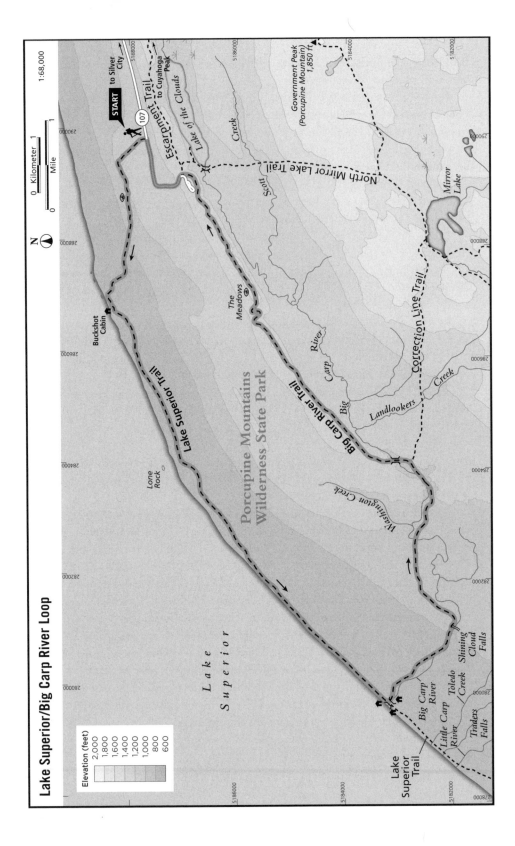

1:68,000

Elevation (feet)
2,000
1,800
1,600
1,400
1,200
1,000
800
600

Lake Superior

Porcupine Mountains
Wilderness State Park

Lake Superior Trail

Buckshot Cabin

Lone Rock

START to Silver City

107

Escarpment Trail

to Cuyahoga Peak

Lake of the Clouds

Scott Creek

North Mirror Lake Trail

Big Carp River Trail

Carp River

Big Carp River

The Meadows

Landlookers Creek

Correction Line Trail

Mirror Lake

Government Peak (Porcupine Mountain) 1,850 ft

Washington Creek

Shining Cloud Falls

Big Carp River

Little Carp River

Toledo Creek

Trailers Falls

Lake Superior Trail

N

Options: A 6-mile out-and-back hike to the shoreline east of the Buckshot Cabin features both high views of Lake Superior from rock ledges and a perfect break spot on the shore. Depart from the Lake Superior Trailhead on M–107.

Another short alternative, at the end of the hike's loop, offers sweeping views and quiet ambience. That outing is a 4-mile round-trip on the Big Carp River Trail to "The Meadows." From the intersection of M–107 and South Boundary Road, drive 7.5 miles west on M–107 to the Big Carp River Trailhead. Then hike 2 miles southwest on that trail.

Key Points

0.0	Lake Superior Trailhead on M-107.
1.3	"Whaleback" conglomerate rock parallels trail.
3.0	Buckshot Cabin spur.
5.5	Lone Rock.
9.0	Mouth of the Big Carp River.
10.4	Shining Cloud Falls.
13.0	Ford of Big Carp River.
14.0	Junction with Correction Line Trail.
17.7	The Meadows.
19.5	Big Carp River Trailhead, end of M-107.
20.5	Lake Superior Trailhead on M-107.

$\mathcal{9}$ Little Carp River Cascades

Highlights: The waterfalls and cascades of the Little Carp River and old-growth forest.
Location: Porcupine Mountains Wilderness State Park (PMWSP).
Type of hike: Point-to-point.
Distance: 9.6 miles.
Difficulty: Moderate.
Fees and permits: Michigan Department of Natural Resources vehicle sticker.
Best months: May through October. River crossings will be more difficult in periods of high water.

Camping: Backcountry camping is available along the trail, within PMWSP regulations. The park's Presque Isle Campground has fifty campsites and is 5 miles west of the Pinkerton Trailhead.
Maps: USGS Tiebel Creek, Carp River quad; PMWSP map by Nequaket Natural History Associates (available at the visitor center).
Trail contact: Porcupine Mountains Wilderness State Park, (906) 885–5275.

Finding the trailhead: From the intersection of M–107 and South Boundary Road, in PMWSP, drive south and west 19.7 miles to the Pinkerton Trailhead.

Special considerations: The Little Carp River Trail fords its namesake stream twice. I found these crossings an easy rock hop during a low-water period in August. At other times they would be a wade. During high-water episodes, they might be dangerous or impossible.

The Hike

This is a poetic route. Elegant old-growth forest begins a few minutes from the trailhead and stays with you until the end of the outing. Three miles down the trail, the sights and sounds of the cascading Little Carp River join in, a near constant companion for the rest of the hike. Another water theme, Lake Superior's shore, is available as a short side-trip.

Begin your hike by walking north on the broad Pinkerton Trail as it drops ever so gradually to the bridge over Pinkerton Creek at Mile 1.0. A bench overlooks the stream, a shady scene of low bedrock ledges and gentle riffles in midsummer.

About a mile later, after threading through memorable hemlock groves, the path reaches another bench. This one is on a bluff high above the swirling cascades of the Little Carp River. The trail swings northward and reaches a junction with the Lake Superior Trail at Mile 2.9. Turn right (east) following the Lake Superior Trail across the bridge over the Little Carp River. You'll reach the junction with the Little Carp River Trail at Mile 3.0.

For a worthy side trip, turn left (northwest) and walk 0.2 mile on the Lake Superior Trail to the cobble and bedrock shoreline of Lake Superior, the Earth's largest freshwater lake. When you are ready, retrace your steps to the junction of the Lake Superior and Little Carp Trails.

From this junction turn right (east) and hike upstream on the Little Carp River Trail. After a quick ascent and descent of a bluff, the trail settles down to follow the

Greenstone Falls, part of the Little Carp River's striking white-water parade.

rushing river and crosses it at Mile 4.1. Now on the west side of the river, the trail winds through a flood plain forest; an overflow channel is nearby. About a mile after the crossing, a scene of subtle beauty unfolds as a series of swirling cascades drops through mossy bedrock formations.

As mesmerizing as the cascades were, I found the next scene to be even more memorable. The river runs down a huge waterslide, roughly 70 feet long and 20 feet high, known as Trappers Falls. Due to the pebbly nature of the conglomerate bedrock, the water shoots up in a zillion small ripples as it races down the slope. When I was there the cascade was backlit, and it was a brilliant, pulsating spectacle.

Just above Trappers Falls the trail crosses the river. About a mile later, the path ascends a low bluff, offering glimpses of cascades 50 yards down slope with picturesque virgin timber framing the view. Watch for some outstanding specimens of white pine trees in this stretch, near a backcountry campsite.

Continue hiking eastward on the Little Carp River Trail as it ascends a low bluff and meets the junction with the Cross Trail at Mile 8.5. Bear right (south); the Cross Trail goes left (north). Soon after the junction the path descends back to the river and a bench by a campsite.

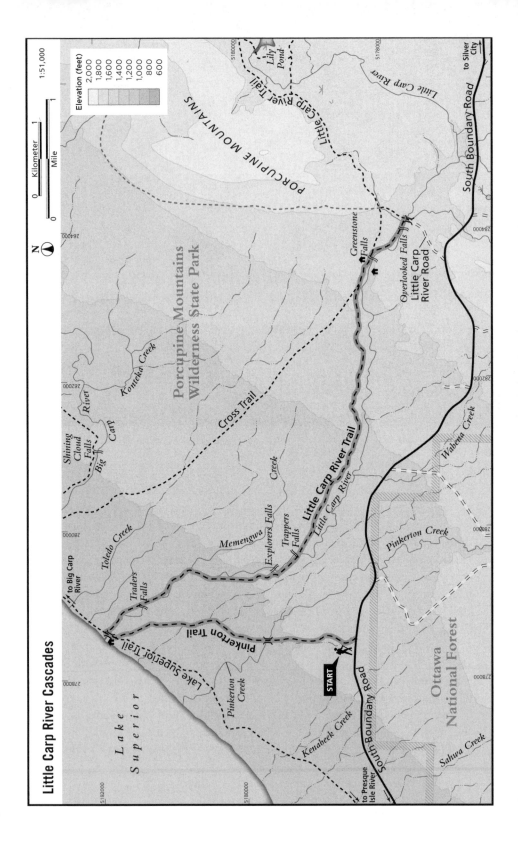

Little Carp River Cascades

A stretch of charming cascades leads past the Greenstone Falls cabin. At Mile 8.9 the trail arrives at Greenstone Falls, a 6-foot drop that is well worth a break. From there hike east, reaching the well-marked junction of the spur trail that leads to the Little Carp River Road at Mile 9.2.

Turn right (south) on the Little Carp River Road spur trail. Just before the spur trail reaches the road, a series of cascades, including Overlooked Falls, warrants a visit. At Mile 9.6 the spur trail reaches the Little Carp River Road, the end of the hike.

Options: A 6.5-mile round-trip hike to the mouth of the Little Carp River from the Pinkerton Trailhead has considerable appeal. This shorter outing features the forest scenes along the Pinkerton Trail, the charming cascades of the Little Carp River, and the Lake Superior shore.

Another compelling alternative is a 1.4-mile out-and-back hike from the Little Carp River Trailhead to Greenstone Falls. This stretch of river, including the 7-foot drop at Overlooked Falls, is a gem.

Key Points

0.0 Pinkerton Trailhead.

1.0 Pinkerton Creek.

2.9 Lake Superior Trail junction.

3.0 Little Carp River Trail junction.

4.1 Little Carp River Trail crosses river.

5.5 Trappers Falls; Little Carp River Trail crosses river.

8.5 Cross Trail junction.

8.9 Greenstone Falls.

9.2 Spur trail to Little Carp River Road.

9.6 Little Carp River Road.

10 Mirror Lake Loop

Highlights: A loop through the wild core of the Porcupine Mountains, virgin forest, wilderness lakes, clear-running streams, and spectacular views.

Location: Porcupine Mountains Wilderness State Park (PMWSP).

Type of hike: Loop.

Distance: 12.4 miles.

Difficulty: Difficult.

Fees and permits: Michigan Department of Natural Resources vehicle sticker.

Best months: May through October.

Camping: PMWSP's Union Bay Campground, with one hundred campsites is 7 miles east of the trailhead. Backpack camping, within PMWSP regulations, is permitted along the trail.

Maps: USGS Carp River quad (inc.); PMWSP by Nequaket Natural History Associates (available at the visitor center).

Trail contact: Porcupine Mountains Wilderness State Park, (906) 885-5275.

Finding the trailhead: From the intersection of M-107 and South Boundary Road in PMWSP, drive 7.5 miles west on M-107 to the North Mirror Lake Trailhead.

The Hike

Picture a hike that begins at a famous viewpoint and then wanders through hemlock cathedrals to a wilderness lake. From that serene pond, aptly named Mirror Lake, the hike immerses itself in a memorable route through impressive old-growth forest. For a grand finale, the hike offers a ridge walk, with long sight lines stretching to Lake Superior.

Begin your hike at the North Mirror Lake Trailhead, at the far eastern end of the Lake of the Clouds Overlook parking area. Walk east, following the North Mirror Lake Trail as it first ascends a low knob and then descends its east side. During that rocky descent, several short, unofficial paths lead off to the right (south) to worthwhile viewpoints overlooking Lake of the Clouds.

When you are ready, resume your hike eastward on the North Mirror Lake Trail, bearing right (south) at a junction with the Escarpment Trail at Mile 0.3. Follow the North Mirror Lake Trail as it descends, sometimes steeply, to the bridge over Lake of the Cloud's outlet, the Big Carp River, at Mile 0.7.

The trail then runs south. It first climbs slowly, then eases into a steep ascent. That steeper stretch, about a mile south of Lake of the Clouds, parallels a memorable scene: A small stream tumbles down a shady gorge set in a hemlock cathedral. Those hemlocks aren't the only notable forest scenery on this hike. Once past Lake of the Clouds, the rest of the route passes through virgin forest.

Continue hiking south as the path reaches the top of the slope and descends to a trail junction at Mile 3.0. Bear right (west) on the North Mirror Lake Trail as the Government Peak Trail goes left (east). The North Mirror Lake Trail runs southwest, crosses a marsh on a boardwalk, and reaches its namesake at Mile 4.0. It then skirts

The Mirror Lake loop's last miles offer spectacular views along the Escarpment to Cuyahoga Peak.

the shoreline, arriving at another junction at Mile 4.3. There, turn right (northwest) onto the Correction Line Trail as the North Mirror Lake Trail goes left (southwest).

Hike northwest as the trail ascends a short, steep slope before passing through a fern garden flanked by a rock wall. This stretch has a well-earned reputation for pleasing forest scenes. Sugar maples, basswood, and yellow birch add to the setting here, but it is a broad swath of hemlock, about a mile west of Mirror Lake, that stands out in my memory. That hemlock stand is old, open forest—elegant and enchanting. This, and other forest scenes in the Porkies, brings a revelation: The whole Northwoods once looked like this. It must have been magnificent.

The Correction Line Trail descends westward, crossing Landlookers Creek at Mile 6.5 and reaching a trail junction at Mile 7.3. There, turn right (north) onto the Big Carp River Trail and follow it across a bridge over its namesake stream.

Soon after that bridge the Big Carp River Trail begins to run along the bottom of the Escarpment's slope. Here too, the hemlock groves are hauntingly delightful. At Mile 9.8 the path offers a unique perspective of the Escarpment's cliffs—a view of Miscowawbic Peak's rock face from its base.

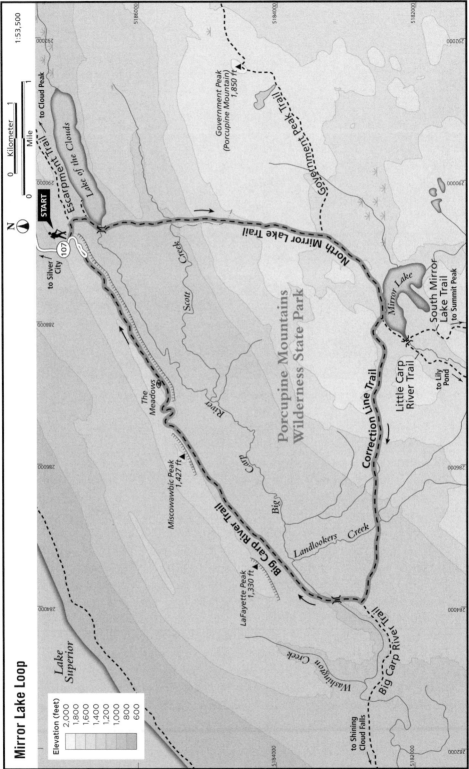

Mirror Lake Loop

Elevation (feet)
2,000
1,800
1,600
1,400
1,200
1,000
800
600

1:53,500

0   Kilometer   1

0   Mile   1

N

Lake Superior

to Silver City

107

START

Escarpment Trail

→ to Cloud Peak

Lake of the Clouds

Government Peak (Porcupine Mountain) 1,850 ft

Government Peak Trail

North Mirror Lake Trail

Scott Creek

Porcupine Mountains Wilderness State Park

Mirror Lake

South Mirror Lake Trail to Summit Peak

Little Carp River Trail

to Lily Pond

Correction Line Trail

The Meadows

Miscowawbic Peak 1,427 ft

Big Carp River Trail

Big Carp River

Landlookers Creek

LaFayette Peak 1,330 ft

Washington Creek

Big Carp River Trail

to Shining Cloud Falls

Now ascending, the path swings into a saddle east of Miscowawbic Peak, switchbacks up to the Escarpment, and arrives at a memorable open area known as "The Meadows" at Mile 10.5. For the next half mile, a parade of sweeping views passes to the right of the trail. Long sight lines stretch east to Lake of the Clouds and Cloud Peak beyond, while Lake Superior appears to the southwest, beyond Lafayette Peak's rise. With the hike rapidly winding down, this is a good place to take a break and enjoy the views.

Continue hiking eastward, reaching the Lake of the Clouds overlook and the Big Carp River Trailhead at Mile 12.3. The Big Carp River Trailhead is at the west end of the Lake of the Clouds overlook parking area. Walk 0.1 mile to the east end of the parking area to reach the hike's starting point, the North Mirror Lake Trailhead.

Option: One enticing alternative is to access The Meadows from the Big Carp River Trailhead at the west end of the Lake of the Clouds overlook parking area. Walk west 1.5 miles on the Big Carp River Trail to reach The Meadows. This option offers comparatively easy access to a notable place with outstanding views.

Key Points

- **0.0** North Mirror Lake Trailhead.
- **0.3** Escarpment Trail junction.
- **0.7** Lake of the Clouds.
- **3.0** Government Peak Trail junction.
- **4.0** Mirror Lake.
- **4.3** Correction Line Trail junction.
- **6.5** Landlookers Creek.
- **7.3** Big Carp River Trail junction.
- **7.5** Big Carp River Bridge.
- **9.8** Miscowawbic Peak cliffs.
- **10.5** The Meadows.
- **12.3** Big Carp River Trailhead.
- **12.4** North Mirror Lake Trailhead.

11 Escarpment

Highlights: A ridge walk offering a parade of sweeping views.
Location: Porcupine Mountains Wilderness State Park (PMWSP).
Type of hike: Out-and-back.
Distance: 6.4 miles.
Difficulty: Moderate.
Fees and permits: Michigan Department of Natural Resources vehicle sticker.
Best months: May through October.

Camping: PMWSP's Union Bay Campground, with one hundred campsites, is 2.5 miles east of the trailhead. Backpack camping, within PMWSP regulations, is allowed along the trail.
Maps: USGS Carp River, Government Peak quads; PMWSP by Nequaket Natural History Associates (available at the visitor center).
Trail contact: Porcupine Mountains Wilderness State Park, (906) 885-5275.

Finding the trailhead: From the intersection of M-107 and South Boundary Road in PMWSP, drive 3.5 miles west on M-107 to the Government Peak Trailhead.
Special considerations: The Escarpment Trail follows an exposed ridgeline. Although often glorious in fine weather, it may not be a pleasant place to be in high winds or thunderstorms.

The Hike

For many Porkies' veterans, the Escarpment is at the top of any "don't miss" list of outings in the park. Open meadows on this ridgetop offer long sight lines and memorable views of the area's landmarks. Far to the west, past Lafayette Peak's craggy south face, Lake Superior sparkles in the distance. Off to the southeast the Trap Hills dimple the horizon. Hundreds of feet below the Escarpment's craggy heights, Lake of the Clouds feeds the headwaters of the Big Carp River.

Begin your Escarpment hike by walking southwest on the broad, rocky Government Peak Trail as it ascends into the woods above the trailhead. One hundred ninety paces later, at Mile 0.1, bear right (southwest) on the Escarpment Trail as the Government Peak Trail goes left (southeast).

The Escarpment Trail soon settles into a steady ascent, reaching the first views at about Mile 0.6. An opening in the woods, a mixture of meadow and bedrock, offers long sight lines to the southeast, where the Trap Hills dot the horizon. Here a pattern develops. Five more minutes of uphill hiking brings you to another viewpoint. It's similar in orientation to the first, but the added elevation adds a new sight to the eastern view: the deep blue of Lake Superior.

Another five minutes of walking, with the trail still rising, brings striking new vistas. For the first time they are to the west. Below the Escarpment's long ridgeline, mile-long Lake of the Clouds appears; beyond the ridge Lake Superior shows. Here, at Mile 1.2 of the hike, Cuyahoga Peak's wooded high point is a little north of the trail.

As you continue walking west, the plateaulike ridge becomes more open and the views broader, stretching east, south, and west. There is an airy feeling to this stretch,

Views from the Escarpment Trail stretch past Lake of the Clouds to Lafayette Peak and beyond.

a delightful sense of height, long sight lines, and a pristine landscape as far as the eye can see.

The path descends into a wooded saddle in the ridgeline, reaching a junction with the M–107 Cutoff Trail at Mile 2.0. Go straight (west) on the Escarpment Trail, as the M–107 Cutoff Trail leads off to the right (north).

Ascending from the saddle, the trail reaches Cloud Peak at Mile 2.3. A tad lower than Cuyahoga Peak, Cloud Peak still offers memorable views. I spotted Copper Peak 15 miles to the southwest. A half-mile off and 500 vertical feet below me, the rhythmic wing beat of a great blue heron caught my attention as the bird cruised along the Lake of the Clouds shoreline.

After Cloud Peak, the trail dips and rolls as it runs west before rising to another high point at Mile 3.2, a crest sometimes known as Peregrine Peak. Hikers visiting in June may spot the peak's namesake falcons, a species famous for their 100-mile-an-hour, stun gun–like dives to knock out prey. Whether or not falcons are nearby, this is another memorable viewpoint and a fine place to linger. It also makes a suitable turnaround spot for the hike. Retrace your steps eastward to return to the trailhead.

Options: Several other choices are available to enjoy the Escarpment's views. From Peregrine Peak, you could continue hiking west, reaching the Lake of the Clouds

Escarpment

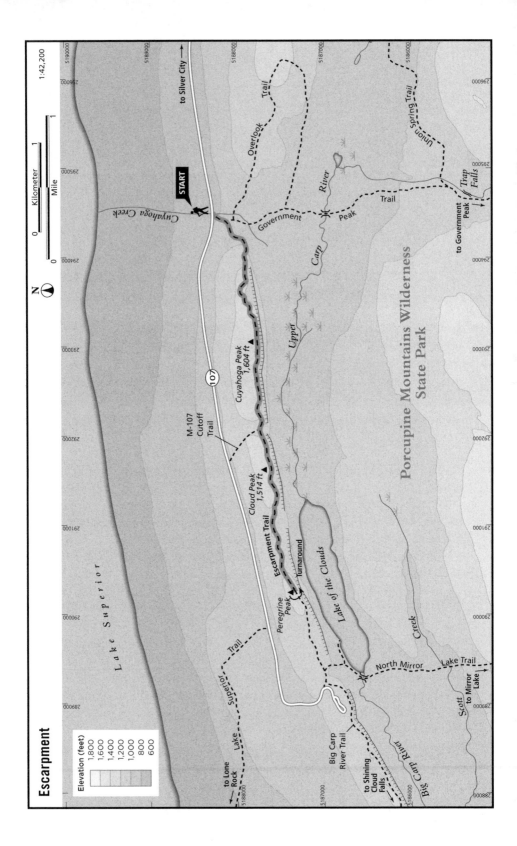

Elevation (feet)
1,800
1,600
1,400
1,200
1,000
800
600

1:42,200

N

0   Kilometer   1
0   Mile   1

Lake Superior

Cuyahoga Creek

START

to Silver City

Overlook Trail

Government Trail

Carp River Peak

to Government Peak

Trap Falls

Union Spring Trail

Cuyahoga Peak 1,604 ft

M-107 Cutoff Trail

Cloud Peak 1,514 ft

Escarpment Trail

Turnaround

Peregrine Peak

Upper Carp River

Lake of the Clouds

North Mirror Lake Trail

Scott Creek

to Mirror Lake

Porcupine Mountains Wilderness State Park

Superior Lake Trail

to Lone Rock

Big Carp River Trail

to Shining Cloud Falls

Big Carp River

107

overlook 0.8 mile later. A major parking lot is nearby; don't expect solitude here on a fine afternoon. What is beyond the Lake of the Clouds overlook is highly motivating, however. The Big Carp River Trail runs west, and for a while the views play peek-a-boo as the trail skirts the forest's edge. About 1.5 miles west of the Lake of the Clouds overlook, the path reaches an open stretch locals call "The Meadows." The next half mile, before the trail switchbacks off the Escarpment, is sublime. Views are outstanding and trail traffic is remarkably light.

One other choice is worth considering. Drive to the trailhead of the Lake of the Clouds overlook by traveling 7.5 miles west on M–107 from the intersection of M–107 and South Boundary Road. From there, walk west 1.5 miles on the Big Carp River Trail to reach The Meadows. This option offers comparatively easy access to a picturesque place, and splendid views.

Key Points

- **0.0** Government Peak Trailhead.
- **0.1** Escarpment Trail junction.
- **1.2** Cuyahoga Peak.
- **2.0** M–107 Cutoff Trail.
- **2.3** Cloud Peak.
- **3.2** Peregrine Peak; turnaround point.
- **6.4** Government Peak Trailhead.

12 Union River Cascades Loop

Highlights: A compact collection of small waterfalls, waterslides, and cascades.
Location: Porcupine Mountains Wilderness State Park (PMWSP).
Type of hike: Loop.
Distance: 1 mile.
Difficulty: Moderate.
Fees and permits: Michigan Department of Natural Resources vehicle sticker.

Best months: May through October.
Camping: PMWSP's Union Bay Campground, 3 miles northwest of the trailhead, has one hundred campsites.
Maps: USGS Government Peak (inc.), White Pine (inc.) quads.
Trail contact: Porcupine Mountains Wilderness State Park, (906) 885-5275.

Finding the trailhead: From the intersection of M–107 and South Boundary Road in PMWSP, drive south a little less than 2 miles. Turn right (west) into the parking area for the Union Mine Trail.

Special considerations: Water levels affect the white-water show here. The Union River's gurgling cascades maintain their charm even in low-water periods. Nearby, the Little Union River Gorge's spectacular waterfall show tends to be a "now and then" event. *The Porcupine Mountains Companion,* a well-grounded reference by Michael Rafferty and Robert Sprague, describes one of these waterfalls, when it is flowing, as the highest in the park, with a 30-foot drop. During dry spells the gorge's mossy nooks and crannies are memorable, but the stream's flow is barely a trickle.

The Hike

Every time I visit the Union River, my usual brisk hiking pace slows to a halt. It is a place reminiscent of an art gallery with a theme of falling water, and it seems counterproductive to rush from display to display.

Begin your hike at the Union Mine Trailhead. Note that a series of numbered posts and a trail guide brochure found at the trailhead suggest a clockwise tour of this loop trail. I'm suggesting the opposite—a counterclockwise direction around the circuit. My premise is that the Union River cascades, not the mine remains, are the major attraction here, and upstream travel offers optimum viewing.

At the southwest corner of the trailhead's parking area, a path runs south and enters the woods. Hike south then east on that path, reaching South Boundary Road at Mile 0.1. Cross the road to its east side and follow the trail into the woods.

To the south of the trail, the mossy cleft known as the Little Union River Gorge begins with a rock wall that is the park's highest waterfall, *when it is flowing.* Continue hiking east, following the Union Mine Trail along the rim of the shady canyon; a giant hemlock marks a turn in the watercourse. At Mile 0.3 of the hike, a trail marker notes an old mining dig, and the path swings north.

Hike north on the Union Mine Trail, arriving at Union River (Mile 0.6) just west of the Union River Outpost Road's bridge. The path swings southwest here,

Long sets of delightful cascades line the Union River.

paralleling the stream and a long, charming waterslide. Continue hiking west, upstream, as the river forms a series of cascades.

Cross South Boundary Road at Mile 0.8, following the Union Mine Trail southwest to one last water show. Miners altered a 4-foot drop here to accommodate a water wheel.

From that last cascade the trail turns south then quickly east, returning to the trailhead at Mile 1.0.

Option: Hikers with confidence in their off-trail hiking skills will find rich rewards if they opt to expand the Union Mine Trail Loop. Downstream of the trail both streams offer notable scenery, cascades, and solitude. This alternative would start at Mile 0.3 of the hike described above. Hike east, along the north side of the Little Union River Gorge (instead of following the Union Mine Trail north).

Key Points

0.0   Union Mine Trailhead.

0.1   First Crossing of South Boundary Road.

0.3   Trail leaves Little Union River Gorge.

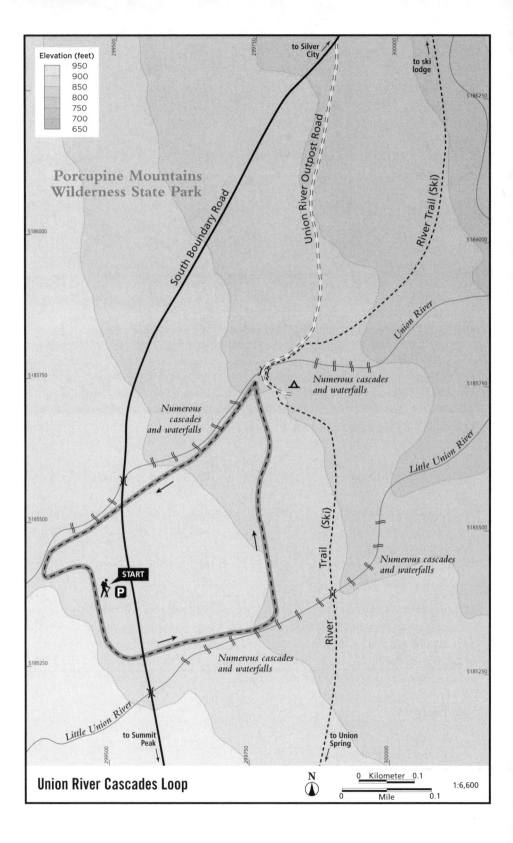

Elevation (feet)
950
900
850
800
750
700
650

Porcupine Mountains
Wilderness State Park

to Silver
City

to ski
lodge

5186250

Union River Outpost Road

River Trail (Ski)

5186000

5186000

South Boundary Road

Union River

Numerous cascades
and waterfalls

5185750

5185750

Numerous
cascades
and waterfalls

Little Union River

5185500

5185500

START

P

Numerous cascades
and waterfalls

Trail (Ski)

River

Numerous cascades
and waterfalls

5185250

5185250

Little Union River

to Summit
Peak

to Union
Spring

Union River Cascades Loop

N

0   Kilometer   0.1

0   Mile   0.1

1:6,600

0.6 Trail meets Union River.

0.8 Second Crossing of South Boundary Road.

1.0 Union Mine Trailhead.

13 Trap Hills Loop

Highlights: Spectacular views, solitude, and a quiet forest setting in the wild core of the Trap Hills.

Location: 4 miles north of Bergland.

Type of hike: Loop.

Distance: 6.1 miles.

Difficulty: Difficult*.

Fees and permits: None, but consider a contribution to the Trap Hills Conservation Alliance, a campaign to gain protection for the Trap Hills, www.traphills.org; or the North Country Trail Association, www.northcountrytrail.org.

Best months: May through October.

Camping: Backpack camping along the trail, within zero-impact guidelines. Bergland Township Park, 4 miles south of the trailhead, has fifteen campsites.

Maps: USGS Bergland NE quad (inc.); North Country Trail Map TMI14; Cascade Falls to Ironwood.

Trail contact: Ottawa National Forest, (906) 932-1330, www.fs.fed.us/r9/ottawa; North Country Trail Association Web site, www.northcountrytrail.org/pwf.

Finding the trailhead: From the town of Bergland, drive north 2.0 miles on M-64 and turn right (east) on old M-64 (gravel). Drive east and north 3.9 miles on old M-64. There, turn right (east) on Forest Road 326 and drive 0.7 mile to the North Country Trail (NCT). About 100 yards west of the NCT crossing, a wide shoulder offers parking.

Special considerations: Note that the spur trail from FR 326 to the hack site is a path that has thin wear marks but viable marking (vertical white paint blazes). A few spots on the NCT are similar. This loop includes a mile of road walking on FR 326, a quiet forest lane. Use caution on the viewpoints, many of which are atop sheer cliffs.

The Hike

I was stunned when I first saw the Trap Hills. Huge, mesmerizing views; a beautiful older forest; soul-satisfying solitude; and a trail that seemed to be the proverbial miles of smiles had me on cloud nine. Part of the attraction was the long views—oceans of trees, forest stretching 50 miles or so to the far-off horizon. Better yet was the sheer mystery of the place, the feeling that in the Trap Hills exploration reaped rich rewards. The open, older forest invited rambling, and I kept finding new overlooks with memorable views—high-rock balconies where the lichen didn't show a single scuff mark from boots. Forest glens, chock-full of subtle ambience, were tucked into the hollows.

This hike offers a convincing sample of the Trap Hills' charms in a bite-size loop. Energetic hikers looking for a few more miles can venture east on the NCT (see

Storm over Lake Gogebic. The Trap Hills loop offers long sight lines and sweeping panoramas from the heights of a remote, pristine headland.

options). Or you may want to sample a classic Trap Hills pastime—looking for new viewpoints. Typically the trail runs a stone's throw "inland," usually north, of the bluff's edge. While walking the trail scan for openings in the forest canopy in the direction of the bluff's rim and investigate.

Begin your outing where the NCT crosses FR 326. Walk southeast, uphill, on the NCT, a narrow but defined footpath entering the woods. Steadily climbing, the path passes a curious reddish boulder before approaching the top of a knoll. A rock outcrop offers northwest views—the Bergland fire tower two miles off and broad ridges of the Porkies beyond.

Descending the knoll's east side, the NCT swings southward. First it crosses a small valley, then it crosses a low ridge, and then it drops to an intersection with the Gogebic Ridge Tail at Mile 1.6. Bear left (south) on the NCT as the Gogebic Ridge Trail goes right (west).

Continue on the NCT, first rock hopping a small creek and then ascending steeply through an older maple forest. At the top of that uphill, watch for a rock outcrop about 15 feet to the right (northwest) of the trail. That ledge offers a worthwhile view to the northwest.

Heading southeast the NCT nears the southern corner of the Trap Hills' high plateau, swings northeast, and begins a miles-long run in that direction. About a half mile later, the trail nears the bluff's edge, and an open slope below the trail, partially screened by stunted trees, offers expansive views.

Continue hiking northeast on the NCT as it dips to a saddle and then ascends in a southerly direction. Topping out, the trail passes over grassy bedrock near a south-facing corner of a knoll, and a faint spur trail leads southwest thirty paces. There, a rock outcrop offers long views to the southwest, where a corner of Lake Gogebic peeks out from what seems to be an endless scene of undulating ridge and forest.

Resume walking northeast on the NCT. About a quarter-mile later the path again nears the edge of the bluff. A faint spur trail leads south, downhill, 50 feet to striking views. A ledge-top opening here, roughly 80 feet wide and clear of trees, offers sweeping vistas southeast, south, and southwest. These are stunning views. However, a little less than a half mile farther east are vistas that rival these. Walk east, passing over the top of the knoll marked 1,772 on maps (the highest point on this headland). As the trail nears the 4.1 mile point, it comes near the bluff's edge. For the first and only time on this hike a narrow opening allows you to stand on the trail and see the views without any partial obstruction from trees. Explore the viewpoint, enjoy the huge views, but make a note of this spot.

As you resume hiking northeastward, count your paces. One hundred sixty-five paces later, at a point where the NCT swings north, is a trail junction (Mile 4.1). Turn sharply left (northwest) on a narrow path known as the Hack Site Trail, marked by white blazes, as the NCT goes right (north). "Hack Site" refers to the release of peregrine falcon chicks on the cliff top nearby. "Hacking" places young falcon chicks on an artificial structure on the top of a cliff that would be a suitable habitat. Human attendants feed them until they are old enough to fly and hunt for themselves. Check the Web site of the NCT Association (www.north countrytrail.org/pwf) to see pictures of the hack box that was previously here. Whether or not the falcons interest you, those pictures serve as a superb preview of this hike and its views.

Peregrine falcons are flying stun guns. They knock out their prey with a lightninglike dive, reaching well above 100 miles per hour in their attack.

Follow the Hack Site Trail north 0.9 mile, through pleasant forest, to FR 326 (Mile 5.0). Then walk north and west, 1.1 downhill miles on FR 326, to the NCT Trailhead (Mile 6.1).

Options: Hiking east on the NCT is an attractive addition. From the junction of the NCT and the Hack Site Trail (listed as Mile 0.0 for this description) walk east on the NCT, at first somewhat near the bluff's edge then further "inland," north. The forest is fine, and the trail leads to a long descent to the Soo Line Railroad tracks at Mile 1.5. Walk east across the tracks and the Bush Creek trail bridge at

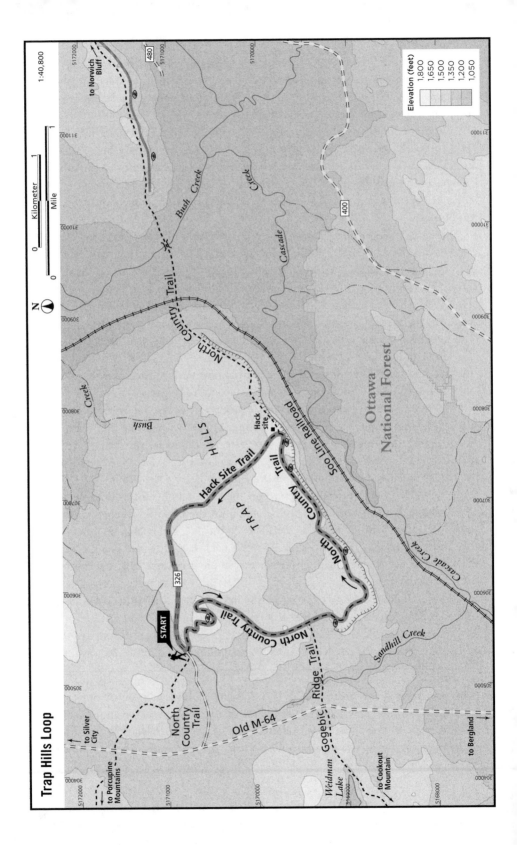

Trap Hills Loop

1:40,800

Elevation (feet)

- 1,800
- 1,650
- 1,500
- 1,350
- 1,200
- 1,050

Ottawa National Forest

TRAP HILLS

Bush Creek

Cascade Creek

Bush Creek

Hack Site Trail

North Country Trail

Soo Line Railroad

Hack site

North Country Trail

Sandhill Creek

Cascade Creek

North Country Trail

Gogebic Ridge Trail

Old M-64

Weidman Lake

START

326

480

400

North Country Trail

to Norwich Bluff

to Silver City

to Porcupine Mountains

to Cookout Mountain

to Bergland

Kilometer

Mile

Mile 1.9. Continue to follow the trail eastward, slowly ascending on an overgrown lane before the trail once again becomes a path and ascends steeply east.

Another escarpment, not as high as the Hack Site cliffs but with a strategic location that makes it well worth exploring, is now south of the NCT. Scan the woods south of the trail for a domelike rock wall, a little less than 1 mile east of Bush Creek. A little scouting will reveal safe routes to scramble to the top of the rock, a location I call "Domeland" (Mile 2.8). This is an extensive mosaic of bedrock slabs and vegetation. Views west show the immense grayness of the Hack Site crag across the Bush Creek valley. Lake Superior's sparkling blue water and the forested ridges of the Porkies are visible to the northwest. When you're ready, retrace your steps to the Hack Site Trail.

One other option is well worth mentioning: a hike from FR 326 east along the NCT to Forest Road 400, a total of 9.3 miles.

Key Points

0.0 NCT Trailhead on FR 326.

1.6 Gogebic Ridge Trail junction.

4.1 Hack Site Trail junction.

5.0 FR 326.

6.1 NCT Trailhead on FR 326.

14 Trap Hills Traverse

Highlights: Spectacular views from a parade of viewpoints, quiet forest, and solitude.
Location: Trap Hills, 4 miles north of Bergland.
Type of hike: Point-to-point backpack.
Distance: 28.3 miles.
Difficulty: Difficult*.
Fees and permits: None, but consider a donation to the Trap Hills Conservation Alliance, a coalition campaigning to gain protection for the Trap Hills, www.traphills.org; or the North Country Trail Association, www.north countrytrail.org.
Best months: May through October.
Camping: Backpack camping is allowed along the trail, within zero-impact guidelines, on forest service land where blue markers are present. Vertical paint blazes indicate private land, where there is no camping (Whisky Hollow and 3 miles east, Lookout Mountain). Bergland Township Park, 5 miles south of the trailhead, has fifteen campsites.
Maps: USGS Bergland NE (inc.), Matchwood NW (inc.), Oak Bluff (inc.), Rockland (inc.) quads; North Country Trail Maps TMI14, Cascade Falls to Ironwood, and TMI13, Alberta to Cascade Falls.
Trail contact: Ottawa National Forest, (906) 932-1330, www.fs.fed.us/r9/ottawa; North Country Trail Association Web site, www.northcountrytrail.org/pwf.

Finding the trailhead: From the town of Bergland, drive north 2.0 miles on M-64 and turn right (east) on Old M-64 (gravel). Drive 2.9 miles east and north on Old M-64 to the Gogebic Ridge Trail trailhead.

Special considerations: Parts of the North Country Trail (NCT) have thin wear marks but viable marking. Use caution on the viewpoints, many of which are atop sheer cliffs. Hikers may want to budget some time to explore Old Victoria. This restored historic mining village is adjacent to the hike's end. Also note the presence of an NCT trail shelter at Old Victoria, 0.9 trail mile east of the end of the hike. That shelter's location makes it useful for pre- or posthike stays.

The Hike

Among all the attractions of this route, and there are many, one thing stands out in my memory of this trip—broad views. A string of rock outcrops offered sweeping vistas of what seemed to be endless forest. Better yet were the sight lines along the ridgeline route, where I could spot a far-off cliff from which I'd enjoyed the sunrise the day before—or look farther east to where I would be the next morning. Sleeping on those high-rock balconies, watching the morning and evening light touch far-off ridges, was the icing on the cake.

Of course you do have to walk between the viewpoints, but that part of the route is hardly disappointing. Much of the Trap Hills forest is older second growth and a pleasure to the eye. Small streams cut mossy clefts in the escarpment. The trail passes dozens of rocky nooks that seem to beg for exploration, and solitude is there for the asking.

The bottom line for backpackers is this: If you are looking for an energetic, adventurous, and highly rewarding three-day outing, take a long look at this one. Three days

Rock slabs east of Bush Creek. The Hack Site cliff is in the center of the skyline.

would be reasonable, but more would be better if you enjoy exploring along the way. Two days would be a bit of a rushed trip, with little time to enjoy the sights.

Begin by hiking east from Old M–64 on the Gogebic Ridge Trail and follow it to its junction with the NCT at Mile 0.8. Turn right (east) and follow the NCT as it ascends through a fine maple forest. As the climb ends watch for a rock outcrop 15 feet northwest of the trail that offers views to the northwest. Typically the NCT runs a stone's throw "inland" from the bluff's edge, but sharp-eyed hikers will have little trouble spotting the openings in the forest canopy that mark the viewpoints.

The NCT then runs southeast, passes the southern corner of the Trap Hills' high plateau, and begins a miles-long run northeast. About a half-mile later, an open slope below the trail offers long views south, before the path dips to a saddle. East of that saddle the path ascends steadily, reaching notable views a little over a half-mile later, where a faint spur trail leads 50 feet south, down the slope to a broad open cliff top. A ledge top opening here, roughly 80 feet wide and clear of trees, offers sweeping vistas southeast, south, and southwest. These are stunning views. However, a little less than a half mile farther east are vistas that rival these. Walk east, passing over the top of the knoll marked 1,772 on maps (the highest point on this headland). As the trail nears the 4.1 mile point, it comes near the bluff's edge. For the first and only time

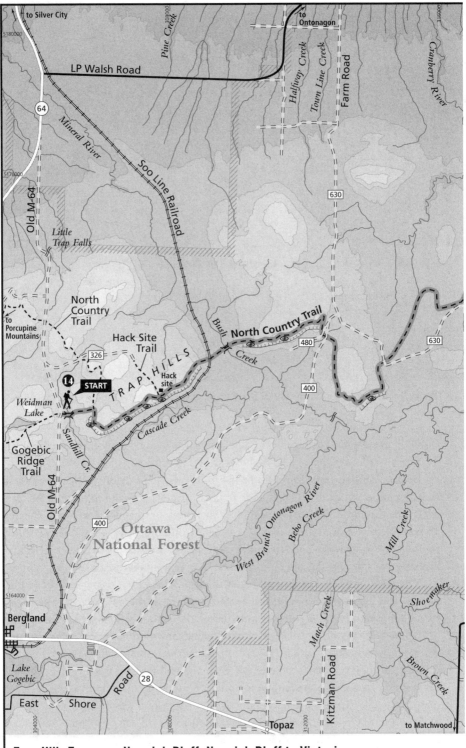

Trap Hills Traverse; Norwich Bluff; Norwich Bluff to Victoria

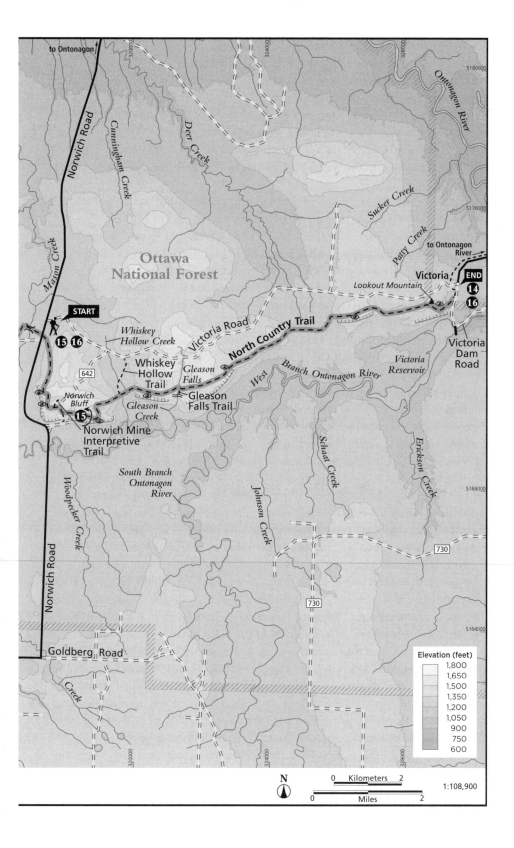

on this hike a narrow opening allows you to stand on the trail and see the views without any partial obstruction from trees. Explore the viewpoint and enjoy the huge views, but make a note of this spot.

On a good day you may notice a headland with a sharp south face, 6 miles due east as the crow flies. That headland is Norwich Bluff, and after you have followed the NCT east for 14 trail miles you will be standing on that spot. When you do reach Norwich Bluff, look to the west. The gray crag of the Hack Site cliff, where you are now, is striking.

Return to the NCT. Hike 165 paces east to an unmarked junction (Mile 3.3) with a white-blazed trail running north a mile to the end of FR 326. This trail, known as the Hack Site Trail, refers to the release of young peregrine falcons on the nearby cliff, a process known as "hacking."

Continue northeast on the NCT as it turns a tad "inland" from the bluff's edge, crosses a saddle, and eases into a long descent to the Soo Line Railroad tracks at Mile 4.8. Cross the railroad tracks and a bridge over Bush Creek at Mile 5.1. About a mile east of the bridge, the trail ascends sharply and begins to parallel a series of rock slabs and domes south of the trail. That swath of bedrock is well worth exploring and offers views west across Bush Creek to the Hack Site cliffs, as well as north to Lake Superior and the Porcupine Mountains.

After enjoying the views continue walking east. Soon a rock ledge along the trail offers views south and west. The trail then runs northeast a bit before turning south then southeast and crossing FR 480 at Mile 8.5, and FR 400 at Mile 8.6. Follow the trail east and south, passing through an area of a recent thinning logging operation. After swinging east, the trail runs along the crest of a "whaleback" stretch of bedrock, offering long views south as well as east to Norwich Bluff and beyond. Descending off that rock ridge, the NCT turns north and crosses FR 630 at Mile 12.0.

Walk east from FR 630, entering a flat gap in the ridgeline. The trail turns north for a bit, passes two remnants of logging cuts, and winds its way east to the marshy headwaters of Mason Creek and shortly thereafter to Norwich Road at Mile 15.7.

Norwich Road, paved but remarkably quiet, marks the trail's approach to an escarpment that offers some of the best views in the Trap Hills—Norwich Bluff. Hike southeast, following the NCT as it steadily ascends that bluff's western slopes. Two rock slabs near its southwestern corner offer views north to Lake Superior and the Porcupine Mountains, as well as west to the Hack Site.

Follow the NCT as it turns east to cross Norwich Bluff's convoluted south face, reaching a junction at Mile 17.7. Go straight (east) as a spur trail goes left (north) to FR 642, as the trail dips into a hollow and arrives at a corner of the headland that holds spectacular views at about Mile 18.9. One hundred feet south of the trail, down a piney slope, a broad opening from the top of the cliff offers sweeping views. Unencumbered by screening ridges, the views stretch 50 miles or so.

Moving on, follow the NCT as it swings north and drops to a junction, unmarked when I saw it, with the Whisky Hollow Trail at mile 19.9. Go straight (east), past the Whisky Hollow Trail, which goes left (north). Next the NCT quickly passes Whisky Hollow Creek and ascends to a series of bedrock ledges that offer broad views south and west to Norwich Bluff.

Following a ridge east the trail arrives at a junction with the Gleason Falls Trail at mile 21.2. Turn right (south) onto the narrow Gleason Falls Trail and follow a ledge on the sidewall of Gleason Creek's steep little gorge to Gleason Falls (Mile 21.3). The 20-foot waterfall has a minimal flow except in wet spells, but the setting, a mossy cleft, is well worthwhile. Retrace your steps to the NCT at Mile 21.4 and turn right (east).

Running steadily eastward the NCT ascends a ridge, reaching a broad rock dome that offers a 180-degree view at about Mile 22.6. The trail then descends eastward, crosses several small drainages, and skirts a rock dome on talus slopes at Mile 24.2.

East of the talus slopes, the NCT crosses a mile-long stretch that is relatively flat. The mellow topography ends abruptly when the path takes a steep route to the top of the ridge marked POINT 1,490T on topographic maps (Mile 25.9). Eye-catching views and long sight lines open to the south, and the Trap Hills ridgeline leads west.

Now descending, the trail drops into a gap in the ridgeline before ascending to the west end of the ridge that includes the viewpoint known as Lookout Mountain. The NCT reaches that landmark vista at Mile 27.9, a good time and place to savor the views before the hike ends. Below, Victoria Reservoir's blue waters nest in forested green hills. To finish the hike follow the NCT northeast, descending 0.4 mile to Victoria Dam Road at Mile 28.3.

Key Points

0.0 Gogebic Ridge Trailhead on Old M-64.

0.8 Junction with NCT.

3.3 Hack Site Trail junction, viewpoint nearby.

4.8 Soo Line Railroad tracks.

5.1 Bush Creek.

8.5 Forest Road 480.

8.6 Forest Road 400.

12.0 Forest Road 630.

15.7 Norwich Road.

17.7 Junction with spur trail to Forest Road 642.

18.9 Southeast corner of Norwich Bluff, viewpoint.

19.5 Junction with Whisky Hollow Trail.

19.9 Whisky Hollow Creek.

21.2 Junction with Gleason Falls Trail.

21.3 Gleason Falls.

21.4 Junction with Gleason Falls Trail.

22.6 Ridge east of Gleason Creek, viewpoint.

24.2 Talus slopes.

25.9 Summit (1,490 feet), viewpoint.

27.9 Lookout Mountain.

28.3 Victoria Dam Road.

15 Norwich Bluff

See Map on page 65

Highlights: Outstanding views from a beautiful escarpment and solitude.

Location: Trap Hills, 14 miles south of Ontonagon.

Type of hike: Out-and-back.

Distance: 6.2 miles.

Difficulty: Difficult*.

Fees and permits: None, but consider a donation to the Trap Hills Conservation Alliance, a campaign to gain protection for the Trap Hills, www.traphills.org; or the North Country Trail Association, www.northcountrytrail.org.

Best months: May through October.

Camping: Backpack camping along the trail is allowed within zero-impact guidelines. Blue diamond trail markers designate forest service land. Vertical blue blazes indicate private land where there is no camping (Whisky Hollow, and east for 3 miles). Bergland Township Park, 21 miles southwest of the trailhead, has fifteen campsites.

Maps: USGS Oak Bluff, Matchwood NW quads; North Country Trail Map TMI13, Alberta to Cascade Falls.

Trail contact: Ottawa National Forest, (906) 932-1330, www.fs.fed.us/r9/ottawa; North Country Trail Association Web site, www.northcountrytrail.org/pwf.

Finding the trailhead: From Ontonagon, drive 1.4 miles west on M-64 and turn left (south) onto Norwich Road. Drive 12.8 miles south on Norwich Road to the NCT trailhead.

Special considerations: Use caution at the viewpoints; many are atop sheer cliffs. Note that clay and mud may make Victoria Road four-wheel drive only when wet. Don't presume that Forest Road 642 is in a condition that would allow a vehicle to pass.

The Hike

Norwich Bluff offers knock-your-socks-off views—vistas that would make the short list for "best in the U.P." Stand on this bluff's southeast corner and the views to the south, east, and west are unencumbered by screening ridges and seem to stretch forever. Another vista, on the headland's western slope, offers views north to Lake Superior's deep blue waters and the Porcupine Mountains.

Odds are you'll have these views to yourself; soulful solitude seems to come with the territory here. Between the views and the peace and quiet, Norwich Bluff is an intriguing and complex crag and can be habit forming.

This route offers 6-mile out-and-back tour of the major attractions on the south and west slopes. Those willing to use the trail as an access tool for off-trail rambling will find an abundance of interesting side-trips available near the trail. Rock ledges

Norwich Bluff, a dazzling rock balcony. Western Trap Hills are on the left skyline.

offer perfect verandas for sunrise and sunset views; shady glens and fern gardens tuck into the corners.

Begin your tour at the NCT trailhead on Norwich Road. Hike southeast and south on the NCT, steadily ascending wooded slopes. At Mile 1.3, the trail reaches the first viewpoint, a broad domelike rock sloping west. Lake Superior is visible to the north, and you can see the easternmost ridges of the Porcupine Mountains to the northwest. To the west the immense gray cliff known as the Hack Site is striking.

Resume hiking east and south, arriving at another viewpoint about a half-mile later. Views are similar to the last lookout, although a little more southerly in orientation. Lake Superior still shows to the north; long sight lines stretch southwest toward the Gogebic Range.

Now swinging eastward the trail traverses the bluff's southern slope, ducking in and out of ravines. At Mile 2.0 it arrives at an intersection with a spur trail (the Norwich Mine Interpretive Trail) that goes north to FR 642. Go straight (east), past the spur trail that goes left (north). The NCT continues eastward, dropping into a hollow where it follows a jeep track southward. Watch for the trail to turn left (east), crossing the drainage as the jeep track continues south.

Ascending steeply from the hollow, about a half mile later the NCT reaches a stretch that holds some of Norwich Bluff's most spectacular views. One hundred feet south of the trail, down a piney slope, a broad opening on the cliff tops offers sweeping views. Vistas here fill 180 degrees of the horizon. Far to the right (west) is the cliffy Hack Site escarpment. Landmarks are harder to come by when you look south and east, but the rolling forestland stretches to the horizon, what seems to be an honest 50 miles. There is an airy feel and a sense of well-being to sitting here. The view from the southern slope appears to be endless forest, with hardly a manufactured item in sight. It's a great break spot and a natural turnaround point for the hike.

Options: Two options are worth considering. First, by walking farther east on the NCT, then taking the Whisky Hollow Trail north to Victoria Road, hikers can construct a 6.5-mile loop. Beginning at the southeastern slope viewpoint (designated Mile 0.0 for this discussion), follow the NCT as it swings north, crosses a hollow, and ascends a ridge. Rock outcrops offer views across Whisky Hollow to the eastern Trap Hills ridgeline.

As the trail descends into Whisky Hollow, watch for the intersection with the Whisky Hollow Trail at mile 0.7. It is near the bottom of the steep part of the slope. I did not find a junction sign here, but white blazes lead north. Turn left (north) onto the Whisky Hollow Trail, as the NCT goes east. The Whisky Hollow Trail is half faint path, half marked route. Wear marks are thin, but I could always find the next blaze. The path runs north and east, crosses Whisky Hollow Creek, and reaches Victoria Road at Mile 1.6. Turn left (west) and walk Victoria Road (dirt) 1.5 miles to Norwich Road (paved). Turn left (south) and walk 0.3 mile to the NCT trailhead.

A second option is attractive and adds 4.6 miles to the round-trip hike. Instead of turning north on the Whisky Hollow Trail, continue walking east on the NCT 2.3 miles to Gleason Falls. Starting at the southeastern slope viewpoint (Mile 0.0 for this description), pass the junction with the Whisky Hollow Trail (Mile 0.7), walk east on the NCT, and cross Whisky Hollow Creek at Mile 0.9.

Continue hiking east on the NCT, ascending the slope east of Whisky Hollow. About a half mile east of the creek, the trail reaches a series of rock ledges that offer prime views south, as well as southwest to Norwich Bluff. Resume walking east, arriving at the junction with the Gleason Falls Trail at Mile 2.2. Turn right (south) on the Gleason Falls Trail, a narrow footpath along a ledge in Gleason Creek's gorge. The path reaches Gleason Falls, set in a beautiful mossy nook, at Mile 2.3. Return to the NCT Trailhead at Norwich Road to complete this 10.8-mile hike.

Key Points

0.0 NCT Trailhead on Norwich Road.

1.3 Norwich Bluff's western slope viewpoint.

2.0 Junction with Norwich Mine Interpretive Trail.

3.1 Norwich Bluff's southeastern slope viewpoint; turnaround point.

6.2 NCT Trailhead on Norwich Road.

16 Norwich Bluff to Victoria

See Map on page 65

Highlights: Spectacular views, a remote stretch of the Trap Hills, Gleason Falls and gorge, and solitude.

Location: Trap Hills, 14 miles south of Ontonagon.

Type of hike: Point-to-point.

Distance: 12.7 miles.

Difficulty: Difficult*.

Fees and permits: None, but consider a donation to the Trap Hills Conservation Alliance, a coalition campaigning to gain protection for the Trap Hills, www.traphills.org; or the North Country Trail Association, www.north-countrytrail.org.

Best months: May through October.

Camping: Backpack camping along the trail is allowed within zero-impact guidelines on forest service lands, where blue diamond trail markers are present. Vertical blue blazes indicate private land where there is no camping (Whisky Hollow and 3 miles east, Lookout Mountain area). Bergland Township Park, 21 miles southwest of the trailhead, has fifteen campsites.

Maps: USGS Oak Bluff (inc.), Matchwood NW (inc.), Rockland quads (inc.); North Country Trail Map TMI13, Alberta to Cascade Falls.

Trail contact: Ottawa National Forest, (906) 932-1330, www.fs.fed.us/r9/ottawa; North Country Trail Association Web site, www.northcountrytrail.org/pwf.

Finding the trailhead: From Ontonagon drive 1.4 miles west on M-64 and turn left (south) on Norwich Road. Drive 12.8 miles south on Norwich Road to the trailhead for the North Country Trail (NCT), which will be on your right (west) just before Forest Road 630 (also on your right). Watch for NCT signs on either side of Norwich Road.

Special considerations: Parts of the NCT have thin wear marks but viable marking. Use caution on the viewpoints, many of which are atop sheer cliffs. Hikers may want to budget some time to explore Old Victoria. This historic restored mining village is adjacent to the hike's end. Also note the presence of an NCT trail shelter at Old Victoria, 0.9 mile east of the end of the hike. That shelter's location makes it useful for pre- or posthike stays. Don't presume that Forest Road 642 is in a condition that would allow a vehicle to pass.

The Hike

This is an outstanding hike, and its list of attractions sounds like a hiker's wish list. Norwich Bluff's sweeping vistas would be on any Trap Hills "can't miss" list; the parade of viewpoints that follows is impressive.

Between the sun-splashed lookouts, a fine forest shades the trail, and clear-running streams tumble off the escarpment. Fern gardens carpet the woodland floor, grouse explode from the shadows, and mossy nooks and crannies invite exploration.

Begin at Norwich Road and hike southeast into the woods on the NCT as it steadily ascends Norwich Bluff's western slope. At Mile 1.3 the path reaches a broad domelike rock sloping west, the first viewpoint. Lake Superior shows to the north, and the broad ridges of the Porcupine Mountains can be seen to the northwest. A large gray rock face known as the Hack Site, a landmark of the western Trap Hills,

is visible off to the west. Hike another half-mile or so south, and another rock dome offers views that are similar but a little more southerly in orientation.

Soon the trail swings east, crossing Norwich Bluff's convoluted southern slope. Go straight (east) at Mile 2.0, past the spur trail that goes left (north) to FR 642. Soon the NCT drops into a hollow and runs south a bit on a jeep road. Watch for the NCT to turn left (east) off that jeep track, climb out of that hollow, and arrive at a corner of the headland that holds spectacular views at Mile 3.1. One hundred feet south of the trail, down a piney slope, a wide opening in the cliff tops offers sweeping views. Unencumbered by screening ridges the views stretch 50 miles or so, with oceans of trees leading to the horizon.

When you are ready resume hiking east on the NCT, which soon swings north and drops to a junction with the Whisky Hollow Trail at Mile 3.8. When I saw this intersection, it was unmarked. Go straight (east) as the Whisky Hollow Trail goes left (north). The NCT then arrives at the hollow's namesake creek at Mile 4.0.

Ascending from Whisky Hollow, the trail reaches a poetic stretch a half-mile later. Spacious ledges on a cliff top offer uncluttered views south and west to Norwich Bluff. As the trail continues to ascend, the vistas continue and improve with height. Peek-a-boo views continue as the trail runs east to Gleason Creek and a junction with the Gleason Falls Trail at Mile 5.5.

Turn right (south) onto the narrow Gleason Falls Trail and follow a ledge on the sidewall of Gleason Creek's steep little gorge to Gleason Falls (Mile 5.6). The 20-foot waterfall has a minimal flow except in wet spells, but the setting, a mossy cleft, is well worthwhile. Retrace your steps to the NCT at Mile 5.7 and turn right (east).

Running steadily eastward the NCT ascends a ridge and reaches an open rock dome, offering a 180 degree view at about Mile 6.7. The trail then descends eastward, crosses several small drainages, and skirts another rock dome on talus slopes at Mile 8.8.

East of the talus slopes, the NCT crosses a mile-long stretch that is relatively flat. The mellow topography ends abruptly when the path takes a steep route to the top of the ridge marked POINT 1,490T on topographic maps (Mile 10.1). Extensive views and long sight lines open to the south, and the Trap Hills ridgeline leads west.

Now descending, the trail drops into a gap in the ridgeline before ascending to the west end of the ridge that includes the viewpoint known as Lookout Mountain. The NCT reaches that landmark vista at Mile 12.3, a good time and place to savor the views before the hike ends. Below, Victoria Reservoir's blue waters nest in forested green hills. To finish the hike follow the NCT northeast, descending 0.4 mile to Victoria Dam Road at Mile 12.7.

◀ *Lookout Mountain's sweeping views include*
Victoria Reservoir's sparkling blue waters.

Key Points

0.0 Trailhead at Norwich Road.

1.3 Norwich Bluff's western slope viewpoint.

2.0 Junction with Norwich Mine Interpretive Trail.

3.1 Norwich Bluff's southeastern slope viewpoint.

3.8 Junction with Whisky Hollow Trail.

4.0 Whisky Hollow Creek.

5.5 Junction with Gleason Falls Trail.

5.6 Gleason Falls.

5.7 Junction with Gleason Falls Trail.

6.7 Ridge east of Gleason Creek, viewpoint.

8.8 Talus slopes.

10.1 Summit (1,490 feet), viewpoint looking south.

12.3 Lookout Mountain.

12.7 Victoria Dam Road.

17 Tibbets Falls/Oren Krumm Shelter

Highlights: Rapids and quiet water of the Sturgeon River, Tibbets Falls, and a pleasant backcountry shelter and campsite.

Location: 5 miles northwest of Covington.

Type of hike: Out-and-back.

Distance: 3.6 miles.

Difficulty: Moderate.

Fees and permits: None, but consider a donation to the North Country Trail Association.

Best months: May through October.

Camping: The Oren Krumm Shelter and two developed backcountry campsites are at this hike's turnaround point. Big Lake State Forest Campground, 4 miles north of the trailhead, has twelve campsites.

Maps: USGS Covington quad (inc.); North Country Trail Map TMI13, Alberta to Cascade Falls.

Trail contact: Michigan Department of Natural Resources, (906) 353-6651; www.michigan.gov/dnr; the Peter Wolfe Chapter of the North Country Trail Web site, www.northcountrytrail.org/pwf.

Finding the trailhead: From Covington, drive west 1.8 miles on M-28. Turn right (north) on Plains Road and drive 3 miles, just past the bridge over the Sturgeon River. Park on the broad shoulder on the east side of the road.

Special considerations: Parts of the North Country Trail (NCT) on this hike can be under water during high-water episodes.

The Hike

This is a short, contemplative hike, full of small scenes that each tell a vignette of time and place. One central theme inhabits most of these scenes and supplies a

Tibbets Falls on the Sturgeon River highlights a long stretch of swift water and rapids.

soothing soundtrack as well—the Sturgeon River, a near constant companion on this outing.

Begin your visit just north of the Sturgeon River bridge on the west side of Plains Road. Thirty paces north of the bridge, a white-blazed spur trail of the North Country Trail enters a narrow opening in the trees. Walk west on that trail, a thin but well-defined path.

Stay straight (west) at mile 0.4 as the NCT enters from the right (north) and the white-blazed spur trail ends. Walk west on the NCT. The river is nearby and running swiftly. The trail swings south, following the river at the beginning of a large oxbow bend. At the southernmost point of that bend, a large creek (Kelsey Creek) enters from the opposite (south) side. This is the beginning of an extensive stretch of rapids.

Both the river and the trail then curve north, reaching Tibbets Falls at Mile 1.1. Slate ledges extend across the river here, and the falls consist of a series of drops over those ledges.

Continue hiking northwest on the NCT as it follows the rushing, rapid river downstream. One last white-water scene plays out as the river runs through a 10-foot-wide chute before bouncing left on the bedrock slabs.

Tibbets Falls/Oren Krumm Shelter

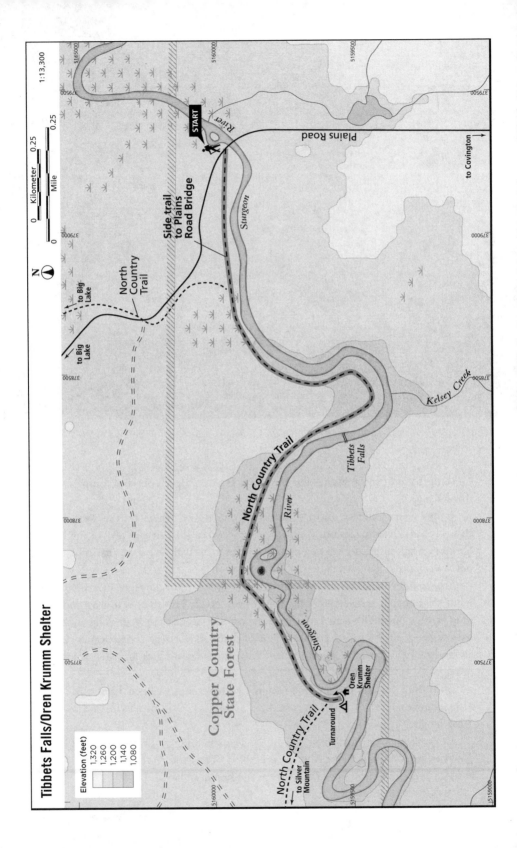

For the first time in the hike, the river current mellows and slows, and the trail enters a stretch of floodplain forest with beaver cuttings nearby. The flat ends and the shelter on a 20-foot-high riverbank comes into sight. During my visit a bald eagle glided off its perch above the shelter as I approached.

To go to the shelter, turn left (south) at mile 1.7, the NCT goes right (west). Walk south 0.1 mile and you will be at the Oren Krumm Shelter. A fire pit, with rustic seating, overlooks the river—a perfect break spot before turning around and hiking back.

Key Points

0.0 Trailhead at Plains Road (by the Sturgeon River bridge).

0.4 North Country Trail junction.

1.1 Tibbets Falls.

1.7 Junction with shelter spur.

1.8 Oren Krumm Shelter; turnaround point.

3.6 Trailhead at Plains Road

18 Canyon Falls

Highlights: Waterfalls and a rocky gorge.
Location: 1 mile south of Alberta.
Type of hike: Out-and-back.
Distance: 1.8 miles.
Difficulty: The official trail is easy; the second segment is difficult.
Fees and permits: None.
Best months: May through October.

Camping: Big Lake State Forest Campground, 10 miles west of the trailhead, has twelve campsites.
Map: USGS Vermilac quad.
Trail contact: Michigan Department of Natural Resources, (906) 353-6651, www.michigan.gov/dnr.

Finding the trailhead: From Alberta, drive 1.1 miles south on U.S. Highway 41 and turn right (west) into the trailhead parking area.

Special considerations: Use caution on wet rocks near the river. The first part of this hike follows an official, maintained trail. The second part ventures off-trail, along segments of an old trail. This second section is very rewarding but requires good judgment. Some of this walking takes place atop massive slabs of bedrock, and some crevices are present in those rock slabs. Moss or leaves cover some of these crevices, creating the possibility of serious injury. Be alert.

Canyon Falls. The Sturgeon River drops into the picturesque cleft known as the Gorge.

The Hike

Aptly named Canyon Falls is a spectacularly scenic little area that can be as mild—or as wild—as you want it to be. An official, constructed trail leads to the namesake waterfall, which is a beauty. As that path ends, the gorge area begins, offering nimble hikers an adventurous outing along its rim.

Begin your hike at the marked trailhead at the southwest corner of the Canyon Falls roadside park. Walk southwest on a broad, graveled path, the Canyon Falls Trail. About 400 paces from the parking area, the trail nears the Sturgeon River and its swift water. A series of low ledge drops—most just a few inches and one waist high—adds to the current's velocity as it nears Canyon Falls.

The river cascades down 15-foot-high Canyon Falls (Mile 0.4) into a rocky slot, locally known as the Gorge. Follow the fence to the right (west) of the waterfall for the best viewing of the falls and a tantalizing look downstream into the rapids and rock walls of the Gorge. Turn around here if maintained trails are your preference. An opening in the railing allows you to step down to a lower ledge and an even better view of Canyon Falls and the canyon below.

If the rim of the Gorge area interests you, take note of a long and low block of rock just west of this railing area. Work your way to the north end (your right as you

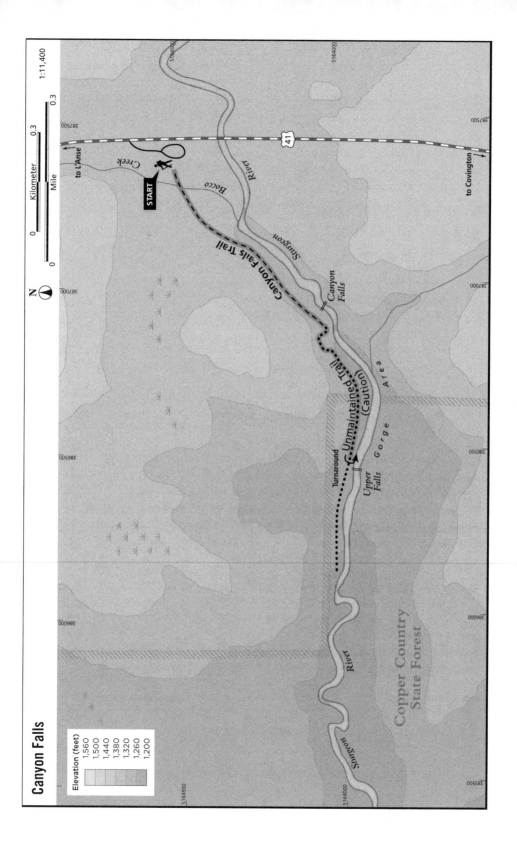

Canyon Falls

Elevation (feet)

1,560
1,500
1,440
1,380
1,320
1,260
1,200

N

1:11,400

Kilometer   0.3
Mile   0.3

to L'Anse

Creek

START

Bocco

Sturgeon   River

Canyon Falls Trail

Canyon Falls

Unmaintained Trail (Caution)

Turnaround

Upper Falls

Gorge Area

Sturgeon   River

Copper Country State Forest

to Covington

41

are facing it) of that rock, then west past its end. There you will see a path, an old trail that leads west, onto the rim of the Gorge. This rim is an almost magical place. It seems as if you stepped through a window and into wilderness. Below you the river churns between huge boulders and gray rock walls 30 feet high. Above, pine needles carpet the bedrock as the path continues southwest and west.

Almost 1 mile west of the trailhead, the walls of the Gorge lower and the river charges into one last white-water display. Upper Falls is a huge ramp, a waterslide that rides a tilting bedrock strata and splits in two just before its final drop. A pleasant break spot, this is also the turnaround point for the hike.

Key Points

0.0 Trailhead.

0.4 Canyon Falls.

0.9 Upper Falls; turnaround point.

1.8 Trailhead.

19 Craig Lake

Highlights: A remote lake, marsh and stream, and quiet forest.
Location: 10 miles northwest of Michigamme.
Type of hike: Loop.
Distance: 7.9 miles.
Difficulty: Moderate.
Fees and permits: Michigan Department of Natural Resources vehicle sticker.
Best months: May through October.

Camping: Craig Lake State Park offers rustic backcountry camping, within zero-impact guidelines. A permit is required, which can be obtained from Van Riper State Park. Sandy Beach campsite, 0.5 mile east of the trailhead, has three tent pads.
Maps: USGS Mount Curwood (inc.), Three Lakes (inc.) quads.
Trail contact: Van Riper State Park, (906) 339-4461.

Finding the trailhead: From Michigamme, drive 1.4 miles west on U.S. Highway 41 and turn right (north) on Craig Lake Road. Drive 3.0 miles on that road and turn left (northwest) continuing on Craig Lake Road. Follow that road, which is at times rough, 3.4 miles to the Craig Lake State Park trailhead.
Special considerations: For identification purposes, some trail intersections on the map are designated by an alphabetical code (Junction A, for example).

The Hike

Craig Lake comes with an attitude check. Persist through 6 miles of rough, bumpy road that winds its way to the trailhead, and the rewards will begin as soon as you

Craig Lake's remote and sparkling waters, where loons linger ▶
and a portage ramp eases the carry to Crooked Lake.

shut off the ignition. Odds are, that will be the last mechanical sound you'll hear during your visit to Michigan's most remote state park.

Round a gate at the parking area's east end and you enter a nonmotorized zone, a designated state wilderness area. Craig Lake State Park's 6,984 acres feature two lakes—Craig Lake and Crooked Lake, each nearly 2 miles in length—and a mosaic of marshes, streams, and quiet forest. Seeing loons and eagles is pretty much a sure thing. Members of the U.P.'s resurgent moose population put in an appearance now and then as well.

A loop trail circles the park's namesake lake, visiting the lake's quiet north end, the park's back of beyond. The 8-mile circuit tour also offers a short side-trip to remote Clair Lake.

Begin your hike by walking on a gated dirt road 310 paces east from the parking area to an intersection designated Junction A (Mile 0.2). Go straight (north), as the eastern segment of the Craig Lake Trail (also the North Country Trail, or NCT, here) splits off to the right (east).

Continue hiking north and northwest on the dirt road. You will pass a put-in and a bay of sparkling Craig Lake and arrive at Junction B at Mile 0.4. Go straight (northwest), as the NCT departs left (west). About 1 mile north of that intersection, the Craig Lake Trail, which is still a dirt road, utilizes a sturdy bridge to pass over a large marshy creek. This is a good place to scan for herons and other wildlife. Next the trail arrives at a clearing by the lake and a lodge (available for rental) left from the days when Frederick Miller, of the brewing family, owned Craig Lake. Check the north side of the lodge's clearing for the trail's continuation, as it becomes a path entering the woods. The path winds its way, occasionally nearing the lake's rocky shore, and reaches a junction with the Clair Lake Portage Trail at Mile 2.7. Turn left (north) and hike 0.2 mile to sample Clair Lake's quiet ambience or perhaps its excellent smallmouth bass fishery.

Retrace your steps south and turn left (east) on the Craig Lake Trail (Mile 3.1). Hike east, crossing a sturdy bridge over Clair Lake's little outlet stream and arriving at a rock outcrop that offers narrow views of Craig Lake's northeast inlet. Then the path wanders east, swinging north a bit to skirt wetlands before arriving at Craig Lake's outlet (Mile 4.3), a branch of the Peshekee River.

Cross the outlet to its south side on a sturdy, 30-inch-wide log. I was startled as several smallmouth bass, one a hefty 18 inches long, attempted to jump up in the riffle below the log. Hike south, following the Craig Lake Trail as it nears Craig Lake's northeast bay, dips and rolls through some hilly terrain, and arrives at Junction C at Mile 5.6. Turn right (west), following a sign for Craig Lake, as another trail goes south (signed for Crooked Lake and the NCT). Follow the Craig Lake Trail southwest to a junction with the Crooked Lake Portage Trail at Mile 6.2. Turn right (west) and walk ninety paces to Craig Lake, where a constructed portage ramp leads up a slope from the shoreline. Loons were offshore during my visit. This is a pleasant break spot.

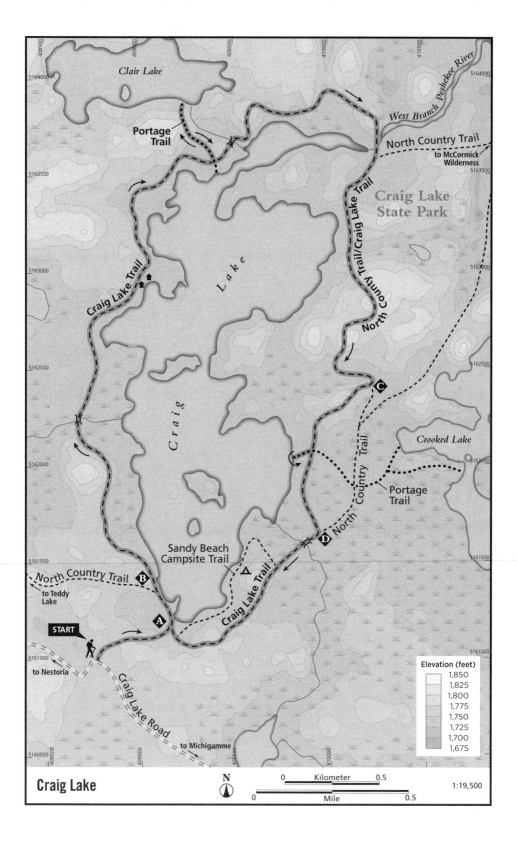

Clair Lake

Portage
Trail

West Branch Peshekee River

North Country Trail
to McCormick
Wilderness

Craig Lake
State Park

Craig Lake Trail

North Country Trail/Craig Lake Trail

Craig
Lake

Crooked Lake

North Country Trail

Portage
Trail

C

Sandy Beach
Campsite Trail

D

Craig Lake Trail

North Country Trail
to Teddy
Lake

B

A

START

to Nestoria

Craig Lake Road

to Michigamme

Elevation (feet)
1,850
1,825
1,800
1,775
1,750
1,725
1,700
1,675

Craig Lake

N

0	Kilometer	0.5

| 0 | Mile | 0.5 |

1:19,500

Retrace your ninety steps eastward and turn right (south) on the Craig Lake Trail. Hike south and southeast to Junction D at Mile 6.9. Turn right (south), as the NCT and Crooked Lake Trail come in from the left (north). Hike south and west on the Craig Lake Trail (now part of the NCT and a jeep trail in width), crossing a sturdy bridge over a large inlet creek. Go straight (southwest) at Mile 7.2 as a spur goes right (northwest) to a camping area on the lakeshore.

Continue hiking southwest on the Craig Lake Trail, arriving at Junction A at Mile 7.7. Turn left (southwest) and walk some 310 paces to the trailhead parking area.

Key Points

0.0 Trailhead.

0.2 Junction A.

0.4 Junction B.

2.0 Cabin Meadow.

2.7 Clair Lake Portage Trail junction.

2.9 Clair Lake.

3.1 Clair Lake Portage Trail junction.

4.3 Craig Lake Outlet.

5.6 Junction C.

6.2 Crooked Lake Portage Trail junction.

6.3 Craig Lake Shore.

6.4 Crooked Lake Portage Trail junction.

6.9 Junction D.

7.2 Campsite spur.

7.7 Junction A.

7.9 Trailhead.

20 White Deer Lake

Highlights: A quiet, remote wilderness; forest; lakes; cliffs; and history.
Location: 10 miles northwest of Champion.
Type of hike: Out-and-back.
Distance: 7.8 miles.
Difficulty: Moderate.
Fees and permits: None.
Best months: May through October.

Camping: Backpack camping is allowed along the trail within zero-impact guidelines. Van Riper State Park, 10 miles south of the trailhead, has 188 campsites.
Map: USGS Summit Lake quad.
Trail contact: Ottawa National Forest, (906) 852-3500, www.fs.fed.us/r9/ottawa.

Finding the trailhead: From Champion drive 2.3 miles west on M–28 and turn right (north) on Marquette County Road 607 (also known as the Peshekee Grade). Drive 9.1 miles north on CR 607, and turn right (north) into the trailhead parking area.

Special considerations: This hike passes through the McCormick Wilderness, a special place. Treat it well.

The Hike

The McCormick Tract is a living vision of what the land was like when it was whole—and what it could be again. Logging hit many of the acres within this backwoods almost a century ago, but the time since then has been kind to this place. The McCormick family, descendants of the inventor of the reaping machine, bought land here for a family retreat. These days the McCormick Tract is a federal wilderness and a notable example of a forest's ability to heal itself, if allowed to do so.

Sprinkled around the broad swath of forest is a mosaic of sparkling lakes, clear-running streams, and rock outcrops. A few miles of trails penetrate the remote interior of this 16,000-acre wilderness.

Begin your hike by walking east from the trailhead on the White Deer Lake Trail, immediately crossing a sturdy bridge over the Peshekee River. The trail follows the old road, now overgrown in spots, which went to the McCormick family lodge at White Deer Lake.

Once past the Peshekee the trail turns north, running through a scrubby stretch, and then threads its way between a cliffy headland and the marshy waters of Baraga Creek. At Mile 1.0, the trail crosses Camp 11 Creek, typically an easy rock hop, and runs northeast to the unmarked junction with the Lower Baraga Lake Trail at Mile 1.2. From this direction, the spur path, almost a 180-degree turn to your left, can be easy to miss. It is 450 paces past the creek crossing. Make a mental note of its location for your return trip.

Continue hiking northeast on the White Deer Lake Trail. Soon the path ascends a slope, and the ambience of the McCormick forest begins. Maples are the upland hardwood here, and the forest is open and older, untouched by logging for nearly a century.

Tranquil White Deer Lake—a time-honored backwoods retreat.

About a half-mile later the trail dips to run along a marshy section, framed by cliff-hugging white pines. Now returning to the rolling hardwood hills, the path runs northeast to White Deer Lake (Mile 3.2). Just before reaching the lake, the White Deer Lake Trail passes a flat, open spot, where remnants of the foundations of the McCormick lodge buildings remain. You can also see vestiges of foundations of the old McCormick buildings on an island just offshore. In the early 1900s an extensive trail system branched out from this spot. One of those constructed paths, the Bentley Trail, led to the Huron Mountain Club on the Lake Superior shore. Today it is possible to find traces of those old paths here and there in the McCormick backcountry, but they are relics of trails long gone. Off-trail hikers that know of the old trails' locations see them as valuable route clues, fascinating hints of the life of those who walked this land before us.

White Deer Lake is now a peaceful spot. Loons dive for minnows in the shallows around the island; their wailing call echoes across the water at twilight. Eagles pass overhead, and the hustle and bustle of modern life seems far away.

When you are ready retrace your steps to the junction with the Lower Baraga Lake Trail, Mile 5.2 of the outing. Turn right (west) and follow the narrow path as

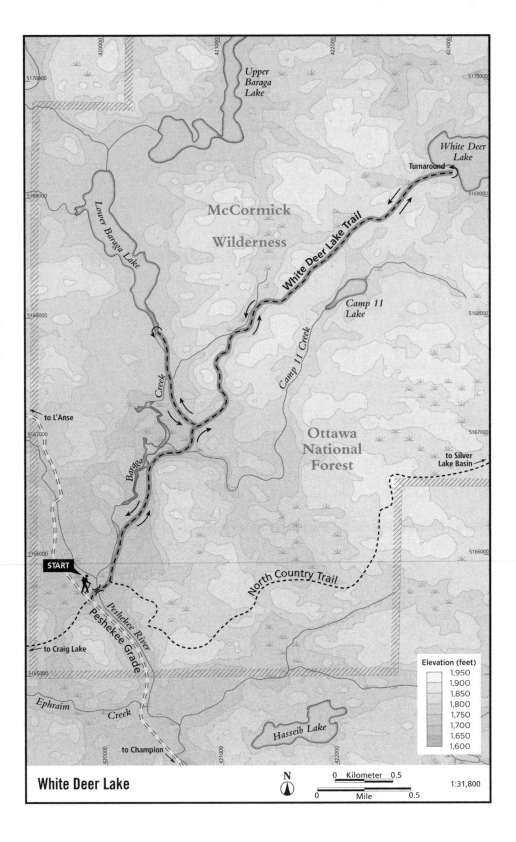

Upper
Baraga
Lake

White Deer
Lake

Turnaround

McCormick

Wilderness

Lower Baraga Lake

White Deer Lake Trail

Camp 11
Lake

Camp 11 Creek

Creek

to L'Anse

Ottawa
National
Forest

to Silver
Lake Basin

Baraga

START

North Country Trail

Peshekee River

Peshekee Grade

to Craig Lake

Ephraim

Creek

Hasseib Lake

to Champion

Elevation (feet)
1,950
1,900
1,850
1,800
1,750
1,700
1,650
1,600

White Deer Lake

N

0   Kilometer   0.5

0   Mile   0.5

1:31,800

it swings north through the woods. About a quarter mile later, the path nears Baraga Creek, a scene of subtle but powerful beauty and a nice spot to linger.

Resume hiking north, arriving at the outlet of Lower Baraga Lake at mile 5.8. Lower Baraga Lake is a mile long, and the outlet is on a narrow, out-of-the-way arm of the lake. I would suggest hiking another 0.1 mile to get more of a view. A faint path makes its way along the eastern shoreline to a peninsula, Mile 5.9 of the hike.

Retrace your steps to the outlet (Mile 6.0) and south on the Lower Baraga Lake Trail to the junction with the White Deer Lake Trail at Mile 6.6. Turn right (southwest) onto the White Deer Lake Trail, hiking to Camp 11 Creek (Mile 6.8) and back to the trailhead.

Key Points

0.0 Trailhead.

1.0 Camp 11 Creek.

1.2 Lower Baraga Lake Trail junction.

3.2 White Deer Lake.

5.2 Lower Baraga Lake Trail junction.

5.8 Lower Baraga Lake outlet.

5.9 Peninsula on Lower Baraga Lake.

6.0 Lower Baraga Lake outlet.

6.6 Lower Baraga Lake Trail junction.

6.8 Camp 11 Creek.

7.8 Trailhead.

21 Falls of the Yellow Dog

Highlights: A remote series of cascades in a beautiful forest setting.
Location: 20 miles west of Big Bay.
Type of hike: Out-and-back.
Distance: 4.8 miles.
Difficulty: Difficult*.
Fees and permits: None.
Best months: May through October.

Camping: Backpack camping is allowed along the trail within zero-impact guidelines. Big Eric's Bridge State Forest Campground, 14 miles northwest of the trailhead, has twenty campsites.
Map: USGS Bulldog Lake quad (inc.).
Trail contact: Ottawa National Forest, (906) 852–3500, www.fs.fed.us/r9/ottawa.

Finding the trailhead: This is a remote trailhead. Consider the advantages of having an accurate map and compass with you in your vehicle. Presume that intersections mentioned are unmarked. Most vehicles, handled with care, can make this drive under good conditions. Poor conditions may make this route impassable.

From the town of Big Bay, drive 2 miles south on Marquette County Route 550 (paved) and make a right (south) on Marquette County Route 510 (graded dirt). Follow that road southwest 3.2 miles and turn right (west) on Triple A Road (graded dirt).

Drive west and south on Triple A Road. After 3.1 miles bear left (south), continuing on Triple A Road as Northwestern Road goes right (west). Drive another 10.9 miles, first south and then steadily west, on Triple A Road to Anderson's Corner.

Go straight (west) as Ford Road goes right (north). After going west past Anderson's Corner, Triple A Road curves south. Follow that curve south and, after driving 0.5 mile from Anderson's Corner, go straight (south), ignoring a hand-painted DEAD END sign as Triple A Road goes right (west).

Continue driving south another 0.5 mile and bear left (south), entering a two-track lane, as the road swings right (west) and uphill. Follow that lane south 0.1 mile to the marked trailhead.
Special considerations: This hike passes through the McCormick Wilderness, a special place. Treat it well. The trail leads to the two branches of the Yellow Dog River. Travel off-trail or along faint, rough paths is necessary upstream to view the cascades and waterfalls on both streams.

The Hike

The headwaters country of the Yellow Dog River holds a hallowed spot in U.P. lore. Approached only by a long, dusty drive, the whole upper drainage resides within a wilderness area, the McCormick Tract. There, on a high plateau inhabited by a remarkable forest, the waters of White Deer Lake, Lake Margaret, and dozens of brooks flow north. At the north end of that plateau, the pace quickens. That pristine water tumbles downward hundreds of vertical feet in the cascades known as the Falls of the Yellow Dog. This hike visits these waterfalls on two separate branches of the river, a mile apart.

Start your hike by walking south from the trailhead on an overgrown woods road that quickly becomes a footpath. The path is pleasant. The forest is older and charming with maple and beech and a scattering of hemlock groves.

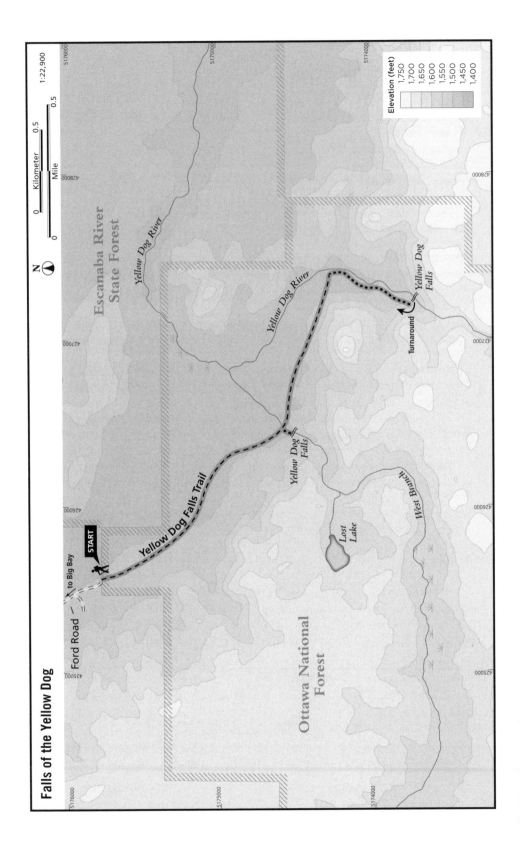

Falls of the Yellow Dog

N

1:22,900

Kilometer 0   0.5   0.5
Mile   0   0.5

Elevation (feet)
1,750
1,700
1,650
1,600
1,550
1,500
1,450
1,400

Escanaba River
State Forest

Yellow Dog River

Yellow Dog River

Yellow Dog
Falls

Turnaround

Yellow Dog Falls Trail

START

to Big Bay

Ford Road

Yellow Dog
Falls

Lost
Lake

West Branch

Ottawa National
Forest

After a mile the trail reaches the West Branch of the Yellow Dog River. Turn right (south) and work your way upstream about 150 feet to where the cascades begin. A long sliding cascade on a large rock slab is the main feature here, but small waterfalls and cascades continue upstream.

When you are ready retrace your steps north, downstream, to the trail (Mile 1.2). I crossed the West Branch on a log, slippery with moss, with vital assistance from my trekking poles. Follow the path east as it ascends a short, rocky stretch near the West Branch. The path continues to run east, at times a bit faint, and reaches the main branch of the Yellow Dog River at Mile 2.0.

The cascades here are farther off the trail, and rougher to get to, than the West Branch's waterfalls. That said, I think they are exceptionally appealing and worthwhile.

Work your way upstream along the west bank of the river. The river is pleasant here, but there is a good quarter mile to go before the cascade show begins. Watch for a remnant from the days when this land was the retreat of the McCormick family: two wooden bridges bracketing a small island in the stream.

Just south of those bridges, the valley narrows, the pitch of the stream steepens, and the cascades begin. It is quite a show—a long series of drops as the Yellow Dog River bounces down more than 150 vertical feet in less than a quarter mile's length.

Footing is often rough, and somehow that seems appropriate. This is a place to take your time and soak in the sights and sounds of an exceptional stream in a notable forest setting. The top of the cascades (Mile 2.4) is the turnaround point for this hike.

Key Points

0.0 Trailhead.

1.0 Trail crosses West Branch of the Yellow Dog River.

1.1 Top of cascades on West Branch of the Yellow Dog River.

1.2 Trail crosses West Branch of the Yellow Dog River.

2.0 Yellow Dog River (main branch).

2.4 Top of cascades on Yellow Dog River (main branch), turnaround point.

4.8 Trailhead.

22 Little Garlic River

Highlights: Little Garlic River and its cascades, attractive forest, ancient hemlocks.
Location: 10 miles northwest of Marquette.
Type of hike: Out-and-back.
Distance: 8.0 miles.
Difficulty: Moderate.
Fees and permits: None, but consider a donation to the North Country Trail Association, www.northcountrytrail.org.

Best months: May through October.
Camping: Marquette Tourist Park, 11 miles south of the trailhead, has 110 campsites.
Maps: USGS Negaunee quad (inc.); North Country Trail Association Map TMI11, Au Train Lake to Little Garlic Falls.
Trail contact: Michigan Department of Natural Resources, (906) 346–9201, www.michigan.gov/dnr.

Finding the trailhead: From the intersection of Sugarloaf Avenue and Hawley Street, on Marquette's north side, drive west and north 10.4 miles on Marquette County Route 550. Turn left (south) into the trailhead parking area (just west of the bridge over the Little Garlic River).

Little Garlic Falls, gurgling cascades in a charming forest setting.

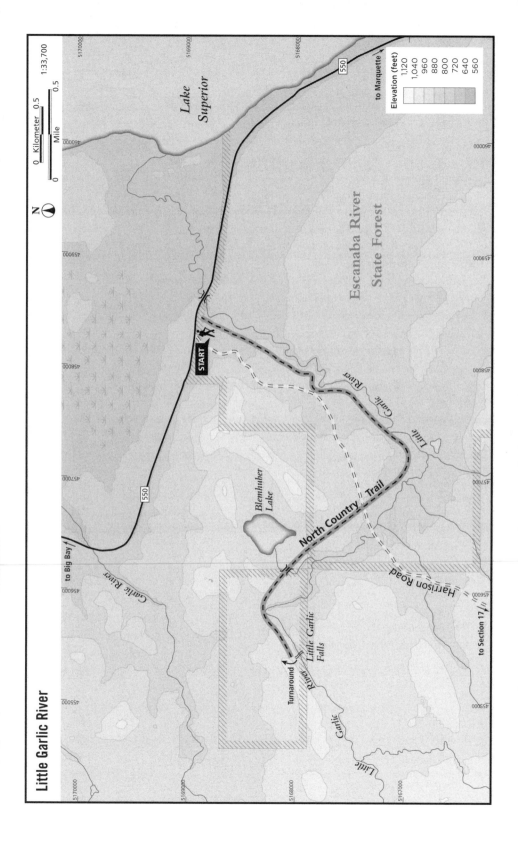

Little Garlic River

N

1:33,700

0 Kilometer 0.5

0 Mile 0.5

Elevation (feet)
1,120
1,040
960
880
800
720
640
560

Lake Superior

to Marquette

550

Escanaba River State Forest

START

Little Garlic River

North Country Trail

Blemhuber Lake

550

Garlic River

to Big Bay

Harrison Road

to Section 17

Turnaround

Little Garlic Falls

Little Garlic River

The Hike

Little Garlic River is one of those quiet hikes that steadily grows on you, one subtle scene at a time. Both the Little Garlic River, a pristine brook trout stream that the trail follows, and the surrounding forest are a pleasure to the eye. Four serene miles from the trailhead, the path arrives at Little Garlic Falls, a scenic stretch of cascades, rapids, and swift water running through a rocky cleft.

Begin your visit along the Little Garlic River by hiking south from the trailhead on the North Country Trail (NCT), through a damp fern garden. The river is just 30 feet to the east. Soon the riverbank rises into a bluff, and the trail ascends into a fine beech–maple forest. About 1 mile from the trailhead, the NCT passes through an ancient stand of hemlocks and a short spur trail leads south, onto a sharp promontory, high above the river.

Continue hiking southwest on the NCT as the path descends to run along the river, rises once more to cross a bluff, and returns to river level. As the terrain flattens out, the trail crosses Harrison Road (dirt) at Mile 2.9, and reenters the woods, passing a line of mossy boulders each the size of a small truck.

Now running northwest the trail passes through open forest. A rock dome shows to the north. After utilizing a plank bridge to cross a marshy spot, the trail winds over several open rock slabs before turning southwest and reaching Little Garlic Falls at Mile 4.0.

I was at Little Garlic Falls at a low water time and discovered a charming setting beyond the end of the official trail. I worked my way upstream along the north side for fifty paces and found a memorable scene: a cascade dropping 4 feet into a pool bordered by a 30-foot-high cliff.

Option: Nimble hikers may want to cross to the stream's south shore if conditions allow. I was able to rock hop across, finding a faint path leading upstream for 400 yards. Even at low water the small river retained its charm, rippling over rock slabs and gurgling its way downstream.

Key Points

- **0.0** Trailhead.
- **2.9** Harrison Road.
- **4.0** Little Garlic Falls; turnaround point.
- **8.0** Trailhead.

23 Clark Lake Loop

Highlights: One of the largest stands of virgin forest in the upper Midwest and a quiet, non-motorized lake.
Location: 8 miles southwest of Watersmeet.
Type of hike: Loop.
Distance: 7.6 miles.
Difficulty: Moderate.
Fees and permits: A daily fee of $5.00 per vehicle (or $20.00 for a season pass) is collected May 15 through September 30. Camping fees are $10.00 per night for designated backcountry campsites. There are no fees for day hikes, but registration is requested.

Best months: May through October.
Camping: Six designated backcountry campsites border this route. A permit is required to use them. The Sylvania Campground, a half-mile east of the trailhead, has forty-eight drive-in campsites.
Maps: USGS Black Oak Lake (inc.) quad; Sylvania Wilderness Trail Map (Ottawa National Forest).
Trail contact: Sylvania Wilderness, (906) 358-4551, www.fs.fed.us/r9/ottawa.

Finding the trailhead: From Watersmeet, drive 4.1 miles west on U.S. Highway 2 and turn left (south) on Gogebic County Road 535. Drive 4 miles south and turn left (south) onto Sylvania's entrance road. Stop at the A-frame office. Drive south 0.2 mile and turn right (west), following signs to the boat launch on Clark Lake. Drive west 1 mile and turn left (south). Drive another 0.3 mile to the boat launch and trailhead.
Special considerations: This hike travels through an outstanding wilderness area. Treat it with respect.

The Hike

When hikers stand at the north end of Clark Lake, with its picnic area and boat ramp, they could easily imagine they were at any one of a number of northern lakes. By the time they arrive at the south end of the lake however, it is obvious they are someplace special—the core of a wilderness area sheltering 17,000 acres of virgin forest.

Paul Bunyan's ax swung hard and wide across our northern forests in the late 1800s. Sylvania is one of a handful of large chunks of old-growth forest that escaped that onslaught, and this hikes takes your through notable stands of hemlock, sugar maple, and white pine elders. Two-hundred-year-old trees are common, and some hardy specimens here are 400 years old.

Begin your circuit of Clark Lake on the southeast corner of the boat ramp parking lot where a sign indicates the beginning of the Clark Lake Trail. Follow the trail southeast as it skirts the shoreline, rounding bays and cutting across piney peninsulas. After a little more than a mile, it ducks inland to make its way around aptly named Golden Silence Lake, a placid pond.

Along the way the myth that Midwest forests are thick and brushy dies. Sylvania's forest, like most old-growth, tends to be open and parklike under its tall

Sixteen thousand acres of stunning virgin forest surround Clark Lake's pure waters.

canopy. Below, the ground shows the pleasant lumpiness of fallen trees, aging into mulch and duff.

Continue following the path southeast and bear right (southeast) onto an old road at Mile 2.2. Walk along that old road to a meadow at Mile 2.4, the far eastern corner of Clark Lake. Stay straight (southeast) as a portage trail crosses, and 5 feet later turn right (southwest) on a path that crosses the meadow. This path quickly enters the woods and joins an old road that runs southwest near Clark Lake's southern shore. Stay straight (southwest) a quarter mile later, as a portage trail crosses. That old road remains close to the lake for almost 1.5 miles before beginning a straight, westward course. Watch for a key signed intersection at Mile 4.3. Turn right (north) on a footpath that is faint at times but features abundant blue blazes.

Walk north, following the path through the forest for a mile before emerging once again on Clark Lake's shoreline. Another mile of shoreline walking brings you to the picnic area and beach at the north end of the lake at Mile 6.9. From there just continue another half mile along the shoreline to the boat ramp and trailhead at Mile 7.6.

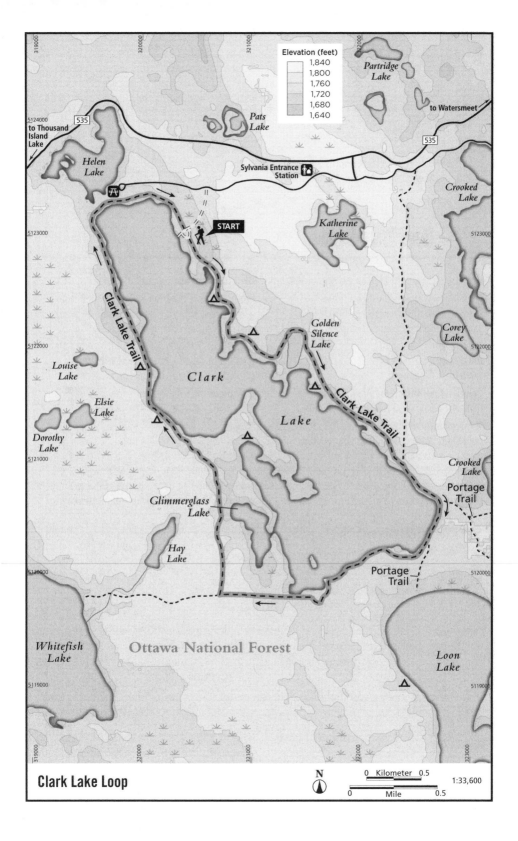

Elevation (feet)
1,840
1,800
1,760
1,720
1,680
1,640

Partridge
Lake

to Watersmeet

535

to Thousand
Island
Lake

Helen
Lake

Pats
Lake

Sylvania Entrance
Station

Crooked
Lake

START

Katherine
Lake

Clark Lake Trail

Golden
Silence
Lake

Corey
Lake

Clark

Lake

Clark Lake Trail

Louise
Lake

Elsie
Lake

Dorothy
Lake

Glimmerglass
Lake

Crooked
Lake

Portage
Trail

Hay
Lake

Portage
Trail

Whitefish
Lake

Ottawa National Forest

Loon
Lake

Clark Lake Loop

N

0   Kilometer   0.5

0   Mile   0.5

1:33,600

Key Points

0.0 Trailhead.

0.9 Golden Silence Lake.

2.4 Clark Lake east end junction.

4.3 Clark Lake Trail.

6.9 Beach and picnic area.

7.6 Trailhead.

24 Deer Island Lake

Highlights: A quiet trail through one of the largest stands of virgin forest in the upper Midwest; loons on wilderness lakes.

Location: 6 miles south of Watersmeet.

Type of hike: Lollipop.

Distance: 21.2 miles.

Difficulty: Difficult*.

Fees and permits: Camping fees are $10 per night for designated backcountry campsites. There are no fees for day hikes, but self-registration at the trailhead is requested.

Best months: May through October.

Camping: Backcountry camping within the Sylvania Wilderness is allowed only at designated sites. A permit is required.

Maps: USGS Black Oak Lake (inc.) and Land O'Lakes (inc.) quads; Sylvania Wilderness Map (Ottawa National Forest).

Trail contact: Sylvania Wilderness, (906) 358-4551, www.fs.fed.us/r9/ottawa.

Finding the trailhead: Start at the intersection of Vilas County Road B and Airport Road in downtown Land O'Lakes, Wisconsin (south of Watersmeet). Drive north on Gogebic County Road 539. After 0.7 mile go straight (west), as CR 539 turns right (north) on Fischer Road. Drive west 0.2 mile and park at the end of the lane.

Special considerations: This hike travels through an outstanding wilderness area. Treat it with respect.

The Hike

Sylvania, with its 17,000 acres of virgin forest and thirty-six named lakes, is no stranger to savvy nature lovers. Most of those folks, though, enter the area from the north, paddling canoes. Few of Sylvania's visitors know of the quiet footpath that enters from the southeast from Land O'Lakes. This trail quickly takes hikers into one of the most remote corners of the wilderness—the Deer Island Lake area. For ambitious hikers that is just the beginning. If you continue walking northwest and round Clark Lake on its loop, you create a prime route. For a brief moment, at the north end of Clark Lake, there are some minor signs of civilization. Other than that this hike is a 21.2-mile-long walking tour of old-growth forest and pristine lakes.

Hauntingly picturesque old-growth forest scenes line the Deer Island Lake Trail.

Start the hike by walking west from the Land O'Lakes trailhead. Follow the path northwest, arriving at a junction with an old woods road just east of Deer Island Lake's south end, at Mile 3.2. This is a key intersection and unmarked when I saw it. Turn right (northeast) and follow the old road north. About 1 mile later go straight (north), ignoring a spur that goes left to the north end of Deer Island Lake.

Follow the old road as it swings northwest, offering a last glimpse of Deer Island Lake, and arrives at an intersection with the Mountain Lake Trail at Mile 5.6. Turn left (west), following another old road to yet another intersection north of Loon Lake, at Mile 6.5. Turn right (northwest) and walk to a meadow at the far east end of Clark Lake (Mile 6.8). Turn left (southwest), following a path that enters the woods and joins an old woods road running southwest near Clark Lake's southern shore. Stay straight (southwest) a quarter mile later, as a portage trail crosses.

The old road remains close to the lake for almost 1.5 miles before beginning a straight, westward course. Watch for a signed intersection at Mile 8.7. Turn right (north) onto the Clark Lake Trail, a footpath that is faint at times but features abundant blue blazes. Walk north, following the path through a forest for a mile, before emerging once again on Clark Lake's shoreline. Another mile of northward walking

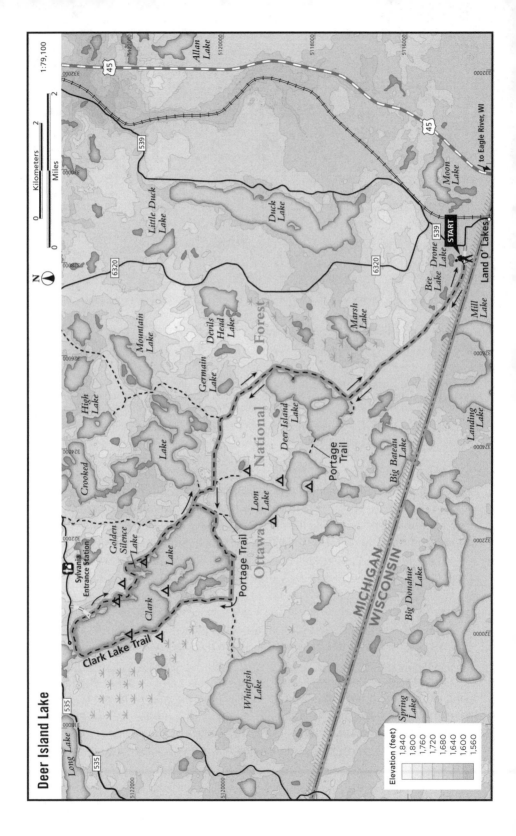

Deer Island Lake

1:79,100

Elevation (feet)
1,840
1,800
1,760
1,720
1,680
1,640
1,600
1,560

Kilometers
Miles

N

Long Lake
Allan Lake
Little Duck Lake
Duck Lake
Moon Lake
to Eagle River, WI

Crooked Lake
High Lake
Mountain Lake
Germain Lake
Devils Head Lake
Forest
Marsh Lake
Bee Drone Lake
START
Land O' Lakes

Sylvania Entrance Station
Golden Silence Lake
Clark Lake
Lake
National
Deer Island Lake
Loon Lake
Portage Trail
Big Bateau Lake
Mill Lake
Landing Lake

Clark Lake Trail
Portage Trail
Ottawa
MICHIGAN
WISCONSIN
Big Donahue Lake

Whitefish Lake
Spring Lake

brings you to a picnic area. Walk eastward, past a swimming beach and along a trail that curls southward to a boat ramp at Mile 12. At the southeast corner of the boat ramp parking area, a sign marks the Clark Lake Trail.

Follow the Clark Lake Trail southeast as it skirts the shoreline, rounding bays and cutting across piney peninsulas. After a little more than a mile, the trail ducks inland to make its way around aptly named Golden Silence Lake, a sylvan pond.

Continue following the path southeast and bear right (southeast) at a junction with an old road at Mile 14.2. Walk along that old road to the meadow at the far eastern corner of Clark Lake (Mile 14.4), the same spot we saw at Mile 6.8. From here retrace your steps of the first part of the hike to return to the Land O'Lakes trailhead.

Options: This route has two attractive options. The first involves following the described route to Mile 6.8, the eastern corner of Clark Lake. From that point hike southwest on the Clark Lake Trail another 0.3 mile, and turn left (south) on the portage trail leading to Loon Lake. Walk south a quarter mile to Loon Lake's shore, then east along a sandy beach. As the shore curves south, look for an informal path in the open woods that parallels the lakeshore. Follow that path and Loon Lake's east shore south and east for 2 miles to the portage trail that leads to Deer Island Lake. Hike southeast a quarter mile on the portage trail to Deer Island Lake. There, a three-quarter-mile off-trail segment begins. Hike south through open woods, keeping Deer Island Lake in sight to your left (northeast) to the Deer Island Lake Trail junction that you saw at Mile 3.2. Total distance for this hike, out-and-back from Land O' Lakes would be about 13.5 miles.

Backpackers looking for an optimum base camp would do well to consider a multinight stay at the Mallard designated campsite on the north end of Loon Lake. That location puts you in excellent position to do the Clark Lake Trail loop as a day trip, as well as explore north to Mountain Lake or west to Whitefish Lake. This plan would require a 6-mile backpack on the first and last day.

Key Points

0.0	Land O'Lakes trailhead.
3.2	Deer Island Lake junction.
5.6	Mountain Lake Trail junction.
6.8	Clark Lake junction.
8.7	Clark Lake Trail (turn north).
11.3	Beach and picnic area, Clark Lake.
12.0	Boat ramp, Clark Lake.
12.9	Golden Silence Lake.
14.4	Clark Lake junction.
21.2	Land O'Lakes trailhead.

25 Piers Gorge

Highlights: A series of booming drops on the Menominee River, Misicot Falls earns a "don't miss" rating.
Location: 3 miles south of Norway.
Type of hike: Out-and-back.
Distance: 2.6 miles.
Difficulty: Moderate.
Fees and permits: None.

Best months: May through October.
Camping: Carney Lake State Forest Campground, 23 miles north of the trailhead, has sixteen campsites.
Map: USGS Norway quad (inc.).
Trail contact: Dickinson County Chamber of Commerce, (906) 774-2002, www.dickinsonchamber.com.

Finding the trailhead: From the town of Norway, drive south 1.9 miles on U.S. Highway 8 and turn right (west) on Piers Gorge Road. Drive 1.2 miles west to the trailhead.
Special considerations: Use caution on wet rocks near the river.

The Hike

Most times the Menominee River runs deep and slow and stretches almost 100 yards across. At Piers Gorge it gets rowdy. Bedrock walls channel the flow into an 80-foot-wide sluice, part of a mile-long stretch of swift water and rapids topped off by a crescendo of thundering ledge drops. It is a striking scene of big water throwing its weight around, the roaring soundtrack a not-too-subtle warning to stand clear, or else.

Quieter scenes also play out here. One could spend hours musing over the current's patterns etched in the bedrock. The forest is a pleasure to the eye, and eagles and ospreys scan from above for an easy meal.

A relatively benign trail leads upstream from the trailhead, periodically marked by posts that announce FIRST PIER and so on. Branching off from these posts are much rougher trails that nimble hikers use to approach the river. Piers refers to bedrock reefs that extend into the current. The Third and Fourth Piers also possess names as waterfalls.

Begin your tour by walking west from the trailhead, quickly crossing two wood bridges that span a damp cedar stand, bisected by a clear-running brook. The broad trail arrives at the First Pier's signpost at Mile 0.1. Hike south, off the maintained trail, for one hundred paces here and a broad bedrock dome borders the first white water, a 2-foot drop.

Return to the main trail and hike up a rocky rise, arriving at the post for the Second Pier at Mile 0.4. This one is louder, and if you hike twenty-five paces south, you learn why. Huge wave trains scour the river's southern shore, while a series of ledge drops inhabit the near side of the river.

Backtrack to the main trail and resume walking west, arriving at the Third Pier's post at Mile 0.5. The Third Pier is Misicot Falls, a 5-foot drop, followed by powerful rapids featuring fearsome standing waves. A large, automobile-size boulder below

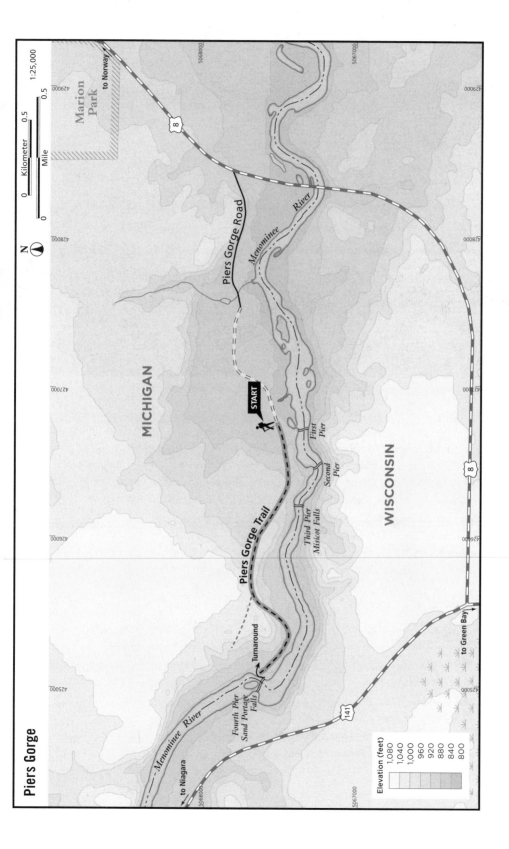

Piers Gorge

1:25,000

N

| Kilometer | 0 | 0.5 |
| Mile | 0 | 0.5 |

to Norway

Marion Park

to Niagara

Menominee River

MICHIGAN

Piers Gorge Road

Menominee River

8

Piers Gorge Trail

START

First Pier

Second Pier

Third Pier
Misicot Falls

WISCONSIN

Turnaround

Fourth Pier
Sand Portage Falls

141

to Green Bay

8

Elevation (feet)

1,080
1,040
1,000
960
920
880
840
800

Misicot Falls. The Menominee River gets rowdy at Piers Gorge.

the drop splits the wave trains, forming a foamy bulge. The trail here is perched on the hillside, offering a memorable high view of the falls and rapids.

When you are ready continue hiking west on the Piers Gorge Trail, arriving at a split at Mile 0.8, where a signpost points the way to the Fourth Pier. Bear left (southwest), walking a trail that becomes a narrow footpath and leads to the Fourth Pier's post at Mile 1.3.

The Fourth Pier, Sand Portage Falls, is a 5-foot cascade, a narrows between bedrock. Legend has this as the beginning of the Great Sand Portage, a prudent alternative to canoeing the rapids and a route that stretched from here to below the First Pier's unnamed falls. Knowing of the legend, I wondered who had used this portage and what stories they told of this place.

Key Points

- **0.0** Trailhead.
- **0.1** First Pier.
- **0.4** Second Pier.
- **0.5** Third Pier, Misicot Falls.
- **0.8** Junction with path to Fourth Pier, Sand Portage Falls.
- **1.3** Fourth Pier, Sand Portage Falls; turnaround point.
- **2.6** Trailhead.

Eastern Region of the Upper Penninsula

The Eastern Upper Peninsula, although lower than the western half, is hardly a landscape without drama. Sand dunes on a gigantic scale border the deep blue waters of Lake Superior west of Grand Marais. To their west aptly named Twelvemile Beach leads to a wild and craggy coast—the Pictured Rocks. There water and ice carved a sandstone plateau into arches, sea caves, and turrets, streaked in yellow, brown, and green. That same sandstone geology lends itself to an arcing free fall form seen in some eastern U.P. waterfalls such as Tahquamenon's Upper Falls and Spray Falls.

Vast swaths of wetlands shelter wildlife and cover much of the interior. Here and there along the Lake Michigan and Lake Huron coasts, bedrock limestone forms cliffs and broad slabs between boulder-dotted beaches.

Hikers can walk through the striking virgin forest between the falls of the Tahquamenon, greet the rising sun at the remote headland known as Marble Head, and spot rare Trumpeter Swans at Seney National Wildlife Refuge. Those seeking solitude will find remote shorelines and patrolling eagles if they explore the quiet corners of the coasts.

26 Laughing Whitefish Falls

Highlights: A famous waterfall, quiet woods, and a hidden chasm.
Location: 10 miles west of Chatham.
Type of hike: Out-and-back, with two stems.
Distance: 3.4 miles.
Difficulty: Moderate*.
Fees and permits: None, but consider a donation to the North Country Trail Association, www.northcountrytrail.org.

Best months: May through October.
Camping: Forest Lake State Forest Campground, 16 miles east of the trailhead, has twenty-three campsites.
Maps: USGS Sand River quad (inc.); North Country Trail Map TMI11, Au Train Lake to Little Garlic Falls.
Trail contact: Michigan Department of Natural Resources, (906) 346–9201.

Finding the trailhead: From Chatham, drive 7.7 miles west on M-94 and turn right (north) on North Sundell Road. Drive 2.3 miles north and turn right (east) into the Laughing Whitefish Falls Scenic Area. Drive 0.4 mile east to the trailhead.

Special considerations: This hike takes place within the Laughing Whitefish Falls State Natural Area. Please treat this special area well.

The Hike

Laughing Whitefish Falls, plunging 100 feet into a scenic gorge, earns mention as the most spectacular waterfall in Michigan. Certainly it is on the short list for that honor.

Picture a 15-foot free fall that sets the stage for the main act, an 80-foot-high bridal train of white water tumbling down a rock apron. The striated texture of the rock bounces a zillion small ripples skyward, each sparkling in midday light.

Below the falls the river settles into a scenic gorge, lined with springs, mossy corners, and old-growth white pine and hemlock. A fine maple-beech forest graces the plateau above.

Take a moment to read the educational signboard at the north end of the trailhead parking loop, then hike north on the broad Laughing Whitefish Falls Trail. Go straight (east) at Mile 0.3, as a spur trail of the NCT goes left (north). Continue walking east, descending past a brook gurgling over small ledge drops; a fern garden is nearby.

The falls kind of sneak up on you. A railing appears at Mile 0.6, the river flowing beside it to the right. As you approach, a huge hole opens beyond the railing, to the north, and spray and sound announce the waterfall.

A set of sturdy stairs leads some 150 steps to a viewing platform at the bottom of the falls. This is the best place to view the flowing symmetry of the Laughing Whitefish Falls. Descend the stairs, past intimate views of mossy nooks and crannies, to the viewing platform. This is a superb place for a break.

When you are ready ascend the stairs and retrace your footsteps to the junction with a spur trail of the NCT, at Mile 0.9 of the hike. Turn right (north) onto the

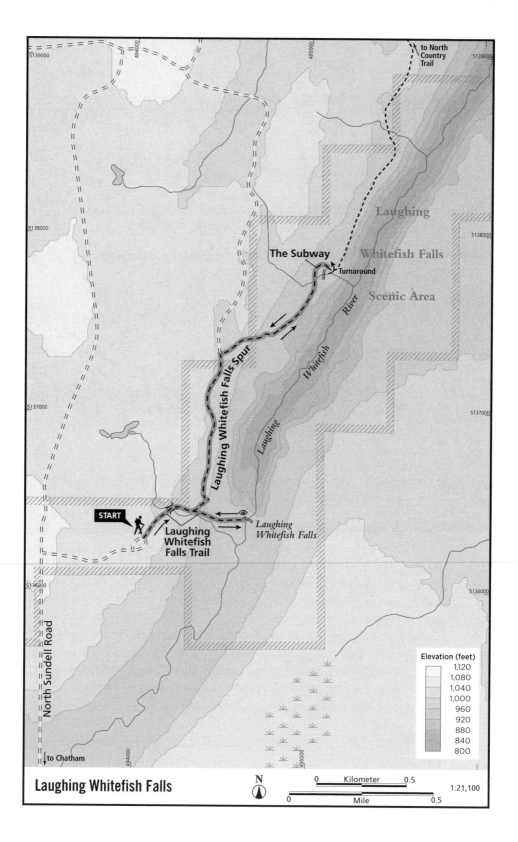

to North
Country
Trail

Laughing

The Subway

Whitefish Falls

Turnaround

Scenic Area

Whitefish River

Laughing Whitefish Falls Spur

Laughing

START

Laughing
Whitefish
Falls Trail

Laughing
Whitefish Falls

North Sundell Road

to Chatham

Elevation (feet)

1,120
1,080
1,040
1,000
960
920
880
840
800

Laughing Whitefish Falls

N

0   Kilometer   0.5

0   Mile   0.5

1:21,100

Laughing Whitefish Falls, a long and sparkling bridal veil.

spur trail. A narrow path leads north and fifty paces later becomes an old woods road. This trail is marked with vertical white blazes and blue diamonds. After following the old woods road for about 0.7 mile, the NCT spur trail turns right (east) on a narrow, faint path. Watch for the markings.

Follow this path east and north. At Mile 2.0 it curls around the lip of a small, but striking, canyon scene. A brook feeds a thin little waterfall, a 25-foot drop that features cascades, both top and bottom, bracketing an 8-foot free fall. An undercut stretch below the falls led me to label this the "Subway." Beyond, hemlocks line the brook's descent to the river.

I was here during a wet spell. The brook was flowing nicely, and I stayed for a while. The little cove was good company. I couldn't help wondering what other gems lay hidden nearby, tucked in the corners of the Laughing Whitefish River's gorge. To return to the trailhead, retrace your steps south, arriving at Laughing Whitefish Falls Trail at Mile 3.1. Turn right (west) and walk 0.3 mile to the trailhead.

Key Points

0.0 Trailhead.

0.3 Junction with North Country Trail (NCT) spur.

0.6 Laughing Whitefish Falls.

0.9 Junction with NCT spur.

2.0 The Subway, a rock overhang.

3.1 Junction with Laughing Whitefish Falls Trail.

3.4 Trailhead.

27 Rock River Falls

Highlights: A delightful waterfall in a quiet, wilderness setting.
Location: 5 miles northwest of Chatham.
Type of hike: Out-and-back.
Distance: 1.8 miles.
Difficulty: Moderate*.
Fees and permits: None.
Best months: May through October.

Camping: Backpack camping is allowed along the trail within zero-impact guidelines. The Hiawatha National Forest's Au Train Lake Campground, 11 miles east of the trailhead, has thirty-seven campsites.
Map: USGS Rock River quad (inc.).
Trail contact: Hiawatha National Forest, Munising Ranger District, (906) 387-2512, www.fs.fed.us/r9/hiawatha.

Finding the trailhead: From Chatham drive 3.3 miles north on Rock River Road. Turn left (west) on Forest Road 2276 (also known as Sandstrom Road). Drive 3.6 miles northwest on FR 2276 and turn left (south) on Forest Road 2293. Drive 0.7 mile south on FR 2293 to the trailhead for the Rock River Falls Trail.

Special considerations: Waterproof boots and trekking poles help at a few damp spots near the falls. Rock River Falls is within the Rock River Canyon Wilderness. Treat it well.

The Hike

Having a waterfall to yourself is a mighty fine thing. The ambience only increases when the waterfall is set in a quiet wilderness valley.

Rock River Falls is an enchanting experience, and the hike to reach it is only a mile. Somewhat obscure, it is a vivid reminder of the rich rewards awaiting those who explore the U.P.'s hidden nooks and crannies.

Begin your hike by walking west from the trailhead on an old two-track woods road, gently descending through a pleasing hardwood forest. A wilderness boundary sign marks entry into the Rock River Canyon Wilderness, a 4,640-acre preserve.

Quickly swinging southwest, then south, the two-track runs along the rim of a ravine that branches off the Rock River and then descends south into the shady river valley. Watch for a path branching off to the east when the old road reaches the valley floor (Mile 0.8). Turn left (east) on that path, finesse one challenging wet spot, and follow the trail as it swings around to the south and arrives at the base of Rock River Falls at Mile 0.9.

Rock River Falls, perched on a wide and multitiered ledge, drops some 20 feet

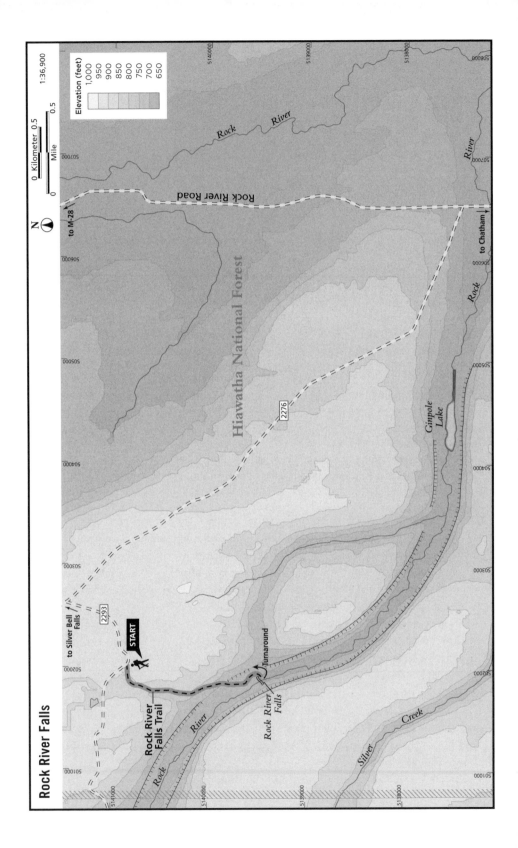

Rock River Falls

Rock River Falls, a hidden gem in the Rock River Canyon Wilderness.

into a dark pool, a cove lined with ferny, mossy walls. At moderate flows the left side free falls, while the center and right side tend to step down, bouncing off a terrace or two during their descent and creating a series of sparkling horsetails.

Key Points

0.0   Rock River Falls Trailhead (on FR 2293).

0.8   Path leaves two-track.

0.9   Rock River Falls; turnaround point.

1.8   Rock River Falls Trailhead.

28 Grand Island Loop

Highlights: Pristine Lake Superior shoreline on an offshore island, quiet forest, cliff top views of Pictured Rocks.
Location: 2 miles north of Munising.
Type of hike: Loop, with two short stems.
Distance: 10.9 miles.
Difficulty: Difficult due to distance; the hiking is moderate.
Fees and permits: There is a daily entrance fee of $2.00 per person.
Best months: May through October.
Camping: Grand Island features remote camping at designated sites only.
Maps: USGS Munising (inc.) quad; Hiawatha National Forest Map.
Trail contact: Grand Island National Recreation Area, (906) 387-2512, www.fs.fed.us/r9/hiawatha.

Finding the trailhead: From Munising, drive 2.9 miles north and west on M-28 and turn right (north). Drive 0.3 mile north to the ferry dock.
Special considerations: A passenger ferry offers service to Grand Island from late May to early October. Call (906) 387-3503 for ferry information. Grand Island's fabled black flies and mosquitoes can be a considerable factor from mid-May through mid-July.

The Hike

Grand Island, aptly named and 8 miles long, is an offshore version of Pictured Rocks. Its quiet north end features miles of scenic sea cliffs, a near mirror image of its mainland sibling. While Grand Island has no shortage of its own attractions, as a Pictured Rocks veteran I found the views of that craggy mainland coast from Trout Bay Overlook remarkable.

This hike features an abundance of junctions; most have directional signs. These intersections do not have names, however, so on the map they have been designated as Junction A, Junction B, and so on, to avoid confusion.

Begin your tour at Williams Landing, walking north on a sandy dirt road to Junction A at Mile 0.1. Turn left (west) on a grassy road that runs a tad inland from the island's shore through a hardwood forest with a sprinkling of hemlocks. About a mile from Junction A, the lane touches the shoreline near a sandy cove and begins a scenic run north. Long sight lines stretch west to little Williams Island and north to the looming cliffs of Grand Island's remote north end.

As the road runs north, the shoreline bluff rises into a cliffy crag, lowering as the lane reaches Junction B at Mile 2.9. Go straight (north); a connector road goes right (east). Walk north, past a campsite to a junction with the Thunder Coves Trail at Mile 3.3. Turn left (west) following the narrow footpath one hundred paces west to the shore, a low cliff. Continue north, past two benches that allow you to soak up the considerable ambience in style, to a point sixty paces north of the second bench, a good turnaround point. Savor the views and retrace your steps to the Thunder Coves Trail junction (Mile 3.9) and Junction B (Mile 4.3).

Trout Bay Overlook offers long views to the craggy Pictured Rocks shoreline.

Turn left (east) and hike along a dirt road that ascends into the island's interior, and begins a compact series of intersections at Junction C (Mile 5.1). Turn right (southeast) on a sandy road that quickly arrives at Junction D (Mile 5.3). Turn left (east) on another sandy woods road that leads to Junction E at Mile 5.4. At Junction E bear left (east) and hike east to Junction F (Mile 5.6), the last of this string of intersections.

Turn left (north) at Junction F and walk a shady mile north and east, following a sandy lane to Junction G (Mile 6.6). Go straight (northeast) as a trail that connects to Trout Bay goes right (south).

Walk a quarter-mile east to Trout Bay Overlook, which may well be the highlight of the day's outing. I visited on a crystalline fall day, and the view from this perch 150 feet above the bay was sublime, even mesmerizing. My notes list the sights visible, then a comment, "Wow!"

Below, the waters of Trout Bay and the open lake beyond were as blue as can be. Sweeping views led across the sparkling water to the Pictured Rocks cliffs, some 5 miles off. I spotted a white strand over there, on the mainland, and decided it was Miner's Beach. Miner's Castle was visible just south of the beach, as was Indian Head

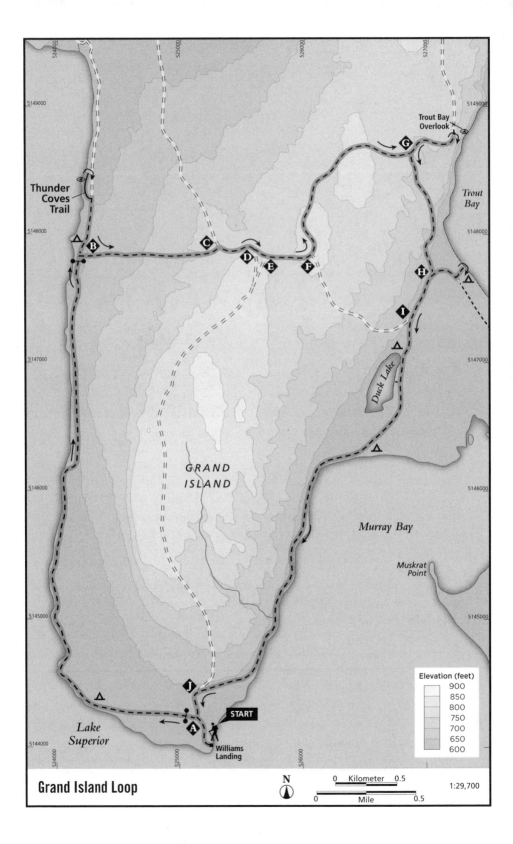

Thunder
Coves
Trail

Trout Bay
Overlook

G

Trout
Bay

△

B

C

D

E

F

H

△

I

△

Duck Lake

△

*GRAND
ISLAND*

Murray Bay

△

*Muskrat
Point*

J

START

△

A

*Lake
Superior*

Williams
Landing

Elevation (feet)
900
850
800
750
700
650
600

Grand Island Loop

N

0   Kilometer   0.5

0   Mile   0.5

1:29,700

and Grand Portal to the north. Past those last two promontories, the shoreline stretched east to the far-off horizon and Au Sable Point.

From the Trout Bay Overlook, retrace your steps to Junction G (Mile 7.0) and turn left (south) on a trail that connects to Trout Bay and follows the route of an overgrown road. Descending off the bluff to the forest floor below, the trail reaches Junction H at Mile 7.7. Turn left (north) onto a sandy lane that quickly arrives at a signboard near Trout Bay at Mile 7.9. At the signboard a boardwalk leads a stone's throw north to benches and Trout Bay's beach, a scenic break spot.

Trout Bay's beach, part of the isthmus that stretches from Grand Island's "mainland" to its "thumb," is an example of the creative power of lake currents and waterborne sand. The isthmus is a tombolo, a land bridge that connects two previously isolated bodies of land.

After visiting Trout Bay return to Junction H (Mile 8.1). Go straight (south) and follow the sandy lane south to Junction I (Mile 8.5). Bear left (south). About a quarter of a mile south of Junction I, the lane enters a long hemlock grove; Duck Lake is visible to the left. A short side-trip is available here—a spur trail leads west eighty paces to a viewing platform on that pond's shore.

After passing Duck Lake the lane continues south, soon running along Murray Bay's western shore and arriving at Junction J at Mile 10.7. Turn left (south) and 0.1 mile later go straight (south) at Junction A. Past that final intersection, the hike arrives at the Williams Landing trailhead at Mile 10.9.

Key Points

0.0 Williams Landing trailhead.

0.1 Junction A.

2.9 Junction B.

3.3 Thunder Coves Trail junction.

3.6 Turnaround point on Thunder Coves Trail.

3.9 Thunder Coves Trail junction.

4.3 Junction B.

5.1 Junction C.

5.3 Junction D.

5.4 Junction E.

5.6 Junction F.

6.6 Junction G.

6.8 Trout Bay Overlook.

7.0 Junction G.

7.7 Junction H.

7.9 Trout Bay Beach (west end).

8.1 Junction H.

8.5 Junction I.

10.7 Junction J.

10.8 Junction A.

10.9 Williams Landing trailhead.

29 Olson Falls

Highlights: Two beautiful waterfalls set in memorable sandstone glens.
Location: Munising.
Type of hike: Out-and-back.
Distance: 0.8 mile, in two segments.
Difficulty: Moderate.
Fees and permits: None, but consider a donation to Michigan Nature Association, www.michigannature.org.

Best months: May through October.
Camping: Bay Furnace, a Forest Service campground 5 miles west of Munising on M-28, has fifty campsites.
Map: USGS Munising quad (inc.).
Trail contact: Michigan Nature Association, (517) 655-5655, www.michigannature.org.

Finding the trailhead: From Munising drive 1.3 miles east and north on Alger County Road H-58, then turn left (north) on Sand Point Road, drive 0.1 mile, and park. Do not park on the shoulder of CR H-58.

Special considerations: This hike travels through the Twin Waterfalls Plant Preserve, a property of the Michigan Nature Association. Treat it well. A loose, erosion-prone slope lies between the two trails described. Let your karma add to the future charm of this lovely place, and don't walk on that slope or other fragile spots.

The Hike

I had driven by the wooden steps that lead to Olson Falls for years. When I finally stopped to investigate, I was stunned. Olson Falls is a gem, and falling water is only part of the story; the sandstone cove setting is hauntingly picturesque. Better yet, Olson Falls' attractive twin, Memorial Falls, is nearby.

Begin segment one of your hike by crossing CR H-58 eastward and ascending the wooden stairs. Take a few moments to read the blue Michigan Nature Association signboard, and pay your respects to those who were here before us—those who protected this place.

Continue hiking eastward on the trail, entering a striking hemlock and fern lined sandstone canyon. The trail runs along the base of a cliff, then dips to cross the creek on a bridge. Here is a scene that seems transported from southern Utah. An arc of overhanging rock leads to Olson Falls, a sparkling bridal veil that begins in cascading steps and then free-falls 40 feet.

Memorial Falls. Olson Falls' around-the-corner twin is a delicate veil in a quiet sandstone glen.

The path, now much narrower and less constructed, swings around to the north side of the canyon, ascending to just below the rock band, and follows it west. As the cliff band ends, the trail climbs the spur ridge's shoulder, drops into the next drainage, and turns west to CR H–58.

Return to your vehicle and drive 0.3 mile northeast on CR H–58 and turn right (south) on Nestor Street. Drive almost 0.2 mile south and park on the right (west) side of the street. This is the start of segment two.

A sign here reads TO MNA MEMORIAL FALLS, OVERLOOK TRAIL. From that sign walk west on a graveled footpath. One hundred thirty paces later, the trail is directly above Memorial Falls; not a good spot to stumble. Crossing the creek on a bridge, the path swings southwest along the lip of the gorge and 145 paces later swings sharply east and descends into the canyon. Now the trail runs east to Memorial Falls, along the base of the cliff.

Memorial Falls, a narrower plume but roughly the same height as Olson Falls, plunges off a deeply undercut sandstone shelf. That broad overhang rivals the falls as an attraction; the two together have an effect that is both subtle and powerful. I found myself fascinated with the different perspectives that came from moving just a few feet, as one would in composing a landscape photograph. When you're ready, retrace yours steps to Nestor Street to complete the hike.

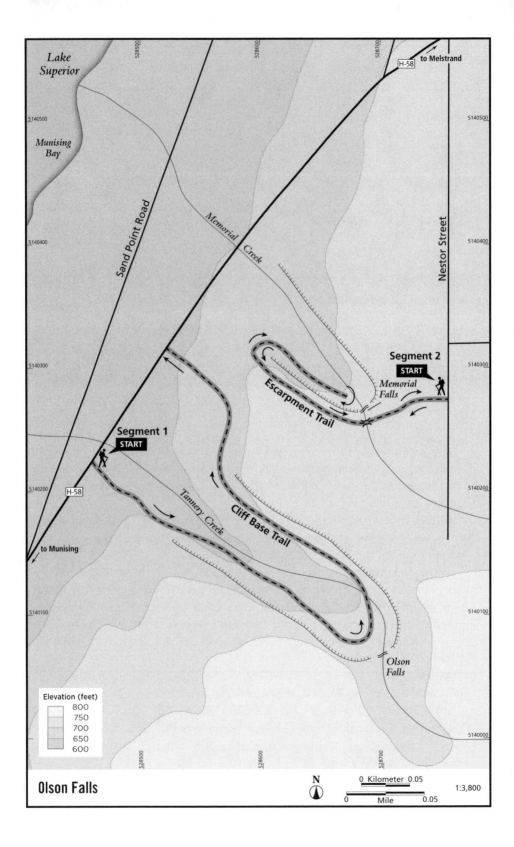

Lake
Superior

Munising
Bay

Sand Point Road

Memorial Creek

H-58
to Melstrand

Nestor Street

Segment 2
START

Memorial
Falls

Escarpment Trail

Segment 1
START

H-58

to Munising

Tannery Creek

Cliff Base Trail

Olson
Falls

Elevation (feet)

800
750
700
650
600

Olson Falls

N

0   Kilometer   0.05

0   Mile   0.05

1:3,800

Key Points

Segment 1:

    0.0   Cliff Base Trailhead on CR H-58.

    0.2   Olson Falls.

    0.4   Cliff Base Trail returns to CR H-58; end of first segment of hike.

Segment 2:

    0.0   Escarpment Trailhead on Nestor Street.

    0.2   Memorial Falls; turnaround point for second segment of hike.

    0.4   Escarpment Trailhead.

30 Miners Falls

Highlights: A notable waterfall and fine maple-beech forest.

Location: 7 miles northeast of Munising.

Type of hike: Out-and-back.

Distance: 1.2 miles.

Difficulty: Easy.

Fees and permits: None.

Best months: May through October.

Camping: Pictured Rocks National Lakeshore's (PRNL) Little Beaver Lake Campground, 20 miles east of the trailhead, has eight campsites.

Map: USGS Indian Town quad.

Trail contact: PRNL, (906) 387-3700 or (906) 387-2607, www.nps.gov/piro.

Finding the trailhead: From Munising, drive 5.3 miles east on Alger County Road H-58. Turn left (north), drive 3.6 miles north, and turn right (east). Drive 0.6 mile east to the Miners Falls Trailhead parking area.

The Hike

Miners Falls, a 50-foot free fall tumbling into a mossy nook, is a big payoff for a short walk. The visual beauty of the falling water is only part of the story here. A shady alcove behind the falls, and potholes carved into the bedrock below, offer a kind of etch-mark history of this place. Access is by way of a smooth constructed trail that winds through a fine maple-beech forest. This is an apt prelude for the show to come.

Begin at the southeast area of the trailhead parking area. The broad Miners Falls Trail heads south and immediately curves around to the east. Hike east, through pleasing open woodland, as the trail slowly descends.

Halfway to the falls the slope eases as the trail travels along an east-west–oriented ridge. Steep slopes fall away on either side, offering a glimpse into treetops, as well as peek-a-boo views north of the forest-swathed Miners River Valley and the deep blue of Lake Superior. At Mile 0.6 the trail reaches a viewpoint and a stairway of eighty-some steps that lead down to another view of the falls. When you are ready, retrace your steps to the trailhead.

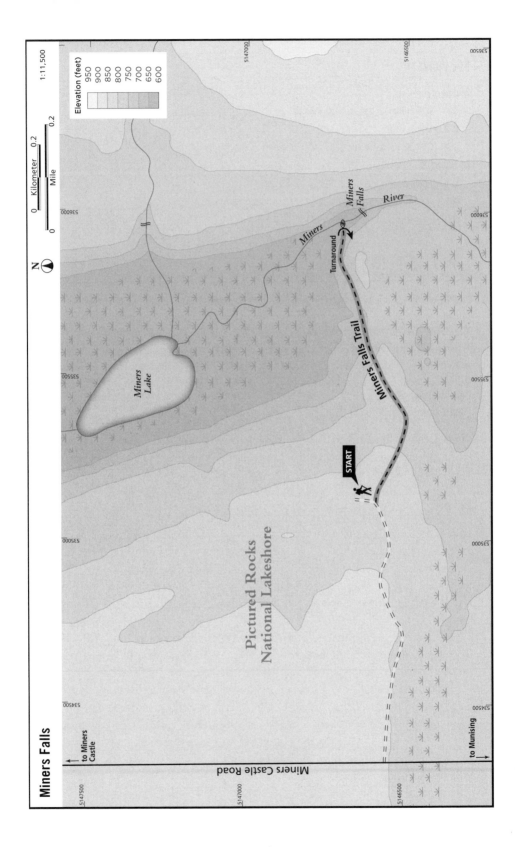

Miners Falls

1:11,500

Elevation (feet)
950
900
850
800
750
700
650
600

N

0   Kilometer   0.2

0   Mile   0.2

Pictured Rocks
National Lakeshore

Miners Lake

Miners
Falls

Miners   River

Turnaround

Miners Falls Trail

START

to Miners
Castle

Miners Castle Road

to Munsing

Key Points

0.0 Trailhead.

0.6 Miners Falls; turnaround point.

1.2 Trailhead.

31 Pictured Rocks

Highlights: A spectacular walk along the lip of the Pictured Rocks cliffs, broad Lake Superior views, and a parade of sandstone rock formations.

Location: 10 miles northeast of Munising.

Type of hike: Point-to-point.

Distance: 13.3 miles.

Difficulty: Difficult.

Fees and permits: None for day hikes. There is a fee for backcountry camping permits within Pictured Rocks National Lakeshore (PRNL).

Best months: May through October.

Camping: Backpack camping is allowed at designated backcountry campsites with a permit from PRNL. Its Little Beaver Lake Campground, 24 miles east of the trailhead, has eight campsites.

Maps: USGS Indian Town, Wood Island SE, Grand Portal Point, Trappers Lake quads; Pictured Rocks National Lakeshore trail map.

Trail contact: PRNL, (906) 387-3700 or (906) 387-2607, www.nps.gov/piro.

Finding the trailhead: From Munising, drive 5.3 miles east on Alger County Road H-58, and turn left (north) onto Miners Castle Road. Drive 5.5 miles north and bear right (east) on Miners Beach Road. Drive east and north 1.0 mile and turn right (east). Drive 0.3 mile east to the trailhead parking.

Special considerations: This hike follows the Lakeshore Trail, part of the North Country Trail (NCT), along the Pictured Rocks shoreline. As a shoreline route it can be glorious in fine weather, but windy and exposed in poor conditions. Sometimes the Lakeshore Trail runs right along the top of the cliffs, other times it is a stone's throw inland. Along the latter stretches, unofficial spur paths often lead to the cliff tops and worthwhile views. Use caution near the edges of the cliffs. The Pictured Rocks cliffs consist of undercut and honeycombed sandstone, and often if you stand close to the cliff edge, you may not be on solid rock. Within PRNL, many trails, with the exception of the Lakeshore Trail, have no official names. Trail junctions, however, tend to be well marked with directional arrows and mileage to landmarks, other trail junctions, and so on.

The Hike

What would you do if you had only one day to hike at Pictured Rocks? Ask me this most pointed of questions, and I have a confession to make. I don't buy into the conventional wisdom that the Chapel Loop is the obvious choice. Rather I believe the spectacular route from Miners Beach to Beaver Lake is well worth consideration. Yes, you need a shuttle, but they are available. Even the briefest glance at what the hike offers reveals compelling reasons to see it for yourself.

Spray Falls, one scene from a peerless 12-mile promenade along the craggy Pictured Rocks coast.

For 12 spectacular miles this route traces the rim of the Pictured Rocks escarpment, one of the truly iconic landscapes of the U.P. Mile after mile of sandstone landscape art passes by, a rich collection of arches, sea caves, and overhangs. Spray Falls cascades off the craggy cliff, clear-running streams rush to the big water, and the view down, into the lake's aquamarine water, is not too shabby either.

Thing is, the sum total of walking this wild and craggy coast is considerably more than a mere list of its components. The long views from the points and promontories offer a strong sense of place, a feeling of traveling along a timeless landscape.

Begin your tour at the Miners Beach trailhead, walking east into the woods on the Lakeshore Trail (also a segment of the NCT). Quickly the trail ascends a short, steep pitch, aiming for a break in a sandstone cliff line. Pause as the trail nears a rock band to your left and notice a faint path descending to your left (northwest), along the sandstone wall, and the pleasant sound of water falling. Follow that path along the base of the stone wall 30 yards to a mossy sandstone cove and a small waterfall free-falling 25 feet off an overhang.

Return to the Lakeshore Trail and ascend the short distance to the plateau above and walk north and east, following the trail through a fine maple forest. Short spur trails lead to the cliff tops. About a mile into the hike, an overlook on a point offers a classic sample of the many long views to come. More high views follow before the trail descends steep manufactured steps and skirts beautiful shoreline ledges. Go straight (northeast) at Mile 3.1, continuing on the Lakeshore Trail as a trail leading to Mosquito Falls goes right (southeast). Follow the Lakeshore Trail on the foot-bridge over the Mosquito River. Then turn left (north) at a junction at Mile 3.2, again following the Lakeshore Trail as another trail goes right (east) to the Chapel trailhead. Hike north on the Lakeshore Trail.

North of Mosquito River's gap in the escarpment, the cliffs and the trail steadily regain their height. Watch for a wooded promontory above a sandstone arch as the Lakeshore Trail winds its way along the coast, arriving at Indian Head Point at Mile 6.2. A sandy ledge there is the perfect veranda for looking back on the long row of cliffs leading southwest.

Indian Head's famous neighbor, Grand Portal Point, a mere 0.3 mile east, marks the escarpment's turn east. Its wooded, plateaulike top offers long views east along the shoreline to Twelvemile Beach and beyond. The best views of Grand Portal Point itself, however, are from another promontory, a half mile farther east. Large chunks of the roof of Grand Portal Point's namesake arch collapsed in the winter of 1999, and the debris is clearly visible.

Continue hiking east. The shoreline is full of scenic nooks and crannies as the plateau slowly descends to Chapel Beach. Go straight (east) at a junction at Mile 7.7, where a trail goes right (south), passing the west side of Chapel Lake. Then follow the Lakeshore Trail farther east, crossing the Chapel Creek Bridge and arriving at another intersection at Mile 7.9. Go straight (east) on the Lakeshore Trail, as a trail goes right (south) to Chapel Falls. Chapel Rock, a Pictured Rocks landmark, is nearby. Waves of a previous, higher, lake era carved arches and windowlike tunnels into the rock. These days Chapel Rock appears fragile, as if its long-term tenure on the coast may be nearing an end.

East of Chapel Rock, the Lakeshore Trail and shoreline cliffs slowly rise, and the path reaches the bridge over Spray Creek at Mile 9.5. You can follow a creek side path to Spray Falls, but the view is poor and the viewpoint severely undercut. Four hundred paces east of the bridge, a promontory offers a spectacular view of the falls as they cascade off the cliff.

Resume hiking east on the Lakeshore Trail. A half-mile east of Spray Creek, the cliffs crest and begin a gradual descent to the east. You may want to linger on one of the viewpoints, savoring the fortification-like profile of Grand Portal Point before the trail loses elevation. A set of steps drops the trail to a shelf close to lake level. After a brief ascent over and around a shoreline headland, the trail settles down into the sandy soil of the low bluff that lines aptly named Twelvemile Beach. At Mile 11.9 turn right (south) on a cutoff trail that leads to Little Beaver Lake as the Lakeshore Trail goes straight (east). Walk south 0.5 mile to a junction and turn right (west) on the Little Beaver Lake Trail.

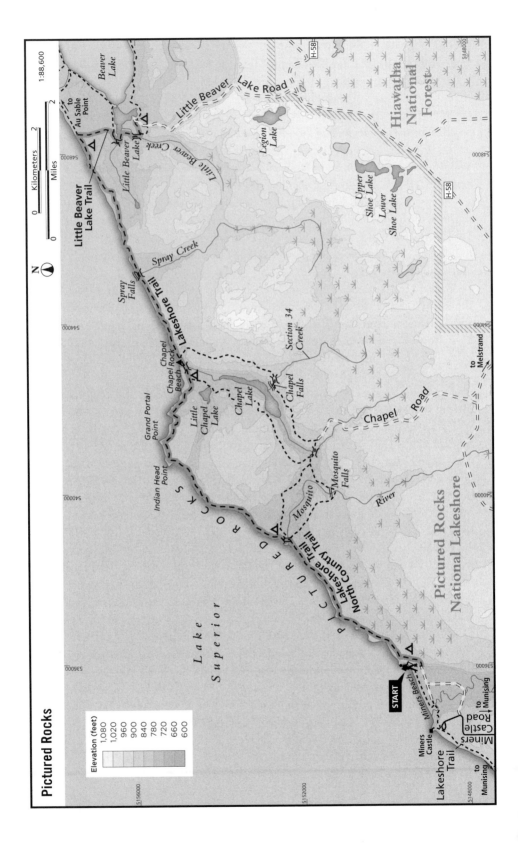

Pictured Rocks

Elevation (feet)

1,080
1,020
960
900
840
780
720
660
600

N

0 Kilometers 2

0 Miles 2

1:88,600

Lake Superior

P I C T U R E D   R O C K S

Indian Head Point

Grand Portal Point

Chapel Rock
Chapel Beach

Spray Falls

Spray Creek

Little Beaver
Lake Trail

Lakeshore Trail

to
Au Sable
Point

Beaver
Lake

Little Beaver
Lake

Little Beaver Creek

Little Beaver Lake Road

Legion
Lake

Hiawatha
National
Forest

Upper
Shoe Lake

Lower
Shoe Lake

H-58

H-58

Section 34
Creek

Chapel
Falls

Chapel Lake

Little Chapel
Lake

Chapel   Road

to
Melstrand

Mosquito
Falls

Mosquito

River

Lakeshore Trail
North Country Trail

Pictured Rocks
National Lakeshore

START

Miners Beach

Miners
Castle

Castle
Road

to
Munising

to
Munising

Lakeshore Trail

Follow the path first west then south on a boardwalk over marshy Arsenault Creek. Next the trail curls east, passing sandstone cliffs and the sea caves of a bygone era. Immediately after Little Beaver Creek's bridge, one last intersection appears. Bear left (east) on the White Pine Trail, as a spur trail goes right (south). Hike east a half-mile to the Little Beaver Lake Campground, the end of the hike.

Key Points

0.0 Miners Beach trailhead.

3.1 Junction with trail to Mosquito Falls.

3.2 Junction with trail to the Chapel trailhead.

6.2 Indian Head.

6.5 Grand Portal Point.

7.7 Junction with trail from Chapel Beach.

7.9 Junction with trail to Chapel Falls.

9.5 Spray Creek.

11.9 Little Beaver Lake Trail junction.

12.4 Junction (north shore of Little Beaver Lake).

12.8 Little Beaver Creek junction.

13.3 Little Beaver Lake Campground trailhead.

32 Chapel Loop

Highlights: Pictured Rocks cliffs, Grand Portal Point, Chapel Rock, and Chapel Falls.
Location: 20 miles northeast of Munising.
Type of hike: Loop.
Distance: 9.7 miles.
Difficulty: Moderate.
Fees and permits: None for day hikes. There is a fee for backcountry camping permits within Pictured Rocks National Lakeshore (PRNL).

Best months: May through October.
Camping: Backpack camping is allowed at designated sites within zero-impact guidelines. PRNL's Little Beaver Lake Campground, 15 miles east of the trailhead, has eight campsites.
Map: USGS Grand Portal Point quad.
Trail contact: Pictured Rocks National Lakeshore, (906) 387-3700 or (906) 387-2607, www.nps.gov/piro.

Finding the trailhead: From Munising, drive 13.9 miles east on Alger County Road H-58 to Melstrand. Turn left onto Chapel Road (gravel) and drive 5.1 miles north to the Chapel trailhead.
Special considerations: This hike follows the Lakeshore Trail, part of the North Country Trail (NCT), along the Pictured Rocks shoreline. As a shoreline route it can be glorious in fine weather, but windy and exposed in poor conditions. Sometimes the Lakeshore Trail runs right along the top of the cliffs, other times it is a stone's throw inland. Along the latter stretches unofficial spur paths often lead to the cliff tops and worthwhile views. Use caution near the edges of the cliffs. The Pictured Rocks cliffs consist of undercut and honeycombed sandstone. What you are standing on, if close to the cliff edge, may not be solid rock. Within Pictured Rocks National Lakeshore, many trails—with the exception of the Lakeshore Trail—have no official names. Trail junctions, however, tend to be well marked with directional arrows and mileage to landmarks, other trail junctions, and so on.

The Hike

One hike stood head and shoulders above all others when I asked hikers for nominations for this book—the Pictured Rocks circuit known as the Chapel Loop. Take even the briefest of glances at this route's attractions, and the reasons for its reputation are obvious.

This hike begins in a quiet forest and continues to a notable waterfall. Next it arrives on the shores of Earth's largest freshwater lake, but not just in any old spot. For 5 eye-catching miles, the path follows what may well be the U.P.'s most spectacular shoreline. A parade of convoluted cliffs, natural arches, and rushing streams line the trail, which hugs the rim of the escarpment between Chapel Beach and the Mosquito River. Grand Island's sharp northern prow marks the western horizon, while the eastern shore arcs to far-off Au Sable Point.

Begin your loop hike on the north side of the parking area at the Chapel trailhead. Hike north on a broad trail signed for Chapel Falls to that cascade (Mile 1.3). Chapel Falls begins with a 10-foot-high free fall that leads into a long waterslide on a steep rock slab. From the falls continue hiking north, reaching a junction with the

The Pictured Rocks shoreline turns south at the promontory known as Indian Head.

Lakeshore Trail (also the NCT), at Mile 3.1. Turn left (west), but before continuing take a moment to view the tunnel-like windows and arches of nearby Chapel Rock. The waves of a previous, higher lake era etched this sandstone landmark.

Hike west on the Lakeshore Trail, crossing a sturdy bridge over the rushing creek that drains Chapel Lake, to the bluff above Chapel Beach. Follow the trail west past the Chapel Beach campsites to a junction at Mile 3.3. Go straight (west) on the Lakeshore Trail at that intersection, as another trail goes left (south) past the west side of Chapel Lake to the Chapel trailhead.

Continue hiking west on the Lakeshore Trail. As that path ascends from the west end of Chapel Beach, it wanders along the rim of several small cliff-bound coves, each a compelling scene. The trail arrives at a significant promontory at about Mile 4.1. This point's west side offers a fine view of Grand Portal Point and its partially collapsed arch, a half-mile farther west.

Follow the Lakeshore Trail west to Grand Portal Point (Mile 4.9). Its wooded, plateaulike top offers memorable views to the east. Savor those eastern views, because the hike's route is about to turn a corner that will leave them behind. From Grand Portal Point hike west to a point known as Indian Head Point at Mile 5.2. A

Chapel Loop

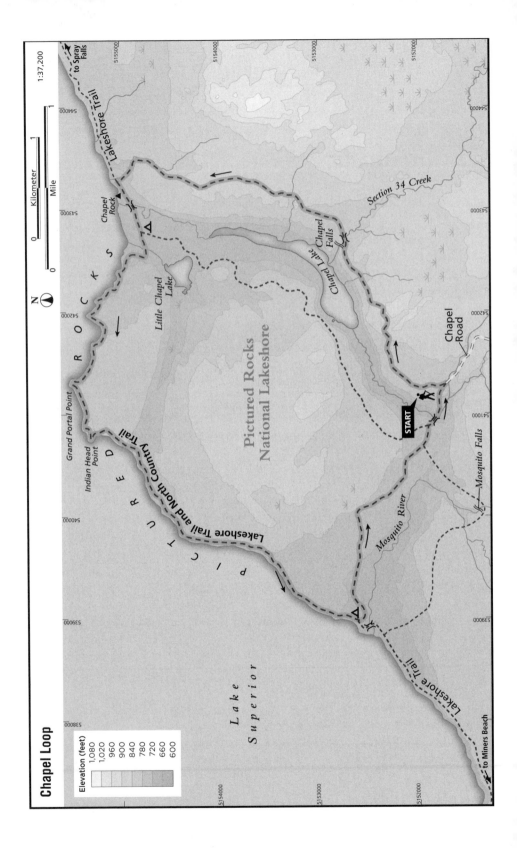

Elevation (feet)
- 1,080
- 1,020
- 960
- 900
- 840
- 780
- 720
- 660
- 600

N

1:37,200

Kilometer

Mile

to Spray Falls

Lakeshore Trail

Chapel Rock

R O C K S

Little Chapel Lake

Grand Portal Point

Indian Head Point

P I C T U R E D

Lakeshore Trail and North Country Trail

Lake Superior

Lakeshore Trail

to Miners Beach

Pictured Rocks National Lakeshore

Chapel Lake

Chapel Falls

Section 34 Creek

Chapel Road

START

Mosquito River

Mosquito Falls

sandy ledge on that headland offers long views along the row of cliffs that lead southwest, the next segment of the hike.

From Indian Head, the cliffs and the Lakeshore Trail ever so slowly descend to meet the Mosquito River at its mouth. Watch for a wooded promontory above a sandstone arch about a half-mile north of Mosquito River. At Mile 7.8 the path arrives at a junction, beside the rushing waters of the Mosquito River. Turn left (east) as the Lakeshore Trail goes right (west) to cross the river on a sturdy bridge. Hike east, following a trail that runs north of the Mosquito River, to the Chapel trailhead.

Go straight (east) at Mile 9.3 as a path from Mosquito Falls enters from the right (south). Then bear right (south) at Mile 9.4, as a path enters from the left (north) from Chapel Beach. Hike south and east, arriving at the Chapel trailhead at Mile 9.7.

Key Points

0.0 Chapel trailhead.

1.3 Chapel Falls.

3.1 Lakeshore Trail junction (Chapel Rock).

3.3 Junction with trail leading south past west side of Chapel Lake.

4.9 Grand Portal Point.

5.2 Indian Head Point.

7.8 Mosquito River.

9.3 Junction with trail from Mosquito Falls.

9.4 Junction with trail from Chapel Beach.

9.7 Chapel trailhead.

33 Beaver Lake Loop

Highlights: A quiet inland lake, forest, wildlife, and beach along Lake Superior shoreline.
Location: 20 miles northeast of Munising.
Type of hike: Loop.
Distance: 10.2 miles.
Difficulty: Difficult due to distance; the hiking is moderate.
Fees and permits: None for day hikes. There is a fee for backcountry camping permits within Pictured Rocks National Lakeshore (PRNL).

Best months: May through October.
Camping: Backpack camping is allowed at designated sites within zero-impact guidelines. PRNL's Little Beaver Lake Campground, at the trailhead, has eight campsites.
Map: USGS Trappers Lake quad.
Trail contact: PRNL, (906) 387-3700 or (906) 387-2607, www.nps.gov/piro.

Finding the trailhead: From Munising, drive 19 miles east on Alger County Road H–58 and turn left (north) onto Little Beaver Lake Road (gravel). Drive 3 miles north on that road to the Little Beaver Lake Campground.

Special considerations: This hike follows Twelvemile Beach and the Lakeshore Trail along the Pictured Rocks shoreline. As a shoreline route it can be glorious in fine weather, but windy and exposed in poor conditions. Within PRNL many trails, with the exception of the Lakeshore Trail, have no official names. However, trail junctions tend to be well marked with directional arrows and mileage to landmarks, other trail junctions, and so on. Some intersections on the map have been designated Junction A, Junction B, and so on, to avoid confusion.

The Hike

East of Spray Falls, the Pictured Rocks cliffs that line the Lake Superior shoreline for 15 miles taper off and Twelvemile Beach begins. The vertical relief of the craggy coast moves inland and becomes the rim of the vast valley known as Beaver Basin.

Not only is Beaver Basin a noticeable healthy bulge in the long, skinny national lakeshore boundary lines, parts of the basin are the lakeshore's quietest corner. Moose wander through, sampling the greens at Trapper Lake; bald eagles and river otters like the fishing at Beaver Lake; and rare coaster brook trout run up Seven Mile Creek.

One dirt road touches the edge of the basin, leading to Little Beaver Lake. There, a loop hike begins that swings around Beaver Lake, winds through a swath of remote forest, and walks the wave-washed beach of Lake Superior for miles.

Begin your circuit at the south end of the Little Beaver Lake Campground by hiking south on the Beaver Lake Trail. That path weaves its way southeast, then east, reaching the shoreline of its namesake at about Mile 0.8. I was there on a morning when the lake was a giant reflecting pool. The stillness was broken only by a kingfisher and an eagle passing by. For about half a mile the trail stays a stone's throw from the shore, then moves inland a tad in an area of meadowlike old fields. Crossing a

Miles of smiles—the scenic route along Twelvemile Beach east of Beaver Creek.

bridge over Lowney Creek, the Beaver Lake Trail heads south and ascends to an intersection at Mile 2.4, designated Junction A.

Turn left (east), following a sign for Trappers Lake. The trail follows an old woods road northeast, along the forested rim of a low plateau that occupies a large wedge of Beaver Basin. About a mile northeast of Junction A, the trail begins an almost due north run to Trappers Lake. Finally it descends to an intersection just southwest of the lake at Mile 5.3, Junction B. Turn right (northeast) and follow the sandy trail 0.1 mile to the Trappers Lake campsite (Mile 5.4) and another intersection. Turn left (north) on a connector trail that runs northwest to Lake Superior.

Walk 0.5 mile northwest to an intersection with the Lakeshore Trail (Mile 5.9), on a bluff above Twelvemile Beach. Take a moment to savor the view from the 40-foot-tall bluff. Then descend a sandy ramp to the beach below and walk southwest toward the distant ramparts of Grand Portal Point, some 8 miles off.

Hike the shoreline to the mouth of Beaver Creek, then turn left (south) and follow a path along the creek a little less than 100 yards, pass a massive log jam, and arrive at a trail bridge at Mile 7.7. Cross the bridge to Beaver Creek's north side and follow the Lakeshore Trail west to an intersection at Mile 7.9. Turn right (west)

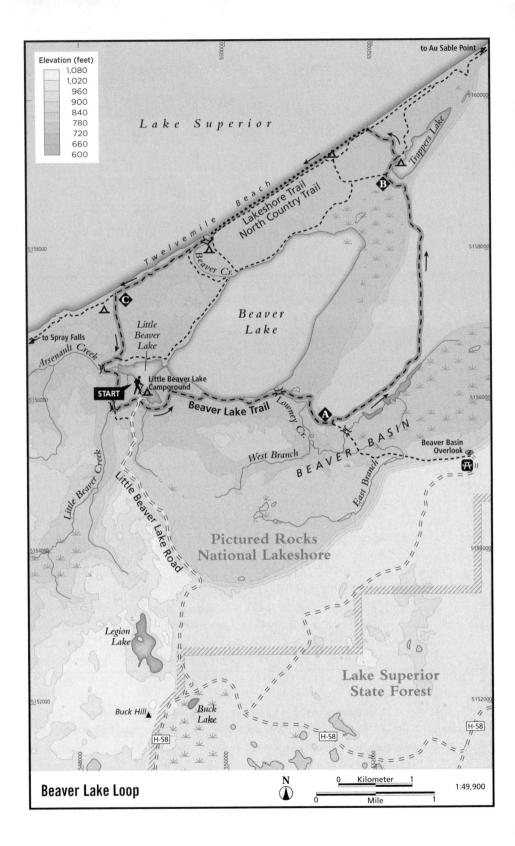

Elevation (feet)

	1,080
	1,020
	960
	900
	840
	780
	720
	660
	600

to Au Sable Point

Lake Superior

Trappers Lake

B

Lakeshore Trail
North Country Trail

Twelvemile Beach

Beaver Cr.

5158000

5160000

C

to Spray Falls

Little
Beaver
Lake

*Beaver
Lake*

Arsenault Creek

START

Little Beaver Lake
Campground

Beaver Lake Trail

Lowney Cr.

A

BEAVER BASIN

Beaver Basin
Overlook

5156000

Little Beaver Creek

Little Beaver Lake Road

West Branch

East Branch

*Pictured Rocks
National Lakeshore*

5154000

Legion
Lake

**Lake Superior
State Forest**

5152000

Buck Hill

Buck
Lake

H-58

H-58

H-58

Beaver Lake Loop

N

0	Kilometer	1
0	Mile	1

1:49,900

there, following the Lakeshore Trail (also the North Country Trail) west as a trail that leads to Beaver Lake goes left (south).

Walk west on the Lakeshore Trail to an intersection at Mile 8.6, designated Junction C. Consider a break on the nearby bluff top (a few feet north) that overlooks Lake Superior, the last lake views on this hike. At Junction C turn left (south), as the Lakeshore Trail continues straight (west), and hike 0.6 mile to an intersection (Mile 9.2) above an inlet of Little Beaver Lake. Turn right (west), following a connector trail that crosses Arsenault Creek on a sturdy bridge, meanders past sandstone cliffs, and arrives at a junction just beyond Little Beaver Creek at Mile 9.9. Turn left (east), following the White Pine Nature Trail to the trailhead at Mile 10.2.

Key Points

0.0   Little Beaver Lake trailhead.

0.8   Beaver Lake.

2.4   Junction A.

5.3   Junction B.

5.4   Trappers Lake campsite.

5.9   Lakeshore Trail/Twelvemile Beach.

7.7   Beaver Creek.

7.9   Beaver Creek junction.

8.6   Junction C.

9.2   Little Beaver Lake junction.

9.9   Little Beaver Creek junction.

10.2 Little Beaver Lake trailhead.

34 Au Sable Point/Log Slide

Highlights: Terraced bedrock, shipwrecks, a lighthouse, a historic log slide, sweeping high views of Lake Superior, and huge sand dunes.
Location: 13 miles west of Grand Marais.
Type of hike: Out-and-back.
Distance: 7 miles.
Difficulty: Moderate.
Fees and permits: None for day hikes. There is a fee for backcountry camping permits within Pictured Rocks National Lakeshore (PRNL).

Best months: May though October.
Camping: PRNL's Hurricane River Campground, at the trailhead, has twenty-one campsites.
Maps: USGS Au Sable Point and Grand Sable Lake quads (inc.).
Trail contact: PRNL, (906) 387-3700 or (906) 387-2607, www.nps.gov/piro.

Finding the trailhead: From Grand Marais, drive about 13 miles west on Alger County Road H-58 (also known as Kingston Lake Road) and turn right (north) onto the Hurricane River Campground road. Drive a quarter mile north on the campground spur road to the picnic area beside the mouth of the Hurricane River.

Special considerations: This hike follows either the Lake Superior shoreline or the Lakeshore Trail, part of the North Country Trail (NCT). Shoreline routes can be glorious in fine weather, but windy and exposed in poor conditions.

The Hike

This hike is a charmer, with a bit of a daydreamlike feeling to it. First there's the stroll down the Lake Superior shoreline, a pleasant beach that turns to gently sloped sandstone bedrock scalloped by waves. Farther down the shore are the ribs of shipwrecks and the Au Sable Point Lighthouse. Then the route follows the Lakeshore Trail to a viewpoint perched 300 feet above the lake, a lookout with a sweeping view of the spectacular Grand Sable Dunes.

Begin at the picnic area just east of the mouth of the Hurricane River. Step down to the shoreline and walk east along the water's edge. As the beach nears a low bedrock cliff, the remains of a shipwreck, the *Mary Jarecki,* appear just below the waterline.

Continue walking east, and soon sandstone bedrock is underfoot and a ledge-filled bluff lines the shore. A north slope, the ledges were green with moss and hanging gardens and dripping with small waterfalls on the day I was there.

Remains of two more shipwrecks, the *Sitka* and *Gale Staples,* lie just offshore 150 yards west of Au Sable Point. Hike east from the wrecks, watching for log steps that lead up the bluff. Ascend those steps to the lighthouse complex, a collection of four buildings and the white tower.

The Lakeshore Trail (also a segment of the NCT) runs by the west side of the buildings. Hike that trail—a charming path just inland from the lakeshore—southeast

Au Sable Point/Log Slide

1:43,200

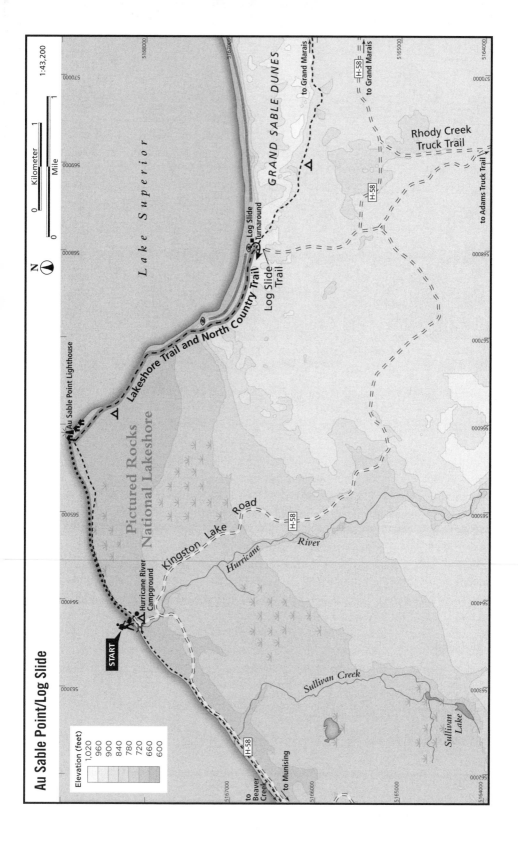

Elevation (feet)

1,020
960
900
840
780
720
660
600

N

Kilometer
0   1

Mile
0   1

Lake Superior

Pictured Rocks
National Lakeshore

Au Sable Point Lighthouse

Lakeshore Trail and North Country Trail

GRAND SABLE DUNES

Log Slide
Turnaround

Log Slide
Trail

Rhody Creek
Truck Trail

to Grand Marais

H-58

to Grand Marais

H-58

to Adams Truck Trail

START

Hurricane River
Campground

Kingston Lake Road

Hurricane River

H-58

Sullivan Creek

Sullivan Lake

to Beaver Creek

to Munising

H-58

A scenic and shipwreck-studded shoreline route leads to Au Sable Point's lighthouse.

as it ascends a wooded bluff. Along this stretch are several viewpoints that may well be the most spectacular perspective of the Grand Sable Dunes. The tall dunes and shoreline sweep east in a graceful arc; sand and tan tones are offset by the lake's deep blue.

Still climbing, the trail reaches a high plateau and runs east, arriving at the Log Slide at Mile 3.5. During the logging era workers slid the cut trees down a steep chute in the dunes to the lake below. A wide spur trail runs north one hundred paces to an overlook that offers sweeping views of Lake Superior and the Grand Sable Dunes. This is the hike's turnaround point.

Key Points

- **0.0** Hurricane River mouth.
- **1.5** Au Sable Point Lighthouse.
- **3.5** Log Slide; turnaround point.
- **7.0** Hurricane River mouth.

35 Grand Sable Dunes Loop

Highlights: Quiet forest, notable sand dunes, and Lake Superior shoreline.
Location: 2 miles west of Grand Marais.
Type of hike: Loop.
Distance: 12.2 miles.
Difficulty: Difficult.
Fees and permits: None for day hikes. There is a fee for backcountry camping permits within Pictured Rocks National Lakeshore (PRNL).

Best months: May through October.
Camping: Grand Marais's Woodland Park, 2 miles east of the trailhead, has 125 campsites. Backpacking camping, with a permit, is allowed at designated sites.
Map: USGS Grand Sable Lake (inc.) quad.
Trail contact: PRNL, (906) 387-3700 or (906) 387-2607, www.nps.gov/piro.

Finding the trailhead: From Grand Marais, drive 1.4 miles west on Alger County Road H-58. Turn right (northwest) into the trailhead parking.

Special considerations: Part of this hike is off-trail, including a descent of Log Slide, a steep and intimidating dune slope. Below, the route follows a Lake Superior shoreline for miles. In high winds or storms, the shoreline is unpleasant and can be dangerous. Near the end of the hike, the route requires a crossing of Sable Creek without the benefit of a bridge. I utilized a handy log jam; alternatively it would be an easy wade. Remote shoreline is important wildlife habitat. While you are hiking be sure to give wildlife lots of elbowroom, especially during the spring and early summer nesting season.

The Hike

When it comes to the realm of sand dunes, the Grand Sable Dunes are a knockout. Three hundred feet high and 5 miles long, this massive tan headland towers over the deep blue of Lake Superior. This hike loops around the dunes, first skirting their inland edge where forest meets sand slopes. Then it plunges from the crest of the dunes to the lakeshore, an adventurous descent that leads to a route along a wild shoreline, beneath the towering dunes. Finally the hike winds along Sable Creek, past Sable Falls.

Begin your hike from the northwest corner of the Sable Falls trailhead parking area, where a broad dirt trail (a segment of the North Country Trail) leads west into the shady woods and a sign reads VISITOR CENTER 1 MILE. Bear left (south) at mile 0.2, as the Dunes Trail goes right (north) over a bridge on Sable Creek. Walk south through a fine beech-maple forest; dunes show across the creek now and then. At Mile 1.0 the path arrives at CR H–58, with the PRNL Grand Marais Visitor Center just to the west.

Cross CR H–58 and hike southwest through meadowlike fields and woodlots. At a boat landing the trail comes back to CR H–58 and runs west along its south shoulder to skirt the north end of Grand Sable Lake. Beyond the road stretch the Lakeshore Trail follows the lake's shoreline southwest before turning west and crossing CR H–58 (Mile 4.1), this time to the northwest.

The immense headland of the Grand Sable Dunes towers above Lake Superior's blue waters.

Now the path runs west through the woods. Dunes sometimes appear to the north and sandy slopes spill past tree trunks. A half-mile or so before you get to Log Slide, the path ascends a wooded dune northward and emerges on an open dune with Lake Superior beyond. The Lakeshore Trail then dives back into the woods, arriving at the Log Slide at Mile 6.8. An exhibit here offers historical notes from the logging era, and a broad path leads north one hundred paces to a viewpoint. To the east the shoreline is an appealing crescent below the immense mass of the Grand Sable Dunes.

While savoring the view, take time for a reality and weather check. Scan the beach below that leads east past the dunes. Typically, waves don't wash completely across the narrow beach, but this is a good time to verify the conditions. Then consider the descent route itself. Just east of this viewpoint is the steep sandy slope where a logging era chute dropped logs to the lake below. Eyeball the Log Slide and see how you feel about it. Note a park service sign that cautions that the base of the route is not pure sand; buried rocks may also be present.

When you are ready descend the Log Slide, step after sliding step. As I dropped down I found myself fascinated with the aquamarine color of Lake Superior's water and its changes.

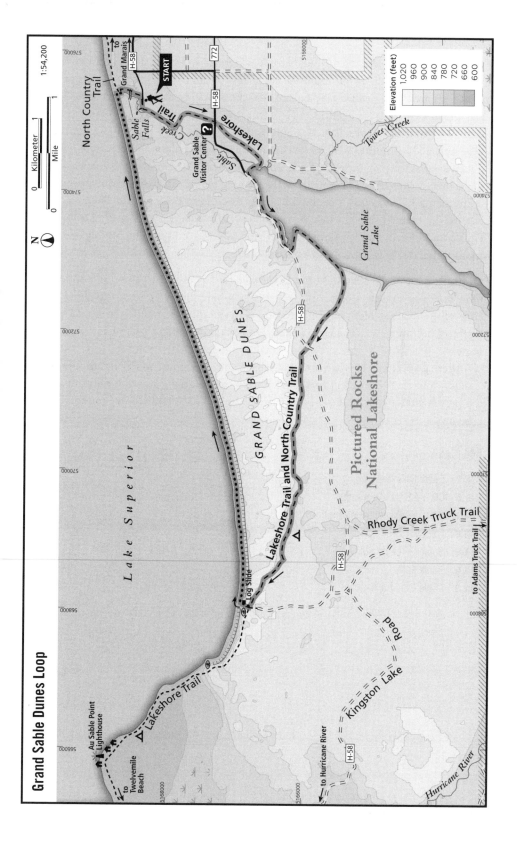

Grand Sable Dunes Loop

1:54,200

N

Elevation (feet)
1,020
960
900
840
780
720
660
600

Kilometer

Mile

START

North Country Trail

to Grand Marais

H-58

772

Sable Falls Trail

Sable Creek

Grand Sable Visitor Center

Lakeshore

Sable Creek

Towes Creek

Grand Sable Lake

Lake Superior

GRAND SABLE DUNES

H-58

Lakeshore Trail and North Country Trail

Pictured Rocks National Lakeshore

Log Slide

Rhody Creek Truck Trail

H-58

to Adams Truck Trail

Lakeshore Trail

Au Sable Point Lighthouse

to Twelvemile Beach

Kingston Lake Road

to Hurricane River

H-58

Hurricane River

Once on the beach, when your "land legs" return, walk east along the shoreline. To your right (south) is the immense slope of the dunes. You'll hear their soundtrack—a pitter-patter of pebbles and small rocks bouncing down to the beach. Several green swaths—vegetated alcoves with gushing spring runs—also run to the shore. As I walked the beach, an eagle flushed out of one of these lush ravines and a deer retreated at another one. Merganser families cruised along the shoreline.

Five miles east of the Log Slide, the dunes' wall lowers as Sable Creek cuts through and runs to the lake (Mile 11.8). Sable Creek is not large, but it is usually more than a hop to cross. I found a log jam to cross to the east side. There, at the base of the ravine's slope, turn right (south) on a maintained trail leading to Sable Falls, a multitiered drop of about 20 feet (Mile 12.0). From the falls continue hiking south to the Sable Falls trailhead at Mile 12.2.

Options: West of the Log Slide, the Lakeshore Trail leads to two appealing options. One would be to walk about a mile northwest, where the trail curls north along the edge of the wooded bluff, offering striking views to the east. I believe this may well be the optimum view of the Grand Sable Dunes and shoreline, a graceful arc stretching east.

Alternatively, hike northwest to Au Sable Point. The point and its lighthouse are 2 miles from the Log Slide. Lighthouse history and nearby shipwreck remnants are the point's attractions; the Lakeshore Trail that winds its way there has considerable charm.

Key Points

- **0.0**   Sable Falls trailhead.
- **1.0**   CR H-58 (first crossing).
- **4.1**   CR H-58 (second crossing).
- **6.8**   Log Slide.
- **11.8** Sable Creek mouth.
- **12.0** Sable Falls.
- **12.2** Sable Falls trailhead.

36 Bruno's Run Loop

Highlights: Undeveloped lakes, an ancient hemlock grove, quiet forest, and river.
Location: 15 miles south of Munising.
Type of hike: Loop.
Distance: 8.6 miles.
Difficulty: Moderate.
Fees and permits: None.
Best months: May through October.

Camping: Hiawatha National Forest's Petes Lake Campground, just east of the trailhead, has forty-one campsites.
Maps: USGS quads Corner Lake, Tie Lakes; Hiawatha National Forest Bruno's Run handout map.
Trail contact: Hiawatha National (906) 387-2512, www.fs.fed.us/r9/hiawatha.

Finding the trailhead: From Munising, drive 3.1 miles south and east on M-28 and turn right (south) on Alger County Road H-13 (also known as Forest Highway 13). Drive 10.3 miles south and turn left (east) on Forest Road 2173. Drive 0.5 mile east. Then turn right (south) on Forest Road 2256 (Petes Lake Campground Road). Drive 0.3 mile south and turn right (south) into the trailhead parking area.

The Hike

Bruno's Run is a loop trail that has a pleasant rhythm about it. It goes like this. Walk a mile or so through fine forest. The terrain is sometimes rolling with hills, but it is not grueling. All the while scan for flashy pileated woodpeckers and other forest delights. Then arrive at a quiet lakeshore and enjoy loons, eagles, breezes, and broad vistas. Repeat the lake rhythm seven times. Ditto the forest part, and throw in an ancient hemlock cathedral for good measure. Did I mention passing clear-running streams several times and enjoying an abundance of peace and quiet?

Begin your circuit tour by walking east through the Petes Lake Campground. At the east end of the campground loop, a blue diamond marker and a hiker sign mark the path's beginning. Walk a woodsy 0.7 mile east and north and cross quiet FR 2173 to its east side.

Hike south and east. Nearby Grassy Lake is visible through the trees. Then walk along the lake's hemlock-lined shore. At the end of the shoreline stretch, the trail passes over the lake's outlet stream on a sturdy bridge. It then again crosses FR 2173 (at Mile 1.6) and immediately arrives at McKeever Lake. For the next half-mile, the Bruno's Run Trail winds along that lake's shore, finally swinging southwest, and crosses Deer Creek on another solid bridge.

Now running steadily westward, the path nears an arm of McKeever Lake, passes Wedge Lake, and curls around little Dipper Lake. Next the trail crosses Forest Road 2258 (Mile 4.0) and nears the Indian River as it approaches Forest Highway H-13 at Mile 4.2. Pay attention here. Walk up the road's embankment and turn left (south). Walk 100 feet south along the highway, utilizing the highway bridge to cross the Indian River. Then turn right (northwest), descending the embankment to the trail.

The Bruno's Run Trail loops past a parade of lakes, including quiet shorelines along Moccasin Lake.

Hike west, then northwest on the Bruno's Run Trail. The river broadens at a place aptly known as Widewaters, and the trail nears the shore and crosses the stream at Mile 5.7.

Hike east as the trail ascends a ridge and arrives at a grove of virgin hemlocks at Mile 6.1. Someone once told me, "Old-growth forest just has a way of making you feel good, making you feel that something is very right here." This is such a place, and a sign offers lyrical comment.

When you feel ready to move on, continue hiking east and north on the Bruno's Run Trail. An educational sign mentions that a trail segment here follows the grade of the Nahma and Northern Railway, a logging-era railroad.

A half-mile of trail along Moccasin Lake's shore precedes a second crossing of Forest Highway H–13 at Mile 7.1. Cross the highway to its east side. Then follow the trail into the woods, hiking southeast to a third crossing of FR 2173 at Mile 7.4. Cross that road and continue walking southeast on the Bruno's Run Trail, arriving at the trailhead at Mile 8.6.

Bruno's Run Loop

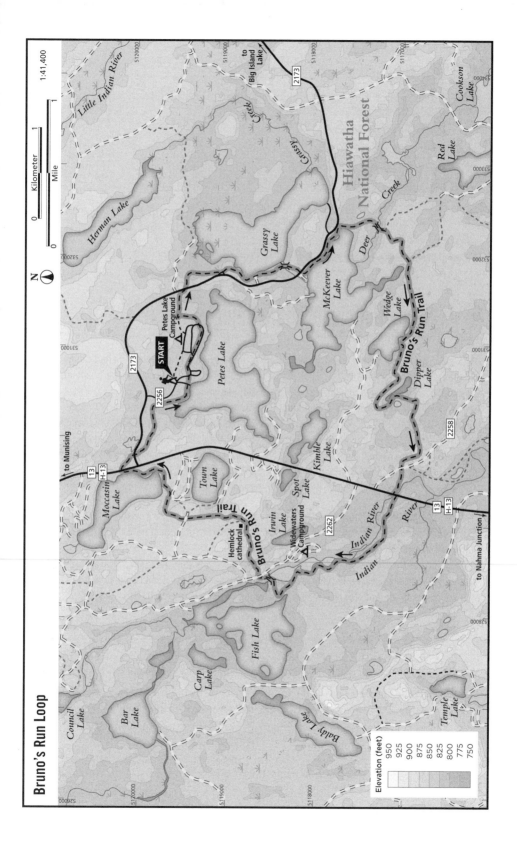

0.0 Trailhead at Petes Lake.

0.7 FR 2173 (first crossing).

1.6 FR 2173 (second crossing).

4.0 Forest Road 2258.

4.2 Forest Highway H–13 (first crossing).

5.7 Indian River footbridge.

6.1 Hemlock cathedral.

7.1 Forest Highway H–13 (second crossing).

7.4 FR 2173 (third crossing).

8.6 Trailhead at Petes Lake.

37 Seney National Wildlife Refuge

Highlights: Trumpeter swans, other wildlife, and quiet forest.
Location: 1 mile southwest of Germfask.
Type of hike: Out-and-back with a side loop.
Distance: 6.3 miles.
Difficulty: Moderate*.
Fees and permits: None.
Best months: May through October.

Camping: Mead Creek State Forest Campground, 5 miles southwest of the trailhead, has ten campsites.
Maps: USGS Seney, Germfask (inc.) quads; Northern Hardwoods Ski Trails Map (available at Seney National Wildlife Refuge headquarters).
Trail contact: Seney National Wildlife Refuge, (906) 586–9851, http://midwest.fws.gov/seney.

Finding the trailhead: From Germfask, drive south 0.5 mile on M–77 and turn right (west) onto Robinson Road. Drive 0.6 mile west on Robinson Road to the trailhead parking for the Northern Hardwoods Ski Trails.

Special considerations: Parts of the Bear Hollow Ski Trail feature an abundance of thigh-high ferns in summer and fall. The ferns are a pleasant sight, but in a few stretches they form a carpet that obscures the trail. These stretches may require a little concentration to navigate.

The Hike

Few and far between are the places where you have a good chance of seeing trumpeter swans. Odds are stacked in your favor, though, if you visit Seney National Wildlife Refuge in the open water months of April through November.

Aptly named, trumpeter swans have a deep, sonorous call. Their long, graceful necks, snow-white bodies, 7-foot wingspan, and status as North America's largest native waterfowl add to their aura.

Rare and graceful trumpeter swans, stars of the Seney National Wildlife Refuge wildlife show.

This hike offers long sight lines, framed by white pines, across the quiet flowages known by the names A Pool and B Pool. There, trumpeter swans, sometimes a dozen at a time, were a common sight during my visit. Preceding that 2-mile-long sojourn with the vast open spaces of Seney's watery landscape, the route follows a ski trail through a beautiful maple-beech forest.

Begin your hike at the Northern Hardwoods Ski Trailhead and walk west, past a gate, on a broad gravel road to a junction where the Bear Hollow Ski Trail begins (Mile 0.3). This intersection has been designated Junction A on the map.

Turn right (north), following the Bear Hollow Ski Trail as it swings east, dips through a hollow or two, and arrives at an intersection at Mile 0.5, designated Junction B. Turn left (north) as the Cub Hollow Ski Trail goes right (east). Walk north on the Bear Hollow Ski Trail to another intersection at Mile 0.6 (Junction C). Bear left (north) here, still on the Bear Hollow Ski Trail, as the Cub Hollow Ski Trail rejoins the route.

Follow the Bear Hollow Ski Trail north and west as it bisects several hemlock stands, now and then pushing through thigh-high ferns. Turn right (west) at Junction D (Mile 1.1) on a broad gravel road as the woodsy ski trail ends. Hike west,

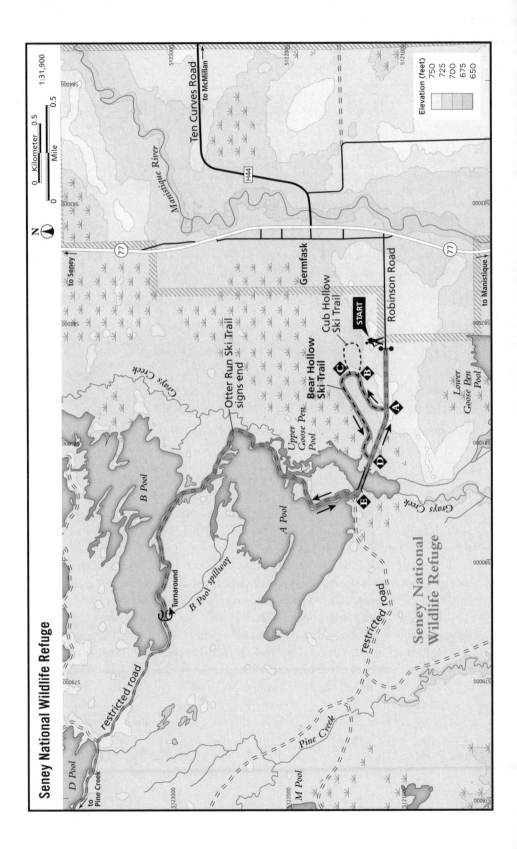

Seney National Wildlife Refuge

1:31,900

Elevation (feet)
750
725
700
675
650

crossing over marshy Grays Creek on a bridge, to an intersection at Mile 1.5 (Junction E).

Turn right (north) onto a two-track dirt road. This lane follows the top of A Pool's dike, wandering north along that flowage's eastern shore. For this stretch it is also called the Otter Run Ski Trail. Broad views open to the west, over A Pool's watery expanse. I saw and heard both trumpeter swans and sandhill cranes here.

Near A Pool's northeastern corner, the lane swings northwest, the Otter Run Ski Trail signs end, and the White Pine Natural Area begins. Now the lane follows low ridges sprinkled with white pines. Harriers patrolled the marshes on either side during my visit. About a half-mile after that decisive turn northwest, B Pool's island-studded waters appear to the right (north).

B Pool sported an abundance of trumpeter swans during my visit, and it seemed that any time spent here was a gift. The open vistas, wildlife, white pines, and abundant peace and quiet lent a special feeling to this place. B Pool's outlet, at the southwest corner of that flowage, is at Mile 3.4 of the hike, a suitable turnaround point. Retrace your steps to Junction D, but don't enter the woods on the Bear Hollow Ski Trail. Instead continue eastward on the gravel road that leads to the trailhead at Mile 6.3.

Key Points

0.0   Northern Hardwoods Ski Trailhead.

0.3   Junction A, begin Bear Hollow Ski Trail.

0.5   Junction B.

0.6   Junction C.

1.1   Junction D, end Bear Hollow Ski Trail.

1.5   Junction E, begin Otter Run Ski Trail.

2.5   End Otter Run Ski Trail.

3.4   B Pool spillway; turnaround point.

5.3   Junction E.

6.3   Northern Hardwoods Ski Trailhead.

38 Mouth of the Blind Sucker River

Highlights: Lake Superior shoreline and mouth of the Blind Sucker River.
Location: 12 miles east of Grand Marais.
Type of hike: Out-and-back.
Distance: 9 miles.
Difficulty: Moderate*.
Fees and permits: None.
Best months: May through October.
Camping: Backpack camping is allowed on state forest land along the trail with a permit from the Michigan Department of Natural

Resources (DNR). The Lake Superior State Forest Campground, 1 mile west of the trailhead, has eighteen campsites.
Maps: USGS Muskallonge Lake West quad (inc.); North Country Trail Map TMI09, Curley Lewis Road to Grand Marais.
Trail contact: Michigan DNR, (906) 293-3293, www.michigan.gov/dnr; The North Country Trail Association Web site, www.northcountrytrail.org.

Finding the trailhead: From Grand Marais, drive 5.9 miles east on Alger County Road H-58. At that point H-58 becomes Luce County Road 433 as it crosses the county line. Continue driving east on CR 433 for 6.3 miles. At that point CR 433 makes a ninety degree turn south, away from the Lake Superior shoreline it has been paralleling. Park in the pullouts adjacent to this turn.

Special considerations: I found the trail's paint blazes older and less distinct, and the trail itself fainter and brushier, as I neared the mouth of the Blind Sucker River. During a September trip, the Blind Sucker River was a knee-deep, 12-foot-wide wade. High-water episodes could make this ford dangerous. This hike's route is along, or just inland from, the Lake Superior shore. While glorious in good conditions, bad weather or high winds could make this route unpleasant.

Remote shorelines are important wildlife habitat. As you are hiking be sure to give wildlife lots of elbowroom, especially during the spring and early summer nesting season.

The Hike

West of the Blind Sucker River, the Lake Superior shoreline forms the gentlest of radiuses, a broad crescent of a bay. Seen from the low bluff above the beach, that coast, ever so slightly curving, is an eye-pleasing line as it stretches to a peninsula some 5 miles off. I happened to be there at the tail end of a hurricane, on a day when the surf was rowdy. The offshore breakers highlighted the symmetry of the long beach.

Shore side the visuals aren't too shabby either. Winding its way through an open white birch forest, the trail offers peek-a-boo views of the lake from a bluff 20 feet above the beach. Between the forest, the shore, and the inland sea, it is an eye-pleasing route and one I would gladly repeat.

Walk east from the trailhead on the North Country Trail (NCT), and the ambience begins immediately as the path winds its way along the lip of the low bluff behind the beach. At Mile 1.6 an opening without any screening tree or brush appears on the edge of the bluff, offering broad views of the lake and shore.

A classic shoreline hike, the North Country Trail follows the Lake Superior shoreline west of the mouth of the Blind Sucker River.

As I walked east from this point, the trail grew fainter and brushier and the markings less distinct. Navigationwise this is hardly a problem. The trail's route here is along a very elongated peninsula, with the lake to the north and the Blind Sucker River to the south. That said, if following the trail becomes problematic, I would suggest dropping down to the beach, a stone's throw north, while marking the spot for your return trip westward.

A little more than a half-mile east of the first viewpoint, the peninsula's plateaulike top narrows to a mere 30 feet in width as a bend of the river swings toward the lake. That topography makes it tempting to think the river mouth is near, but it turns out the peninsula regains its width and there is still a good mile to go.

Eventually I lost the last of the trail's remnants, but by then there was only a short stretch of woods left—the peninsula became a gravel bar at the river mouth. A short wade brought me to the Blind Sucker River's south bank, where a NCT marker post signaled the trail's route.

Ducking into the woods to the south, the trail quickly swings eastward, following an old woods road. About a half-mile east of the crossing, the trail becomes a path just off the beach, running through low wooded dunes. An opening at Mile 4.1 offers a spacious view, and at Mile 4.5 the NCT swings decisively south and inland. This is a good turnaround point for the hike.

Mouth of the Blind Sucker River

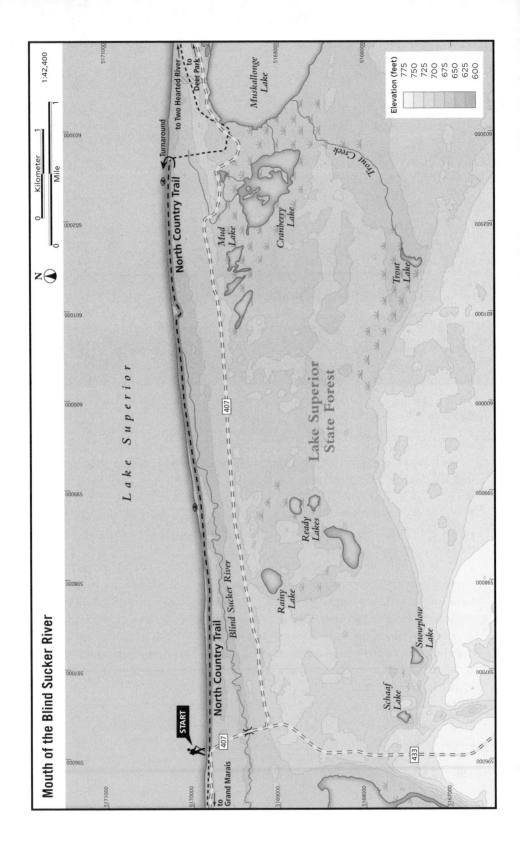

Options: Walking to the mouth of the Blind Sucker River only, and skipping the ford and mile of trail east of the river, is an attractive option. It would be a 6.8-mile round-trip hike. One other tactic is appealing: Walk eastward on the trail, returning on the shoreline. The water's edge and the trail are seldom 50 yards apart.

Key Points

0.0 Trailhead on CR 433.

1.6 First viewpoint.

3.4 Mouth of the Blind Sucker River.

4.1 Second viewpoint.

4.5 North Country Trail turns inland; turnaround point.

9.0 Trailhead.

39 Two Hearted River

Highlights: Lake Superior shoreline and the fabled mouth of the Two Hearted River.
Location: 33 miles north of Newberry.
Type of hike: Out-and-back.
Distance: 5.8 miles.
Difficulty: Moderate.
Fees and permits: None.
Best months: May through October.
Camping: Backpack camping is allowed on state forest land along the trail with a permit from the Michigan Department of Natural

Resources (DNR). The Mouth of Two Hearted River State Forest Campground at the trailhead has thirty-nine campsites.
Maps: USGS Betsy Lake NW quad (inc.); North Country Trail Map TMI09, Curley Lewis Road to Grand Marais.
Trail contact: Michigan DNR, (906) 293-3293, www.michigan.gov/dnr; The North Country Trail Association Web site, www.northcountrytrail.org.

Finding the trailhead: From Newberry, drive 18.2 miles north and east on M–123 and turn left (north) on Luce County Road 500. Drive 6.2 miles north on CR 500 and turn left (west) on Luce County Road 414. Drive 4.8 miles west on CR 414 and turn right (north) on Luce County Road 423. Drive 4.3 miles north to the trailhead at the mouth of the Two Hearted River.
Special considerations: This hike's route is on, or just inland from, the Lake Superior shore. While glorious in good conditions, bad weather or high winds can make this route unpleasant. Remote shorelines are important wildlife habitat. As you are hiking be sure to give wildlife lots of elbowroom, especially during the spring and early summer nesting season.

The Hike

The name *Two Hearted River* is full of mystery and romance. Ernest Hemingway's short story "Big Two Hearted River" gave the river icon status—a back-of-beyond stream of the north where the trout were large and life was good. There is abundant

The North Country Trail hugs the Lake Superior shore west of the Two Hearted River.

evidence that Hemingway was fibbing to camouflage his favorite fishing hole, the Fox River; but the mythology took root and grew.

Today the mouth of the Two Hearted River is a remote outpost. Graded dirt roads lead there, but it is a good 15 miles to the pavement in any direction. A campground, small store, and grass airstrip add to the end-of-the-road character of the place.

The North Country Trail (NCT) runs along the coast on either side of the mouth of the Two Hearted River and bisects the campground. A suspension bridge within the campground carries the trail across the river, leading to a hike along the shoreline to the west.

Begin your hike at the river mouth's parking area and walk west to the nearby suspension bridge, crossing that bouncy span to the river's north bank. There Lake Superior fills the horizon, and the trail makes a sharp left, running west along the top of low dunes. The dunes end quickly, and after a momentary flirtation with the riverbank, the NCT settles into the course that will characterize this hike: a route parallel to and just inland from the beach.

Continue hiking west on the NCT. The trail occasionally ascends a low bluff or dips to touch the beach. At Mile 1.8 the path ascends a series of steep, vegetated dunes before returning to the beach. A short jaunt off-trail at the crest of these wooded dunes brings you to the highest viewpoints of the outing.

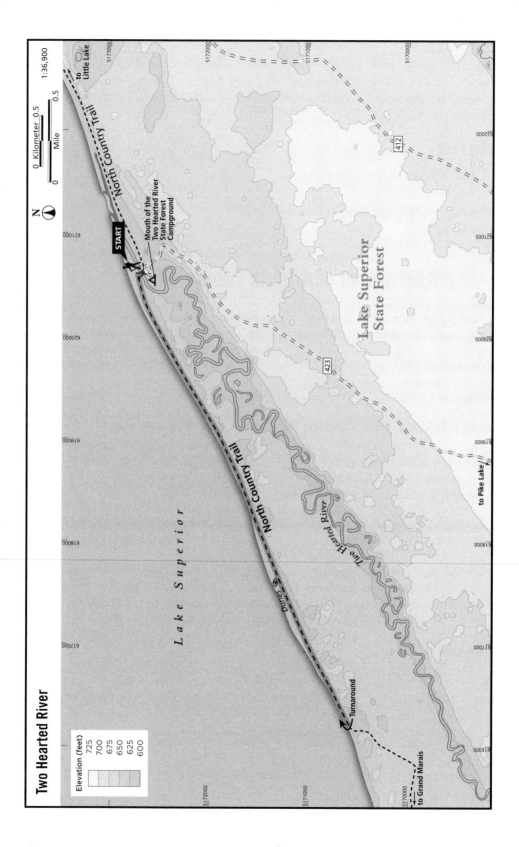

Two Hearted River

Elevation (feet)
- 725
- 700
- 675
- 650
- 625
- 600

1:36,900

N

0 Kilometer 0.5

0 Mile 0.5

Lake Superior

North Country Trail

Lake Superior State Forest

Two Hearted River

Dunes

North Country Trail

START

Mouth of the
Two Hearted River
State Forest
Campground

to Little Lake

412

423

to Pike Lake

Turnaround

to Grand Marais

After another mile beside the wave-washed shore of Lake Superior, the trail turns inland at the base of a large, forested dune (Mile 2.9). This turn marks the first of several miles where the trail spends more time inland than on the shore. It's a good turnaround point for the hike.

Key Points

0.0 Trailhead, mouth of Two Hearted River.

1.8 Steep dunes.

2.9 Large forested dune; turnaround point.

5.8 Trailhead.

40 Tahquamenon West/North Country Trail

Highlights: Solitude, remote sand ridges and marsh, giant white pines, and Tahquamenon Falls.
Location: 15 miles west of Paradise.
Type of hike: Point-to-point.
Distance: 7.3 miles.
Difficulty: Difficult*.
Fees and permits: None, but consider a donation to The North Country Trail Association, www.northcountrytrail.org.
Best months: July through October.
Camping: Backpack camping is allowed along the trail on state forest land with a permit from the Michigan Department of Natural Resources (DNR). Pike Lake State Forest Campground, 7 miles west of the trailhead, has twenty-three campsites.
Maps: USGS Betsy Lake South (inc.) quad; North Country Trail Map TMI09.
Trail contact: Michigan DNR, (906) 293-3293, www.michigan.gov/dnr; The North Country Trail Association, (866) 445-3628, www.northcountrytrail.org.

Finding the trailhead: From the town of Paradise, drive 18.9 miles west on M–123. Then turn right (north) on Luce County Road 500 and drive 2.8 miles north to the North Country Trail (NCT) crossing.

Special considerations: Several short boggy stretches make water levels adventurous when hiking in May or June. Waterproof boots and trekking poles come in handy. Parts of the NCT here have faint or nonexistent wear marks. Trail blazes, though, were adequate, making navigation reasonable but occasionally demanding concentration when searching for the next blaze.

The Hike

Walk a little west and north of Tahquamenon Falls, and the landscape reverts to a pattern that is representative of vast swaths of the eastern U.P. Low sand ridges, arranged in long arcs, overlook flat bogs; the water level in those bogs rises with the snowmelt and falls steadily in summer. That seasonal water level bedeviled me when

A white pine elder along the North Country Trail. ▶

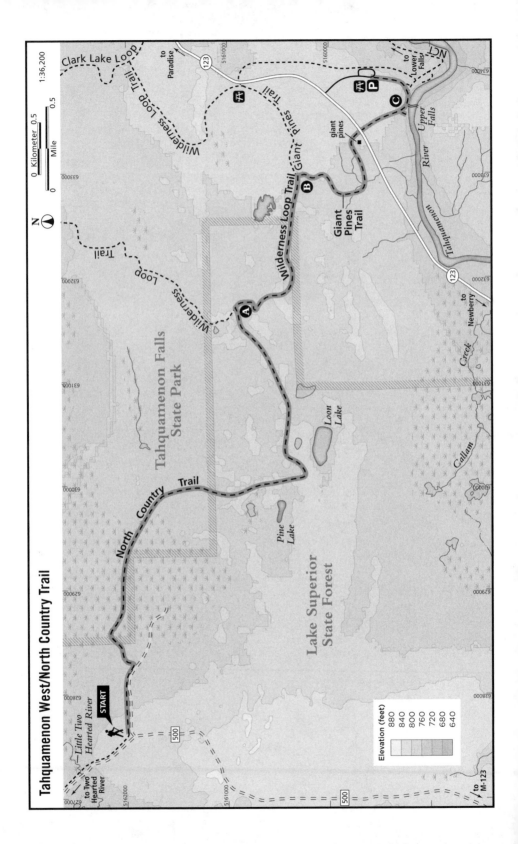

Tahquamenon West/North Country Trail

1:36,200

N

0   Kilometer   0.5
0   0.5   Mile

Elevation (feet)
880
840
800
760
720
680
640

Clark Lake Loop

to Paradise

123

Wilderness Loop Trail

Wilderness Loop Trail

Giant Pines

B

Giant Pines Trail

giant pines

C

Upper Falls

to Lower Falls

NCT

P

Tahquamenon River

123

to Newberry

Callam Creek

Tahquamenon Falls State Park

Wilderness Loop Trail

A

Loon Lake

Pine Lake

North Country Trail

Lake Superior State Forest

Little Two Hearted River

START

to Two Hearted River

500

500

to M-123

I first saw this hike in May. Long stretches of the route intrigued me, but a few short wet areas were almost technical. I hopped from squishy clump to clump for 100 feet. I returned in September and found those short boggy segments reasonable. It all boils down to this. This is a neat hike in quiet, remote country. Skilled hikers, who aren't fazed by following faint trails or having to search for the next blaze, should consider it. In the spring and perhaps early summer, count on water levels that may come over the tops of your boots at the boggy spots.

Still interested? Then begin your hike by walking east, following the NCT, on a dirt lane. About a half mile east of CR 500, the NCT swings north on a lesser two-track and quickly becomes a trail running northeast through a moist bottomland of ferns, moss, and hemlocks. Then the NCT crosses a north-running creek on bundled logs and ascends to a low ridge running eastward.

Hike east on the NCT as it passes impressive old hemlocks on that ridge for about half a mile. When the ridge ends, the trail crosses a short damp stretch and picks up another low ridge. This ridge is drier and sandier than the previous one and features a scattering of lichen-covered meadows. Roughly a mile later two boggy stretches, each about 150 feet long, can be challenging early in the season.

The NCT then swings east, offering a view of Loon Lake south of the trail. Continue hiking east on the NCT. The trail is sometimes faint to nonexistent, with blazes a bit of a hunt at times. About a mile and a half east of Loon Lake, a final boggy stretch tests your mettle. A quarter mile east of that damp spot, the NCT arrives at an intersection designated Junction A on the map to avoid confusion.

Turn right (south) onto the Wilderness Loop Trail of Tahquamenon Falls State Park (also the NCT). The path runs south, then east. The scenery is reminiscent of earlier segments of the hike—broad views from sandy ridges sprinkled with stately red and white pines—but now the trail shows more signs of use. Next the NCT arrives at another intersection at Mile 5.4, designated Junction B. Turn right (south) on a lane that is the Giant Pines Loop Trail as well as the NCT. This lane runs south, then east, arriving at its namesake trees at Mile 6.2. One of these magnificent specimens is an estimated 175 years old, almost 5 feet in diameter, and 120 feet high.

Continue hiking east on the Giant Pines Loop Trail (also the NCT) to M–123 (Mile 6.4). Cross the highway and walk south on a gravel road, then follow the NCT markings onto another woodsy lane that runs south to an intersection designated Junction C (Mile 6.7). Turn right (southwest) and descend steps to a viewpoint (Mile 6.8) that offers a classic view of the Upper Falls of the Tahquamenon River. Sight lines here, along the 50-foot free fall at the lip of the falls, are spectacular.

Retrace your steps to Junction C (Mile 6.9) and turn right (southeast), walking along a broad paved path that follows the rim of the river gorge. Hike about 100 yards southeast and turn left (north) on a broad constructed path. Walk that broad path north to the Upper Falls trailhead, the hike's end (Mile 7.3).

Key Points

0.0 CR 500 trailhead.

0.6 Creek (unnamed, flowing north).

2.2 Loon Lake.

4.1 Junction A.

5.4 Junction B.

6.2 Giant pines.

6.4 M–123.

6.7 Junction C.

6.8 Upper Falls.

6.9 Junction C.

7.3 Upper Falls trailhead.

41 Giant Pines Loop

Highlights: Tahquamenon Falls, virgin forest, and giant white pine trees.
Location: 16 miles west of Paradise.
Type of hike: Loop, with two short stems.
Distance: 4.1 miles.
Difficulty: Moderate.
Fees and permits: Michigan State Park motor vehicle sticker.

Best months: May through October.
Camping: Tahquamenon Falls State Park's (TFSP) Lower Falls Campground, 4.5 miles east of the trailhead, has 188 campsites. TFSP does not allow backpack camping along the trail.
Maps: USGS Betsy Lake South (inc.) quad; Tahquamenon Falls State Park trail map.
Trail contact: TFSP, (906) 492-3415.

Finding the trailhead: From Paradise, drive 15 miles west on M–123 and turn right (west) into the trailhead parking at the Stables Picnic Area.

The Hike

This short loop hike on Tahquamenon Falls State Park's west end offers a compelling sample of the park's attractions. The circuit stops at two vistas to view the Upper Falls, perhaps the preeminent shrine for nature lovers in the eastern U.P. In addition the loop passes a subtle but powerful parade of old-growth forest, an unusual chance to take a journey back in time. To top it all off, the route passes a rare grove of ancient white pine trees.

Begin your hike at the Stables Picnic Area, crossing M–123 and walking southeast on the Giant Pines Trail. Wide as a jeep road, the trail begins a mile-long run south, through a beech-maple forest to the northeast corner of the Upper Falls parking lot (Mile 1.0).

The Giant Pines grove holds a notable specimen that is nearly 175 years old.

Walk south, following the eastern edge of the parking lot to its southeast corner. There hike south for about 0.3 mile, on the Nature Trail, to an intersection with a broad paved trail that runs along the river canyon's rim. Turn left (south) and walk one hundred paces to an intersection (Mile 1.3), designated Junction A on the map. Turn right (west), descending stairs, as the River Trail goes left (east). Descend a little more than one hundred steps and walk north 200 yards to a viewpoint (Mile 1.4). This location offers a frontal view of the Upper Falls' spectacular, almost 50-foot free fall.

When you are ready return to the top of the stairs (Mile 1.5) and turn left (northwest), following the paved path along the rim of the gorge. Now and then the falls peek through the trees along this stretch. Walk a total of 450 paces from Junction A to Junction B (Mile 1.8), where another set of stairs descends left (southwest), as the Giant Pines Trail goes right (northwest). Walk down those stairs to a viewpoint on a ledge beside the top of the Upper Falls at Mile 1.9. Sight lines here, along the lip of the falls' drop, are spectacular.

Retrace your steps up to Junction B and turn left (northwest) on the Giant Pines Trail, a broad jeep road that is also a segment of the North Country Trail (NCT).

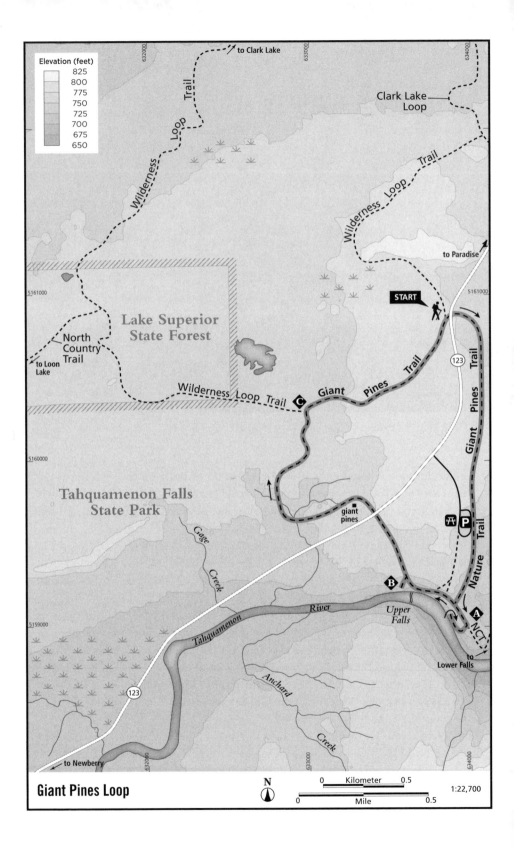

Elevation (feet)

825
800
775
750
725
700
675
650

to Clark Lake

Clark Lake
Loop

Wilderness Loop Trail

632000

633000

634000

Wilderness

Loop

Trail

Wilderness

Loop

Trait

to Paradise

5161000

START

5161000

123

Lake Superior
State Forest

North
Country
Trail

to Loon
Lake

Wilderness Loop Trail **C** Giant   Pines   Trail

Giant Pines Trail

5160000

Tahquamenon Falls
State Park

giant
pines

⅀

P

Gage

Creek

Nature   Trail

B

Upper
Falls

A

NCT

River

5159000

Tahquamenon

to
Lower Falls

123

Anchard

Creek

632000

633000

634000

to Newberry

Giant Pines Loop

N

0   Kilometer   0.5

0   Mile   0.5

1:22,700

Bear left (north) 0.1 mile later, as the trail becomes a graded service road and continues on to cross M–123 at Mile 2.3.

On the north side of the highway, hike north and west on the Giant Pines Trail, arriving at the namesake trees at Mile 2.5. This grove is a haunting reminder of the vast pine stands of the U.P., now long gone. One elder here is estimated to be 175 years old and is almost 5 feet in diameter and 120 feet high.

Continue hiking west and north on the Giant Pines Trail, arriving at an intersection designated Junction C (Mile 3.3). Go straight (north) as the NCT goes left (west). Hike north and east another 0.8 mile, passing impressive specimens of older beech, white pine, and hemlock before arriving at the trailhead, the Stables Picnic Area, at Mile 4.1.

Option: A side-trip west from Junction C is quietly addictive—a route I would gladly repeat. At Junction C turn left (west), following a footpath that is both part of the park's Wilderness Loop and the NCT. That path begins among hemlocks and then follows sand ridges to an intersection 1.3 miles west, a suitable turnaround spot.

Key Points

0.0 Trailhead.

1.0 Upper Falls parking lot.

1.3 Junction A (top of stairs).

1.4 River viewpoint.

1.5 Junction A.

1.8 Junction B (top of stairs).

1.9 Upper Falls.

2.0 Junction B.

2.3 Giant Pines Trail crosses M-123.

2.5 Giant Pines Grove.

3.3 Junction C (Wilderness Loop Trail).

4.1 Trailhead.

42 Tahquamenon Falls

Highlights: Famous waterfalls and cascades of the Tahquamenon River, virgin forest, and wildlife.
Location: 16 miles west of Paradise.
Type of hike: Point-to-point.
Distance: 6.4 miles.
Difficulty: Moderate.
Fees and permits: Michigan State Park motor vehicle sticker.

Best months: May through October.
Camping: Tahquamenon Falls State Park's (TFSP) Lower Falls Campground, 0.2 mile east of the trailhead, has 188 campsites. TFSP does not allow backpack camping along the trail.
Maps: USGS Timberlost (inc.); Betsy Lake South (inc.) quads; Tahquamenon Falls State Park trail map.
Trail contact: TFSP, (906) 492-3415.

Finding the trailhead: From Paradise, drive 11.1 miles west on M-123 and turn left (south) onto the road to the Lower Falls. Drive 0.7 mile south to the Lower Falls trailhead parking area.

The Hike

Mention Tahquamenon Falls State Park, and most Michigan nature lovers think of the famous waterfalls. The Upper Falls, nearly 50 feet high and 200 feet across, is a well-known icon. Its sibling, the roaring series of drops known as the Lower Falls, is a beauty in its own right.

The Upper Falls may well be Michigan's most famous, but it is not the only superlative in these parts. Between the falls, beside the river, is the largest old-growth hardwood forest remnant in the eastern U.P. This virgin forest features 2,300 acres of sugar maple, American beech, eastern hemlock, and yellow birch. Few and far between are the remaining significant chunks of Michigan's old-growth forest. The last large stands are here, along the Tahquamenon River and in the Porcupine Mountains and Sylvania Wildernesses. Add this all together and you have the makings of an outstanding hike. The route begins at the Lower Falls and threads its way through the ancient forest beside the river for 5 miles to the Upper Falls. Better yet, it continues another half mile to visit two giant white pine trees, one of them 175 years old and almost 5 feet in diameter.

Begin your tour by walking west on a broad paved trail from the Lower Falls trailhead. Just 125 paces from the parking area, a broad view of the Lower Falls appears. This is a complex and beautiful series of drops bracketing an island in the river. I visited in early May, and an eagle and osprey were squabbling over fishing rights for the falls.

Walk northwest on a boardwalk that bridges a damp stretch of seeps and springs that is rich with marsh marigolds in May. This is the beginning of the route to the Upper Falls. Known as the Tahquamenon River Trail, or simply the River Trail, this route is also part of the North Country Trail (NCT). It circles a broad pool and arrives beside the Lower Falls, a spectacular white-water show, at Mile 0.3. Three

A remarkable virgin forest lines the Tahquamenon River below the Upper Falls' roaring drop.

thumping, booming drops line the river's north channel here for a descent of about 20 feet.

Continue hiking on the River Trail, now heading south and climbing above the river's rapids. The path stays high for a bit, passing beautiful hemlocks and a cascading brook before descending to a ledge some 10 feet above the river. Below, a cliffy steep drop-off leads to the stream. I found a dramatic, almost lyrical sense of place in this stretch of trail, and I couldn't help wondering who else, perhaps centuries before me, paused to soak in the ambience here. The sights and sounds of the rapids, forest, and brook have an aura of agelessness about them.

About a mile after the beginning of the hike, the river current, as well as the slope beside it, mellow. As the valley widens, the River Trail descends to travel on a flood plain and soon arrives at a bench next to the 2-mile marker.

Continue hiking west on the River Trail, passing huge hemlocks before the trail again bends to the rhythm of the river valley terrain, ascends a bluff and, crosses a flood plain. About Mile 4 of the hike, the trail makes a final ascent onto a headland that holds broad swaths of purple and white spring beauty in May.

Sounds of the Upper Falls drift through the woods as you approach a paved trail junction at Mile 4.5, designated Junction A. The River Trail ends at this junction.

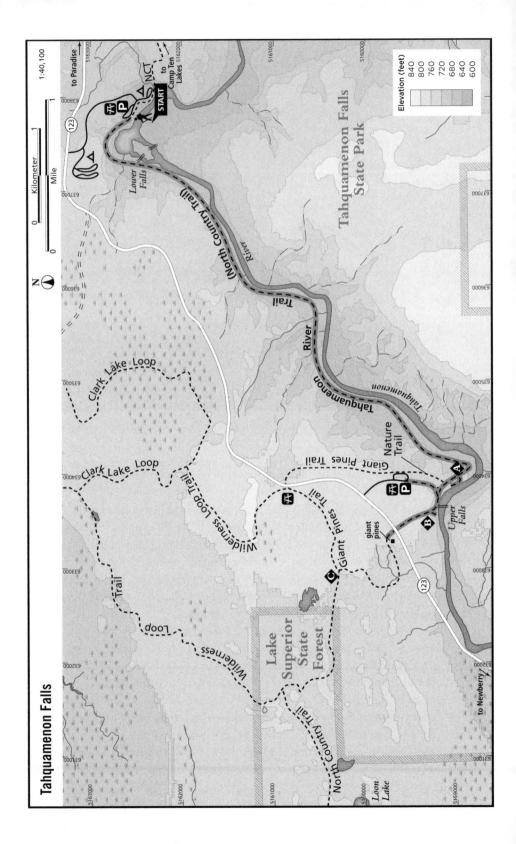

Tahquamenon Falls

1:40,100

Elevation (feet)

840
800
760
720
680
640
600

Tahquamenon Falls State Park

Lake Superior State Forest

to Paradise

to Camp Ten Lakes

123

Lower Falls

NCT

START

North Country Trail

Tahquamenon River

Clark Lake Loop

Wilderness Loop Trail

Giant Pines Trail

Nature Trail

giant pines

Upper Falls

Giant Pines Trail

Wilderness Loop

Trail

Loon Lake

North Country Trail

to Newberry

123

N

Turn left (west), descending stairs to a viewpoint as the NCT goes straight (north) along the rim of the gorge. Descend a hundred some steps, then walk 200 yards north on a boardwalk. At that point (Mile 4.6), there is a frontal view of the Upper Falls, a near 50-foot free fall, almost 200 feet wide.

Retrace your steps, ascending to Junction A (Mile 4.7), and turn left (north), following the NCT, a broad paved path along the rim of the river gorge. Follow the railing along the rim of the canyon northward, the falls playing peek-a-boo through the trees, for 450 paces to Junction B (Mile 5.0). Turn left (southwest) and descend steps to the falls, as the Giant Pines Trail goes straight (northwest). At the bottom of the steps (Mile 5.1) is an oft-photographed view of the falls, a stunning view along the lip of its drop.

When you are ready retrace your steps, ascending to Junction B (Mile 5.2). Turn left (northwest) onto the Giant Pines Trail, a broad jeep road that is also the NCT. Bear left (north) 0.1 mile later as the trail becomes a graded service road and continues on to cross M–123 at Mile 5.5.

On the north side of the highway, hike north and west on the Giant Pines Trail, arriving at the namesake trees at Mile 5.7, a haunting reminder of the vast pine stands of the U.P., now long gone. A sign states that the largest tree is 120 feet high.

From the Giant Pines Trail, retrace your steps to Junction B (Mile 6.2). From that intersection walk southeast about 100 yards on the wide paved trail and turn left (north) on a broad paved trail that leads to the Upper Falls trailhead (Mile 6.4), the end of the hike.

Key Points

0.0   Lower Falls trailhead.

0.3   Lower Falls

2.0   Bench.

4.5   Junction A, spur trail.

4.6   End of spur trail.

4.7   Junction A.

5.0   Junction B, spur trail.

5.1   Upper Falls.

5.2   Junction B.

5.5   M-123.

5.7   Giant pines.

5.9   M-123.

6.2   Junction B.

6.4   Upper Falls trailhead.

43 Naomikong Point

Highlights: A Lake Superior shoreline ramble, wildlife, and views of the Canadian highlands 40 miles across Whitefish Bay.
Location: 20 miles west of Bay Mills.
Type of hike: Out-and-back.
Distance: 7 miles.
Difficulty: Moderate.
Fees and permits: None.
Best months: May through October.

Camping: Hiawatha National Forest regulations allow dispersed camping south of the Curley Lewis Highway only, not on the shoreline. The Forest Service Bay View Campground, 11 miles east of the trailhead, has twenty-four campsites.
Map: USGS McNearney Lake quad.
Trail contact: Hiawatha National Forest, (906) 635-5311, www.fs.fed.us/r9/hiawatha.

Finding the trailhead: From Bay Mills, drive west 19.9 miles on Lake Shore Drive. After 7.2 miles, at Dollar Settlement, this road also goes by the name of the Curley Lewis Highway (Forest Highway 42). Turn right (north) into the trailhead parking area.

Special considerations: This hike's route is along a shoreline. While shoreline hikes may be glorious in good conditions, bad weather or high winds can make this route unpleasant. Changes in lake water levels may have vast influence on the ease of travel on a shoreline route.

Remote shorelines are important wildlife habitat. As you are hiking be sure to give wildlife lots of elbowroom, especially during the spring and early summer nesting season.

The Hike

Time spent along the Lake Superior shore is rarely a loss, and it seems to hold an almost uncanny potential to be a real treat. That was the case the day I hiked the shoreline to Naomikong Point. The lake was in a miragelike calm—a giant reflecting pool dotted with mergansers. Far off on the horizon, some 40 miles distant, the highlands of the Canadian shore loomed above the flat water. Walking along the shore in these conditions was an optical delight, and it seemed that every step offered a wonderful choice. I could scan the nearby shore, enjoying sandbars, white pines, and herons. Or I could practice the fine art of Lake Superior gazing, trying to pick out far-off landmarks or savoring the sheer pleasure of its vast open space. The texture of the shore made foot travel a pleasure. Three-quarters of it was sand beach; the only obstacle was one or two sandbar-and-puddle route puzzles to decipher. The points featured some rock cobble. In those spots, there was a touch of tedious footwork—a reasonable price for the reward.

Begin your hike by walking north from the trailhead through a narrow strip of trees, to the Lake Superior shoreline, a mere stone's throw north. Extensive shallows stretch offshore here, and rocks and boulders pierce the surface far out into the lake. Hike east along the shore, where the beach is a strip 10 to 30 feet wide, until you near the mouth of Naomikong Creek at Mile 0.7. Walk south through low dunes to the North Country Trail, utilizing its sturdy suspension bridge to cross to the creek's east side.

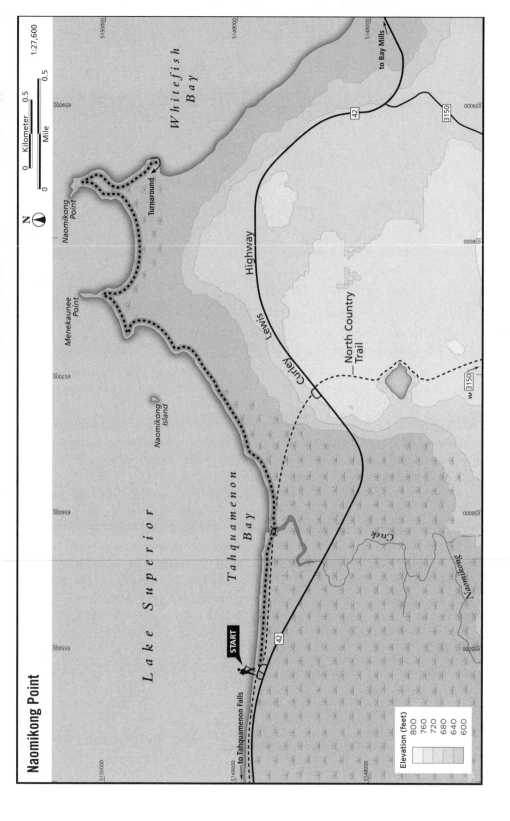

Naomikong Point

1:27,600

N

0   Kilometer   0.5
0   Mile   0.5

Lake Superior

Whitefish Bay

Naomikong Point

Turnaround

Menekaunee Point

Naomikong Island

Tahquamenon Bay

START

to Tahquamenon Falls

42

Lewis

Curley

Highway

North Country Trail

42

3150

3150

to Bay Mills

Naomikong Creek

Elevation (feet)
800
760
720
680
640
600

Along the shoreline route to Naomikong Point—Menekaunee Point and Lake Superior in a mellow mood.

Once on the east side of the creek, turn north to the shore as soon as a dry route is visible. I ended up walking the waterline east of the creek mouth on a long sandbar. Inland from the sandbar a long lagoonlike pond drained into the big lake through a small creek that I hopped.

Slowly the shoreline swings north. Naomikong Island, small and wooded, sits a quarter mile offshore, a mile east of the creek. Then the lakeshore rounds a broad west-facing point before swinging north to Menekaunee Point (Mile 2.3).

East of Menekaunee Point, a half–moon shaped bay features a pleasant sand beach backed by white pines. An eagle flushed as I approached Naomikong Point, the bay's eastern tip. Naomikong Point offers fresh views, and the Mission Hill highlands line the coast 10 miles east. Continue hiking east and south along the shore to a small inlet a quarter-mile past the point. The inlet is the hike's turnaround spot.

Key Points

- **0.0** Trailhead.
- **0.7** Naomikong Creek.
- **2.3** Menekaunee Point.
- **3.3** Naomikong Point.
- **3.5** Inlet south of Naomikong Point; turnaround point.
- **7.0** Trailhead.

44 Cedar River Loop

Highlights: Quiet forest and riverside scenes along the Cedar River.
Location: 8 miles north of Cedar River.
Type of hike: Loop.
Distance: 5.5 miles.
Difficulty: Moderate.
Fees and permits: None.
Best months: May through October.

Camping: Cedar River North State Forest Campground, 2 miles west of the trailhead, has eighteen campsites.
Maps: USGS North Lake quad (inc.); Cedar River Pathway Map, Michigan Department of Natural Resources.
Trail contact: Michigan Department of Natural Resources, (906) 786-2354, www.michigan.gov/dnr.

Finding the trailhead: From the town of Cedar River, drive 1.6 miles north on M-35 and turn left (north) onto River Road (Menominee County Road 551). Drive 5.8 miles north and turn left (west) onto the gravel lane signed for the Cedar River Pathway and Campground. Drive 0.1 mile west and park in the ski trail parking area.

The Hike

Cedar River Pathway is a classic walk in the woods on a cross-country ski trail that works well as a hiking trail. Along the way the route passes picturesque scenes along the placid Cedar River, hemlock groves, and a seemingly endless parade of pleasant woodland panoramas. Life, like the river's current, seems to flow slower here.

A series of numbered intersections marks the ski trails here, which are a series of loops. Note that this hike's route begins with trail marker 9, proceeds to 8, and then arrives at 2. At that point it travels in numerical sequence (2, 3, and so on).

Begin your hike by walking west on the gravel lane that leads to the campground from the ski trail parking lot. Hike west to marker 9 (Mile 0.2) and turn right (north) on a 4 foot-wide ski lane to marker 8 (Mile 0.6). Turn left (west) and walk 0.3 mile to marker 2 (Mile 0.9). Turn right (northwest), following the Loop 2 ski trail through a cedar stand to a scenic bench on the banks of the Cedar River at about Mile 1.4. I was there on a mellow October day and found the break spot irresistible.

From the riverside bench continue walking north to marker 3 (Mile 1.8). Turn left (north), following the Loop 3 ski trail as it wanders west for a few peek-a-boo views of the river before swinging inland. A westward leg brings the trail back to the Cedar River for a final visit and another scenic bench, at about Mile 2.4. Next the trail runs northeast to marker 4 (Mile 2.8).

Turn right (south), following the Loop 3 ski trail south through a hemlock grove. The path, despite a few wiggles, runs steadily south to marker 6 (Mile 3.7). Turn left (east) and hike south and east to marker 7 (Mile 4.5). Bear right (southeast) and a few minutes later the trail rises onto a low ridge, perhaps 30 feet high,

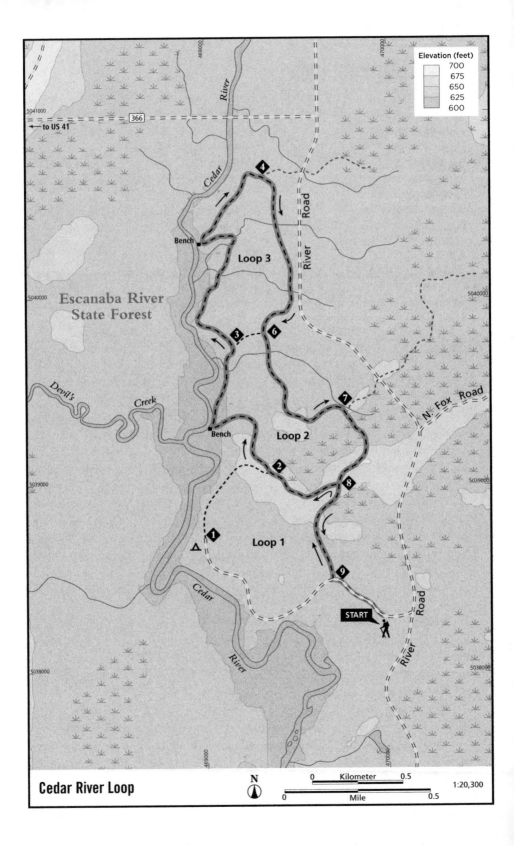

Elevation (feet)
700
675
650
625
600

River

366
← to US 41

Cedar

4

River

Road

Bench

Loop 3

Escanaba River
State Forest

3   6

Devil's

Creek

Bench

7   N. Fox   Road

Loop 2

2

8

1

Loop 1

△

9

START

River   Road

Cedar

River

Cedar River Loop

N

0   Kilometer   0.5

0   Mile   0.5

1:20,300

the major hill of the hike. After miles of flat to rolling terrain, the little ascent is striking.

Hike to marker 8 (Mile 4.9). Bear left (south), retracing your steps from the beginning of the outing to marker 9 (Mile 5.3). Turn left (east) and follow the gravel lane to the ski trail parking area, the hike's end (Mile 5.5).

Key Points

0.0 Trailhead.

0.2 Trail Marker #9.

0.6 Trail Marker #8.

0.9 Trail Marker #2.

1.4 First riverside bench.

1.8 Trail Marker #3.

2.4 Second riverside bench.

2.8 Trail Marker #4.

3.7 Trail Marker #6.

4.5 Trail Marker #7.

4.9 Trail Marker #8.

5.3 Trail Marker #9.

5.5 Trailhead.

45 Portage Bay

Highlights: Remote Lake Michigan shoreline and solitude.
Location: 5 miles south of Garden.
Type of hike: Out-and-back.
Distance: 12.2 miles.
Difficulty: Difficult.
Fees and permits: Michigan Department of Natural Resources (DNR) vehicle sticker.
Best months: May through October.

Camping: Backpack camping is allowed on state forest land, within zero-impact guidelines, with a DNR permit. The Portage Bay State Forest Campground at the trailhead has twenty-three campsites.
Maps: USGS Devil's Corner, Garden, Hiram Point quads.
Trail contact: Michigan DNR, (906) 452-6227, www.michigan.gov/dnr.

Finding the trailhead: From Garden, drive 5.3 miles south and west on M-483. Turn left (south) and drive 1.2 miles south on "08 Road" (gravel). Then turn left (east) on Portage Bay Road and drive 4.6 miles to the Portage Bay boat landing.

Special considerations: This hike is an off-trail shoreline route. While most of this coast is pleasant hiking, occasional rock gardens, cobble, and puddles may be challenging. Be aware that shoreline routes are glorious in good conditions but merciless in their exposure to high winds when the weather is rowdy. Changes in lake water levels may have a vast influence on the ease of travel on a shoreline route.

Remote shorelines are important wildlife habitat. While you are hiking be sure to give wildlife plenty of elbowroom, especially during the spring and early summer nesting season.

The Hike

Portage Bay is literally the end of the road—a quiet shoreline at the terminus of a miles-long dusty gravel road. Every time I visit this inlet's state forest campground, one thought comes to mind: *This is the way it is supposed to be.*

On a fine June evening here, I settled in on the low dunes beyond the beach to watch the evening light. Off to the east the watery horizon had just begun to turn mauve when I realized that I was not alone. A huge snapping turtle was lumbering up the sandy slope in front of me. About 20 feet out she stopped and began a timeless ritual: She scooped out a tunnel-like hole in the sand with a rear leg, laid an egg, pushed the egg into the hole, covered the egg with some sand, and repeated this again and again.

Things only get quieter as you walk the beach north from the campground. Known to few except locals, 7 miles of state forest land lines the Lake Michigan shoreline here.

Begin your hike at the boat landing just south of the Portage Bay State Campground. Walk the open beach north to a broad protrusion (Mile 1.3) I call Portage Bay Point. I found pleasant travel here; the shore is a combination of sand and a sprinkling of rock cobble.

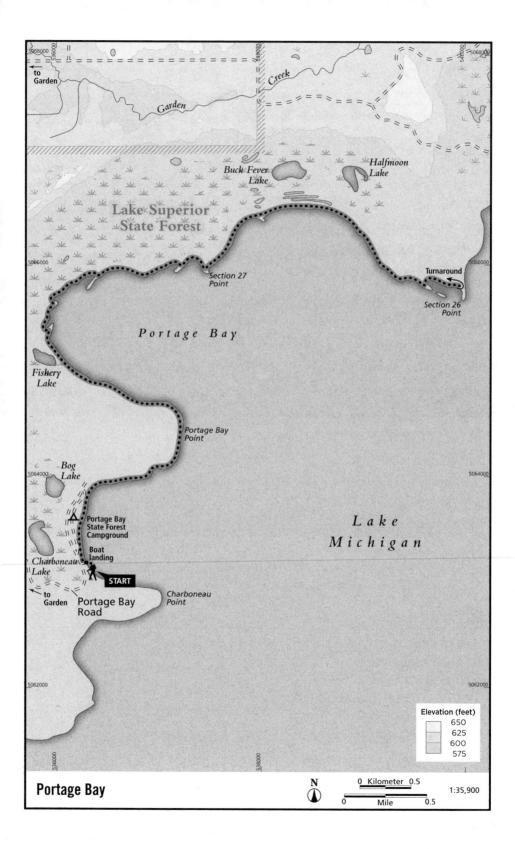

to
Garden

Garden   Creek

Buck Fever
Lake

Halfmoon
Lake

Lake Superior
State Forest

Section 27
Point

Turnaround

Section 26
Point

Portage Bay

Fishery
Lake

Portage Bay
Point

Bog
Lake

Portage Bay
State Forest
Campground

Charboneau
Lake

Boat
landing

Lake
Michigan

START

to
Garden

Portage Bay
Road

Charboneau
Point

Elevation (feet)

650
625
600
575

Portage Bay

N

0   Kilometer   0.5

0   Mile   0.5

1:35,900

On Portage Bay's quiet shoreline.

Continue hiking along the Lake Michigan shoreline, following the waterline as it swings west, the beginning of a bay. I found vast damp flats—part firm wet sand, part puddles—as I rounded this inlet to its north side. There the shoreline returned to the familiar mix of dry sand and rock cobble, and I walked eastward to Section 27 Point (Mile 3.8).

East of Section 27 Point, I followed low dunes, just off the beach, eastward toward the hike's turnaround spot, Section 26 Point.

Key Points

0.0   Trailhead.

1.3   Portage Bay Point.

3.8   Section 27 Point.

6.1   Section 26 Point; turnaround point.

12.2   Trailhead.

46 Birch Point

Highlights: Secluded Lake Michigan shorelines, beaches, dune and swale topography, wildlife, and solitude.
Location: 10 miles south of Gould City.
Type of hike: Out-and-back.
Distance: 5.2 miles.
Difficulty: Moderate.
Fees and permits: None.
Best months: April through October.

Camping: Backpack camping is allowed on state forest land, within zero-impact guidelines, with a Michigan Department of Natural Resources (DNR) permit. Gould City Township Park features a rustic camping area 100 yards northwest of the parking area.
Map: USGS Point Patterson quad.
Trail contact: Michigan DNR, (906) 477-6048, www.michigan.gov/dnr.

Finding the trailhead: From Gould City, drive 9.6 miles south on Gould City Road. Turn left (northeast) into the parking area of Gould City Township Park.

Special considerations: This hike is an off-trail shoreline route. While most of this coast is pleasant hiking, occasional rock gardens and cobble may be challenging. Be aware that shoreline routes are glorious in good conditions but merciless in their exposure to high winds when the weather gets rowdy. Changes in lake water levels may have vast influence on the ease of travel on a shoreline route.

Remote shorelines are important wildlife habitat. As you are hiking, be sure to give wildlife lots of elbowroom, especially during the spring and early summer nesting season.

The Hike

This coast, arguably some of the most remote mainland shoreline on Lake Michigan, has a way of growing on you. A feeling of spaciousness pervades this place—a sense that you could wander these shores for days, and there would always be another wave-washed point and soul-satisfying solitude ahead.

An immense swath of nearly 20 miles of public shoreline brackets Gould City Township Park. Except for a small private section just west of Birch Point, the stretch from Hughes Point in the west to several miles north of the mouth of the Crow River is state forest. Thanks to a strategic move by The Nature Conservancy (TNC) in the 1990s, this chunk of prime habitat, home to wolves and loons, is intact. TNC bought some 10,000 acres near the mouths of the Cataract and Crow Rivers, then transferred title to the state of Michigan. Two locations, near Seiner's Point and the Crow River, have protective status as state natural areas.

Any visit to these shores will be memorable, but one stretch draws me back time and again. That is the ramble west toward Birch Point from Gould City Township Park, a simple, rustic facility blessed with location. This is a scalloped shoreline, a series of shallow indentations in the coast. Passing the points that separate those bays reminds me of turning the page in a magazine that features both striking landscape photographs and text. Immediately your eye goes to the new broad view of the bay

Bedrock and boulders along the shoreline route to Birch Point.

(the photograph) and then to the text (the detail noticed as you walk). During my visits to this coast, bald eagles and osprey seemed to fly by on an almost hourly basis. Eagles often flushed from roosts on snags located on the points.

Begin your hike by walking southwest, along the shore, from Gould City Township Park. A quick 0.2 mile later, round a broad point and notice the low sand dunes north of Scott Point at Mile 0.4 ahead. Walk west, scanning for a worn path that ascends into the dunes in a southwesterly direction. Follow that path west and south to the sandy beach west of Scott Point.

Halfway around this bay, a stretch of cobble and rock begins, at about Mile 0.6. Persevere. The footing improves, and what is ahead is well worth the effort.

Continue hiking the shoreline west, swinging around another bay, to another large point at about Mile 1.0. Beyond this point, a long stretch of sand beach stretches to Hudson Creek, an easy jump. Wide expanses of dolomite bedrock slabs are on the shore here.

Two points punctuate the shoreline a quarter mile west of Hudson Creek. I would suggest choosing the old jeep track that runs west through the woods, a viable shortcut, rather than rounding them on the shore. Look for the old jeep track at the edge of the woods, west of Hudson Creek.

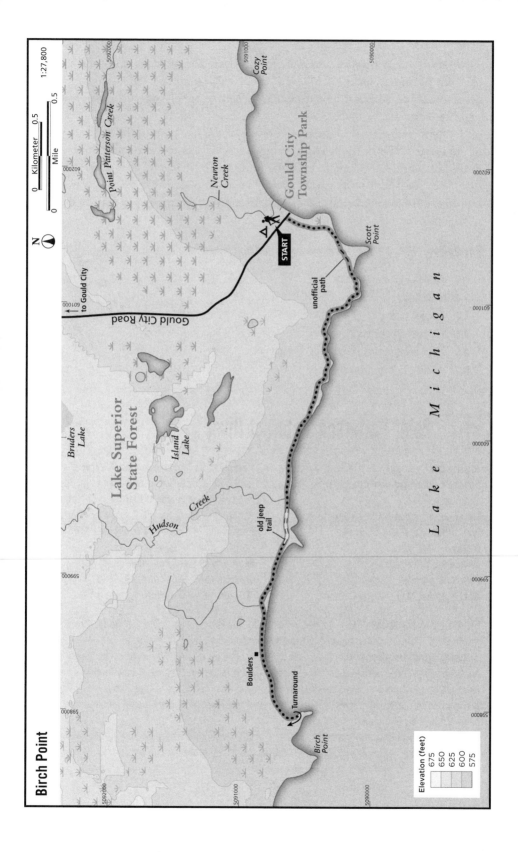

Birch Point

1:27,800

N

0   Kilometer   0.5

0   Mile   0.5

Point Patterson Creek

Newton Creek

to Gould City

Gould City Road

Lake Superior State Forest

Bruders Lake

Island Lake

Hudson Creek

old jeep trail

Boulders

Turnaround

Birch Point

START

unofficial path

Scott Point

Gould City Township Park

Cozy Point

L a k e   M i c h i g a n

Elevation (feet)
675
650
625
600
575

West of these two points, a mile–long bay begins. The shore is a sandy beach dotted with occasional rocks. At Mile 2.1, about halfway around the bay, these rocks become notable. Several dolomite boulders, the size of Volkswagen Beetles, feature vegetated tops.

Resume hiking west, and the sand beach of the bay ends in the rocky cobble of the eastern lobe of Birch Point. Footing is a tad tedious, but it is a short walk out to the point. From here most of the route you have just hiked is visible to the east. Scan the south-southeast horizon. On a good day you can see the dark smudges of the Beaver Island archipelago, 15 miles off. Retrace your steps to return to the trailhead.

Key Points

0.0 Gould City Township Park.

0.4 Scott Point.

1.5 Hudson Creek.

2.1 Limestone boulders.

2.6 Birch Point (eastern prong); turnaround point.

5.2 Gould City Township Park.

47 Point Patterson/Cataract River

Highlights: Remote Lake Michigan shoreline, beaches, dune and swale topography, wildlife, and solitude.
Location: 10 miles south of Gould City.
Type of hike: Out-and-back.
Distance: 7.2 miles.
Difficulty: Moderate.
Fees and permits: None.
Best months: May through October.

Camping: Backpack camping is allowed on state forest land, within zero-impact guidelines, with a Michigan Department of Natural Resources (DNR) permit. Gould City Township Park features a rustic camping area 100 yards northwest of the parking area.
Map: USGS Point Patterson quad.
Trail contact: Michigan DNR, (906) 477-6048, www.michigan.gov/dnr.

Finding the trailhead: From Gould City, drive 9.6 miles south on Gould City Road. Turn left (northeast) into the parking area of Gould City Township Park.

Special considerations: This hike is an off-trail shoreline route. While most of this coast is pleasant hiking, occasional rock gardens and cobble may be challenging. Be aware that shoreline routes are glorious in good conditions, but they can be merciless in their exposure to high winds when the weather is rowdy. Changes in lake water levels may have a vast influence on the ease of travel on a shoreline route.

Remote shorelines are important wildlife habitat. As you are hiking be sure to give wildlife lots of elbowroom, especially during the spring and early summer nesting season.

Low dunes line the vast open spaces of the beach north of Point Patterson.

The Hike

If you like shoreline hikes, and I do, it is pretty hard to go wrong when your outing starts at the rustic parking area known as Gould City Township Park. Walk east or west from there, along the Lake Michigan coast, and peace and quiet are as commonplace as the broad lake vistas, waves, and eagles. In this walk you'll find a stretch of cobble to travel over near Point Patterson. That stretch is at times slow going but a reasonable price for the hike's rewards—miles of Lake Michigan shoreline and typically complete solitude. I would encourage you to size it up for yourself. The short walk past Cozy Point works well as a reconnaissance and is hardly a disappointment as an outing itself.

Begin by walking east from the parking area at Gould City Township Park. Hop little Newton Creek, find firm sand near the water's edge, and follow the beach east. Just before Cozy Point (Mile 0.9), the shoreline changes from sand beach to a mixture of sand and rock cobble.

As I approached Cozy Point, a bald eagle flushed. A few moments later, as I rounded a small cove east of the point, a second eagle took wing. Past that sandy

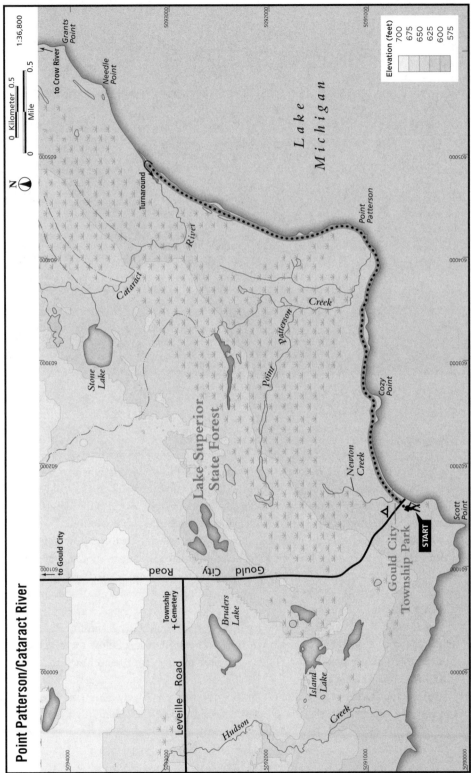

Point Patterson/Cataract River

1:36,800

N

Elevation (feet)
- 700
- 675
- 650
- 625
- 600
- 575

Lake Michigan

Grants Point

Needle Point

to Crow River

Turnaround

Cataract River

Point Patterson

Stone Lake

Point Patterson Creek

Cozy Point

Lake Superior State Forest

Newton Creek

to Gould City

Gould City Road

Township Cemetery

Bruders Lake

Leveille Road

Island Lake

Hudson Creek

Gould City Township Park

START

Scott Point

cove the beach becomes rocky with a few boulders the size of compact cars accenting the cobble. At times the cobble here is a tad tedious, but an alternative is at hand. Check the edge of the tree line for an old jeep trail, which offers easier footing.

Continue hiking east, following the shoreline to Point Patterson Creek (Mile 1.8). I was able to rock hop it, but trekking poles came in handy. Yet another eagle flew around the point; a great blue heron stood sentinel at the creek's mouth. Once past the creek make your way east and north, rounding Point Patterson's broad round perimeter.

North of Point Patterson I found broad flats that were part sand and part puddles and a sprinkling of rock. Travel was pleasant, with occasional route finding required around the larger puddles.

About a mile north of the point, the flats slowly became a classic sand beach; marshy ponds were just inland. Sandhill cranes bugled from the marsh. The Cataract River, not much more than a creek at its sandy mouth, bisects the beach at Mile 3.6, a natural turnaround point for the hike.

Options: You don't have to walk long distances to enjoy this tranquil coast. The 2-mile round-trip hike to the sandy cove east of Cozy Point is a convincing sample.

Energetic hikers may want to consider venturing beyond the Cataract River. Crossing that stream may require a short shin-deep wade or an energetic leap. Beyond, miles of state-owned shoreline stretch to the mouth of the Crow River and beyond. The mouth of the Crow River is 7.3 miles from Gould City Township Park.

Key Points

0.0 Gould City Township Park.

0.9 Cozy Point.

1.8 Point Patterson Creek.

2.0 Point Patterson.

3.6 Mouth of the Cataract River.

7.2 Gould City Township Park.

48 Maple Hill

Highlights: A dolomite reef, quiet woods, trillium, a beaver dam, and a boardwalk through a cedar swamp.
Location: 10 miles north of Moran.
Type of hike: Out-and-back.
Distance: 10.6 miles.
Difficulty: Difficult* due to distance; the hiking is moderate.
Fees and permits: None.
Best months: May through October.

Camping: Backpack camping is allowed along the trail, on Hiawatha National Forest land, within zero-impact guidelines. The Hiawatha National Forest's Carp River Campground, 10 miles southeast of the trailhead, has forty-four campsites.
Map: USGS Ozark NE quad (inc.).
Trail contact: Hiawatha National Forest, (906) 643-7900, www.fs.fed.us/r9/hiawatha; The North Country Trail Association Web site, www.northcountrytrail.org.

Finding the trailhead: From Moran, drive 0.2 mile north on M-123 and turn right (east) onto Mackinac County Road 424 (also known as Charles Moran Road). Drive 0.2 mile and turn left (north) on Mackinac County Road 434 (also known as Forest Road 3119 and East Lake Road). Drive 9.6 miles north and park on the wide grassy shoulder where Forest Road 3114 enters from the right (east).
Special considerations: Rare plants and snails inhabit the Maple Hill dolomite reef. Think of them and consider staying off the rocks unless you are a researcher.

The Hike

This stretch of trail is quietly persuasive. An older, open maple forest that is a pleasure to the eye lines the first few miles. The forest leads to a convoluted cliff band rising from a trailside slope, reminiscent of a ghostly gray fortification. A cedar swamp, conveniently crossed on a boardwalk, follows the rock wall. Better yet, a classic North Woods attraction—an impressive 150-foot-long beaver dam—rounds out the day.

Begin your hike by walking 135 paces south on East Lake Road to the signed NCT crossing. Walk east on the NCT, and Guard Lake appears to your right (east) at Mile 0.2. For the next quarter mile, the trail rounds that pond's west side before heading north into a beautiful, open maple forest and reaching FR 3114 at Mile 1.1.

Cross FR 3114 and continue hiking north on the NCT. I saw this stretch in May, and the forest floor was a vast, rolling carpet of white trillium blossoms and bright green leaves. From time to time the profusion of ground cover, trillium, and ferns obscured any trace of the trail below. Trail markings on trees were adequate, though, and hardly gave me a moment's pause.

The first hint of the Maple Hill escarpment is a scattering of boulders on the slope rising west of the trail, followed by a garage-size rock by the trail, complete with a shrubby "garden" top. Upslope, rock outcrops morph into a continual cliff band at Mile 4.0. Here and there the wall may reach an honest 50 feet in height;

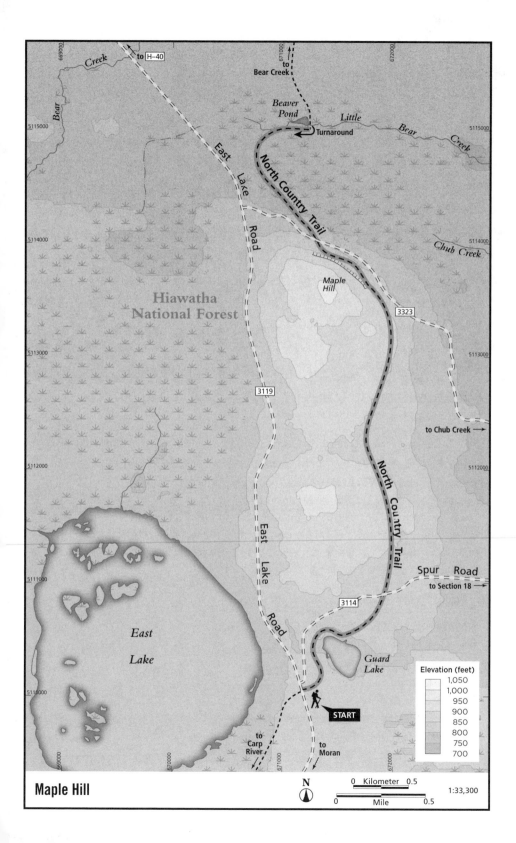

to H-40

Bear Creek

to Bear Creek

Beaver Pond

Little Bear Creek

Turnaround

East Lake Road

North Country Trail

Chub Creek

Hiawatha National Forest

Maple Hill

3323

3119

to Chub Creek →

East Lake

North Country Trail

Spur Road

to Section 18 →

3114

East Lake Road

Guard Lake

START

to Carp River

to Moran

Elevation (feet)
1,050
1,000
950
900
850
800
750
700

Maple Hill

N

0 Kilometer 0.5

0 Mile 0.5

1:33,300

Maple Hill's fortresslike escarpment.

much of it is less. Low and long, the outcrop is part of a dolomite reef that arcs from New York's Niagara Falls (the multistate rock formation goes by the name the Niagara Escarpment) to Wisconsin's Door County peninsula.

Leaving the gray cliff, the NCT drops to FR 3323 at Mile 4.3 and runs north. A well-constructed boardwalk segment carries the path through a damp cedar swamp section before the trail swings east to parallel a marshy pond along Little Bear Creek. Continue hiking east on the NCT, and an extensive beaver dam appears. This is a good break spot and the turnaround point for the hike.

Key Points

- **0.0** North Country Trail at East Lake Road.
- **0.2** Guard Lake.
- **1.1** FR 3114.
- **4.0** Maple Hill escarpment.
- **4.3** Forest Road 3323.
- **5.3** Beaver Pond on Little Bear Creek; turnaround point.
- **10.6** North Country Trail at East Lake Road.

49 Horseshoe Bay

Highlights: A pristine Lake Huron beach to roam and wildlife.
Location: 6 miles north of St. Ignace.
Type of hike: Out-and-back.
Distance: 6.4 miles.
Difficulty: Moderate.
Fees and permits: None.
Best months: May through October.

Camping: Backpack camping is allowed along the trail and shore within zero-impact guidelines. The Foley Creek Campground (at the trailhead) has fifty-four campsites.
Maps: USGS Evergreen Shores quad (inc.); USDA Forest Service Horseshoe Bay Hiking Trail.
Trail contact: Hiawatha National Forest, (906) 643-7900, www.fs.fed.us/r9/hiawatha.

Finding the trailhead: From St. Ignace, drive 3.8 miles north on Interstate 75. Take exit 348, turning right (east) on business I-75. Drive 0.2 mile southeast and turn left (north) on Mackinac County Road H-63 (also known as the Mackinac Trail). Drive north 2.4 miles and turn right (east) into the U.S. Forest Service's Foley Creek Campground. Drive north 0.5 mile on the campground loop to its northern end, where a sign marks the trailhead for the Horseshoe Bay hiking trail. Parking is on either side of the trailhead.

Special considerations: This hike takes place within the Horseshoe Bay Wilderness, a special place. Treat it well. Also, this outing's route is along a shoreline. While shoreline hikes may be glorious in good conditions, bad weather or high winds can make this route unpleasant. Changes in lake water levels may have a vast influence on the ease of travel. I was initially suspicious of the potential impact of the nearby interstate on this outing's soundtrack. That said, I am describing what I found on two separate visits: onshore, easterly breezes and a hike I would gladly repeat. On both occasions, traffic noise faded a half-mile down the trail and soon disappeared.

Remote shorelines are important wildlife habitat. As you are hiking be sure to give wildlife lots of elbowroom, especially during the spring and early summer nesting season.

The Hike

Just around the corner from St. Ignace's hustle and bustle, the Lake Huron shoreline seems like a trip back in time. Eagles roost in white pine trees, otters dot the shore with their splay-footed tracks, and the rattling bark of sandhill cranes carries over the marsh grass inland. Waves gather and rush to the shore, just as they have for hundreds of years.

Seven miles of this coast is within the Horseshoe Bay Wilderness, and the southern third is a sandy beach, which makes for a natural hiking route. Better yet, a maintained trail carries the hiker through the only obstacle in sight—a damp cedar area along the way to the coast.

Begin your hike by walking north from the trailhead on the Horseshoe Bay Hiking Trail, a wide sandy path. After passing a wilderness boundary sign just north of the trailhead, the trail winds its way northeast through the woods to the shore. As the trail nears the beach, the light brightens as the forest canopy thins, and the rhythmic sounds of surf drift inland.

Horseshoe Bay, a timeless beach hike a stone's throw from busy St. Ignace.

The trail blends into open sandy areas here. This is a good time to take a moment to memorize the setting for the return trip before walking east to the wave-washed Lake Huron shore. There, a broad beach, thirty paces wide, stretches north to a miles-off point—the hike's destination. Behind the beach low vegetated dunes lead to other, forested dunes.

A small creek bisects the beach and enters Lake Huron just north of the trail's end. I eyeballed it and considered a running jump, but opted for a bridge of drift-wood. Alternatively it would be the easiest of wades.

Cross the creek and hike north along the shore. On a topographic map this shoreline appears forbidding: a marshy mess. I found fine hiking on a beach some-times damp, but a route that works. I noticed a similar phenomenon on many hikes along the Lake Michigan and Lake Huron shores: Lower lake levels create hiking routes, which may not have been viable for a generation.

Continue walking north along the shore. A strong onshore breeze blew during my visits, and white swans, just far enough off that I couldn't make out the fine details of their heads that might identify them, rode the swells beyond the breakers. At the northern end of the crescent-shaped beach, at about Mile 2.5, a broadly braided, shallow creek ran across the beach to the shore. Having waterproof boots, I

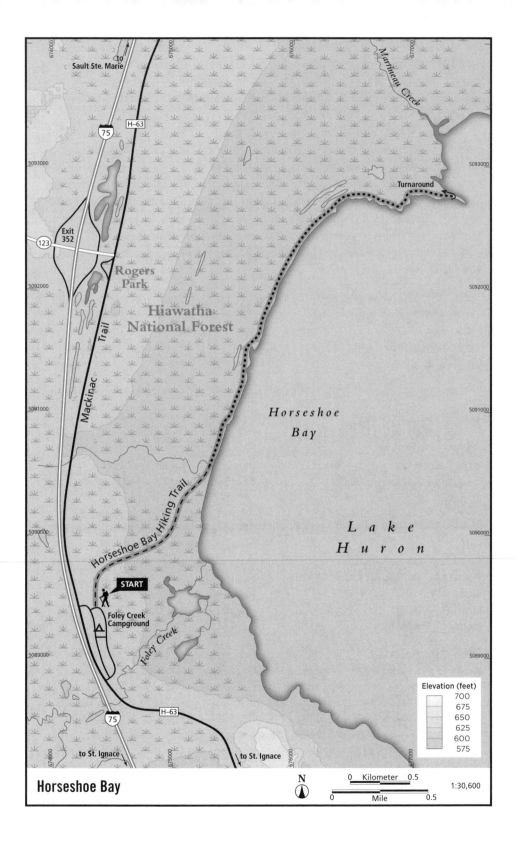

Horseshoe Bay

N

0 Kilometer 0.5

0 Mile 0.5

1:30,600

found a particularly shallow spot and walked through inch–deep water to cross it. Next, I glanced south, puzzled by the sight of a graceful tower on the horizon. It was a few moments before I realized I was looking at the northern tower of the Mackinac Bridge.

Resume hiking along the shore, now turning east to the first of two points, where cedar groves are handy shelter from the wind (Mile 2.9). Continue hiking eastward to a second, more prominent point at Mile 3.2.

Just north of the second point is a secluded bay. It was full of waterfowl on my September visit. Beyond, the shoreline appears intriguing. Martineau Creek empties into the bay, though, and its mouth appears to be a considerable, watery obstacle to further hiking. This second point is the turnaround spot for the hike.

Key Points

0.0 Trailhead at Foley Creek Campground.

1.1 Lake Huron shore (trail ends).

2.9 First point.

3.2 Second point; turnaround point.

6.4 Trailhead.

50 Marble Head

Highlights: Marble Head, a headland that is arguably the first place in the U.P. to be touched by the rising sun. This viewpoint is on a remote Lake Huron shoreline far from the busy shipping lanes to Drummond Island's west.

Location: Drummond Island.

Type of hike: Out-and-back.

Distance: 8.6 miles.

Difficulty: Difficult.

Fees and permits: None.

Best months: May through October.

Camping: Backpack camping is allowed along the trail on state forest land with a Michigan Department of Natural Resources permit. Drummond Township Park, 16 miles west of the trailhead, has fifty campsites.

Maps: USGS Marble Head (inc.); Drummond SE quads.

Trail contact: Michigan DNR, (906) 635-5281, www.michigan.gov/dnr.

Finding the trailhead: From the Drummond Island ferry terminal, drive east 7.8 miles on M-134 to a four-way intersection known as Four Corners. Drive straight (east) on Johnswood Road for 7 miles. At that point turn left (east) onto a gravel road (a sign there designates this SHEEP RANCH ROAD). Drive east and north 0.8 mile and turn right (east) at an unmarked four-way intersection. Now on Glen Cove Road, drive east and northeast 5.5 miles to a point where the road surface becomes cobble in a clearing. Pull off here and park.

Special considerations: Driving to Drummond Island requires a short ferry ride. For schedules and fares visit www.drummondislandchamber.com or call (906) 297-8851.

Marble Head offers sweeping views of Lake Huron's remote North Channel.

Timing may be the key ingredient to enjoying a Marble Head hike. I visited in early May and camped at the viewpoint. The trail was wet, with major puddle obstacles, but I would gladly repeat the trip. The view is exceptional, and I had the trail and Marble Head to myself. This hike, however, follows a designated off-road vehicle trail that shows signs of abundant use. I don't think I'd care to do this hike on Memorial Day.

Remote shoreline is important wildlife habitat. As you are hiking be sure to give wildlife lots of elbowroom, especially during the spring and early summer nesting season.

The Hike

Drummond Island, a 20-mile-long chunk of land at the far eastern end of the U.P., has a remote east end that looks intriguing on a map. Vast swaths of state land, including long miles of Lake Huron shoreline, and a lack of good roads drew my interest. As I studied the maps, Marble Head, a headland on the island's easternmost point, moved onto my short list of must-do trips. It was a blank spot on the map that I had to fill in. When I went there I found a view that was everything I hoped it would be.

I suggest beginning your hike at the clearing where Glen Cove Road turns to cobble. It is possible to drive farther—in fact you can drive all the way to Marble Head—but that driving becomes a technical, high-clearance, four-wheel drive expedition.

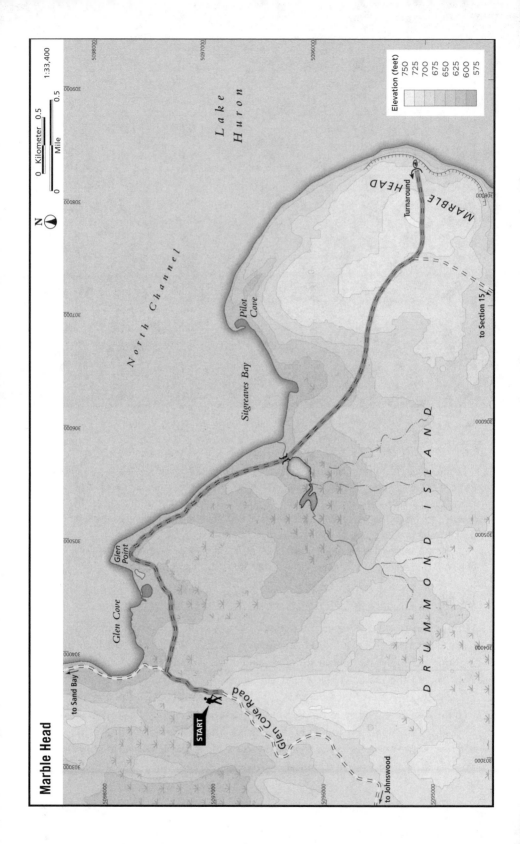

Marble Head

1:33,400

Elevation (feet)
750
725
700
675
650
625
600
575

N

0   Kilometer   0.5
0   Mile   0.5

Lake Huron

North Channel

Pilot Cove

Sitgreaves Bay

Glen Cove

Glen Point

to Sand Bay

START

Glen Cove Road

to Johnswood

MARBLE HEAD

Turnaround

DRUMMOND ISLAND

to Section 15

From the edge of the clearing, hike northeast on Glen Cove Road. It descends through woods to a junction at Mile 0.3. Turn right (east) on a woods road as Glen Cove Road goes left (north). Follow the rough woods road, a designated off-road vehicle route, as it runs east to Glen Point and then southeast, paralleling the Lake Huron shoreline. The jeep trail nears the shore, and a path runs 75 feet northeast to meet it. Loons swam offshore here during my hike.

At Mile 2.2 this rough road reaches an open area, crossing a bridge over a creek that runs into nearby Sitgreaves Bay. Loons and mergansers were offshore here, a harrier worked the grassy meadow upstream, and the primeval bark of sandhill cranes echoed across the marsh. Leaving the shore the jeep trail runs east and south, ascending a low plateau—an area that is half open and half scrubby 30-foot-tall aspens. Grouse broke cover ahead of me; several deer spotted me and ambled off, although I could see them for hundreds of yards. Turn left (east) at a junction at Mile 3.7, where a sign points east to VIEWPOINT. Follow the spur jeep trail 0.6 mile east, descending slightly over ledges, to Marble Head at Mile 4.3.

Marble Head is a low headland 100 feet above Lake Huron. While the elevation may not be impressive, the location is. Sweeping views stretch 40 miles and more, taking in much of Lake Huron's North Channel while Canada's Cockburn Island looms large to the southeast. A series of highlands rise on the Canadian mainland, the north shore of the North Channel.

I was fortunate the day I visited, with crystal visibility and a calm lake. Loons dallied in the lake below me, their calls carrying on the evening air. Both sunset and sunrise were memorable.

Marble Head has a sense of place about it—a feeling of perching on the rim of a vast sound, the North Channel. During my May visit, the view was sweeping, pristine, and mesmerizing. Only a far-off glint hinted of a powerboat. There was a feeling of visiting a timeless panorama. I was reluctant to leave.

Key Points

0.0   Trailhead on Glen Cove Road.

0.3   Off-road vehicle track.

2.2   Bridge over creek at Sitgreaves Bay.

3.7   Spur trail to Marble Head.

4.3   Marble Head; turnaround point.

8.6   Trailhead.

Appendix A: Hike Finder

The hikes listed here are grouped by the types of attractions they offer, such as waterfalls or rivers and streams or the type of hike. If you like to see certain attractions when you hike, use this list as your guide

My favorites, by category, are indicated by an *.

Waterfalls
Black River Waterfalls*, hike 4
Canyon Falls*, hike 18
Chapel Loop, hike 32
Falls of the Yellow Dog*, hike 21
Giant Pines Loop, hike 41
Grand Sable Dunes Loop, hike 25
Lake Superior/Big Carp River Loop, hike 8
Laughing Whitefish Falls*, hike 26
Little Carp River Cascades*, hike 9
Little Garlic River, hike 22
Miners Falls, hike 30
Norwich Bluff to Victoria, hike 16
Olson Falls*, hike 29
Pictured Rocks, hike 31
Piers Gorge*, hike 25
Presque Isle River Waterfalls Loop*,
    hike 5
Rock River Falls*, hike 27
Shining Cloud Falls*, hike 6
Tahquamenon Falls*, hike 42
Tahquamenon West/North Country Trail,
    hike 40
Tibbets Falls/Oren Krumm Shelter, hike 17
Trap Hills Traverse, hike 14
Union River Cascades Loop*, hike 12

Quiet Inland Lakes
Beaver Lake Loop*, hike 33
Bruno's Run Loop, hike 36
Clark Lake Loop*, hike 23
Craig Lake*, hike 19
Deer Island Lake*, hike 24
Grand Sable Dunes Loop, hike 35
Mirror Lake Loop, hike 10
Seney National Wildlife Refuge, hike 37
Tahquamenon West/North Country Trail,
    hike 40
White Deer Lake*, hike 20

Great Lakes Shorelines
Au Sable Point/Log Slide*, hike 34
Bare Bluff*, hike 3
Beaver Lake Loop, hike 33
Birch Point*, hike 46
Chapel Loop*, hike 32
Grand Island Loop*, hike 28
Grand Sables Dune Loop*, hike 35
Horseshoe Bay, hike 49
Horseshoe Harbor*, hike 1
Lake Superior/Big Carp River Loop, hike 8
Lake Superior Shoreline*, hike 7
Little Carp River Cascades, hike 9
Marble Head*, hike 50
Mouth of the Blind Sucker River*, hike 38
Naomikong Point, hike 43
Pictured Rocks*, hike 31
Point Patterson/Cataract River, hike 47
Portage Bay, hike 45
Shining Cloud Falls, hike 6
Two Hearted River, hike 39

Rivers and Streams
Beaver Lake Loop, hike 33
Black River Waterfalls*, hike 4
Bruno's Run Loop, hike 36
Canyon Falls*, hike 18
Cedar River Loop, hike 44
Chapel Loop, hike 32
Craig Lake, hike 19
Falls of the Yellow Dog*, hike 21
Giant Pines Loop, hike 41
Grand Sable Dunes Loop, hike 35
Lake Superior/Big Carp River Loop*, hike 8
Laughing Whitefish Falls, hike 26
Little Carp River Cascades*, hike 9
Little Garlic River*, hike 22
Mirror Lake Loop, hike 10
Mouth of the Blind Sucker River, hike 38
Naomikong Point, hike 43

Loops or Lollipops

Beaver Lake Loop*, hike 33
Bruno's Run Loop*, hike 36
Cedar River Loop, hike 44
Chapel Loop*, hike 32
Clark Lake Loop*, hike 23
Craig Lake, hike 19
Estivant Pines Loop, hike 2
Giant Pines Loop, hike 41
Grand Island Loop, hike 28
Grand Sable Dunes Loop*, hike 35
Lake Superior/Big Carp River Loop*, hike 8
Mirror Lake Loop*, hike 10
Presque Isle River Waterfalls Loop*, hike 5
Trap Hills Loop*, hike 13
Union River Cascades Loop*, hike 12

Long Day Hikes

Beaver Lake Loop*, hike 33
Deer Island Lake*, hike 24
Grand Island Loop, hike 28
Grand Sable Dunes Loop*, hike 35
Lake Superior/Big Carp River Loop*, hike 8
Lake Superior Shoreline*, hike 7
Little Carp River Cascades*, hike 9
Maple Hill, hike 48
Marble Head*, hike 50
Mirror Lake Loop*, hike 10
Norwich Bluff to Victoria*, hike 16
Pictured Rocks*, hike 31
Portage Bay, hike 45
Shining Cloud Falls*, hike 6
Tahquamenon West/North Country Trail, hike 40
Trap Hills Loop*, hike 14
Trap Hills Traverse*, hike 14
White Deer Lake, hike 20

Overnight Backpacking Trips

Au Sable Point/Log Slide, hike 34
Beaver Lake Loop, hike 33
Birch Point*, hike 46
Bruno's Run Loop, hike 36
Chapel Loop, hike 32
Clark Lake Loop, hike 23
Craig Lake, hike 19
Deer Island Lake*, hike 24
Escarpment, hike 11

Falls of the Yellow Dog*, hike 21
Grand Island Loop, hike 28
Grand Sable Dunes Loop, hike 35
Horseshoe Bay, hike 49
Lake Superior/Big Carp River Loop*, hike 8
Lake Superior Shoreline*, hike 7
Little Carp River Cascades*, hike 9
Maple Hill, hike 48
Marble Head*, hike 50
Mirror Lake Loop, hike 10
Mouth of the Blind Sucker River, hike 38
Norwich Bluff*, hike 15
Norwich Bluff to Victoria*, hike 16
Pictured Rocks*, hike 31
Point Patterson/Cataract River, hike 47
Portage Bay, hike 45
Rock River Falls, hike 27
Shining Cloud Falls*, hike 6
Tahquamenon West/North Country Trail, hike 40
Tibbets Falls/Oren Krumm Shelter*, hike 17
Trap Hills Loop*, hike 13
Trap Hills Traverse*, hike 14
Two Hearted River, hike 39
White Deer Lake*, hike 20

Solitude

Bare Bluff*, hike 3
Beaver Lake Loop, hike 33
Birch Point*, hike 46
Bruno's Run Loop, hike 36
Cedar River Loop, hike 44
Craig Lake, hike 19
Deer Island Lake*, hike 24
Falls of the Yellow Dog*, hike 21
Grand Sable Dunes Loop, hike 35
Horseshoe Bay, hike 49
Lake Superior Shoreline*, hike 7
Little Garlic River, hike 22
Maple Hill, hike 48
Mouth of the Blind Sucker River, hike 38
Naomikong Point, hike 43
Norwich Bluff*, hike 15
Norwich Bluff to Victoria*, hike 16
Point Patterson/Cataract River*, hike 47
Portage Bay*, hike 45
Rock River Falls*, hike 27
Seney National Wildlife Refuge, hike 37

Wildlife Viewing Opportunities

Appendix B: Useful Addresses for More Information

Dickinson County Chamber of Commerce
600 South Stephenson Avenue
Iron Mountain, MI 49801
(906) 774–2002
www.dickinsonchamber.com

Grand Island National Recreation Area
Hiawatha National Forest
Munising Ranger District
400 East Munising Avenue
Munising, MI 49862
(906) 387–2512

Hiawatha National Forest
Forest Headquarters
2727 North Lincoln Road
Escanaba, MI 49829
(906) 786–4062
www.fs.fed.us/r9/hiawatha

Munising Ranger District
400 East Munising Avenue
Munising, MI 49862
(906) 387–2512

St. Ignace Ranger District
1798 U.S. Highway 2
St. Ignace, MI 49781
(906) 643–7900

Sault Ste. Marie Ranger District
4000 Interstate 75 Business Spur
Sault Ste. Marie, MI 49873
(906) 635–5311

Michigan Department of Natural Resources
www.michigan.gov/dnr

Baraga Management Unit
427 U.S. Highway 41 N.
Baraga, MI 49908
(906) 353–6651

Escanaba Management Unit
6833 Highway 2, 41, and M–35
Gladstone, MI 49837
(906) 786–2354

Gwinn Management Unit
410 West M–35
Gwinn, MI 49841
(906) 346–9201

Naubinway Field Office
P.O. Box 287, U.S. Highway 2
Naubinway, MI 49762
(906) 477–6048

Newberry Management Unit
Box 428
56666 M–123 S.
Newberry, MI 49868
(906) 293–3293

Sault Ste. Marie Management Unit
Box 798
2001 Ashmun
Sault Ste. Marie, MI 49783
(906) 635–5281

Shingleton Management Unit
M–28 West
P.O. Box 67
Shingleton, MI 49884
(906) 452–6227

Michigan Nature Association
326 East Grand River Avenue
Williamston, MI 48895
(517) 655–5655
www.michigannature.org

The Nature Conservancy
Upper Peninsula Conservation Center
125 West Washington Street, Suite G
Marquette, MI 49855
(906) 225–0399
www.tnc.org

North Country Trail Association
229 East Main Street
Lowell, MI 49331
(866) HIKENCT (445–3628)
www.northcountrytrail.org

Northwoods Wilderness Recovery
P.O. Box 122
Marquette, MI 49855-0122
(906) 226–6649
www.northwoodswild.org

Ottawa National Forest
Forest Supervisor's Office
E6248 U.S. Highway 2
Ironwood, MI 49938
(906) 932–1330
www.fs.fed.us/r9/ottawa

Ottawa Visitor Center
U.S. Highway 2 and Highway 45
P.O. Box 276
Watersmeet, MI 49969
(906) 358–4724

Bessemer Ranger District
500 North Moore Street
Bessemer, MI 49911
(906) 932–1330

Kenton Ranger District
4810 East M–28
Kenton, MI 49967
(906) 852–3500

Ontonagon Ranger District
1209 Rockland Road
Ontonagon, MI 49953
(906) 884–2085

Watersmeet Ranger District
Old U.S. Highway 2, P.O. Box 276
Watersmeet, MI 49969
(906) 358–4551

Pictured Rocks National Lakeshore
N8391 Sand Point Road
P.O. Box 40
Munising, MI 49862-0040
Headquarters: (906) 387–2607

Visitor information: (906) 387–3700
www.nps.gov/piro

Porcupine Mountains Wilderness State Park
412 South Boundary Road
Ontonagon, MI 49953
(906) 885–5275

Seney National Wildlife Refuge
1674 Refuge Entrance Road
Seney, MI 49883
(906) 586–9851
http://midwest.fws.gov/seney

Sierra Club
Mackinac Chapter
109 East Grand River
Lansing, MI 48906
(517) 484–2372
www.michigan.sierraclub.org

Sylvania Wilderness
Ottawa National Forest
Watersmeet Ranger Station
Old U.S. Highway 2, P.O. Box 276
Watersmeet, MI 49969
(906) 358–4551

Tahquamenon Falls State Park
41382 West M–123
Paradise, MI 49768
(906) 492–3415

Trap Hills Conservation Alliance
P.O. Box 223
Marquette, MI 49855
www.traphills.org

Upper Peninsula Environmental Coalition (UPEC)
P.O. Box 673
Houghton, MI 49931
www.upenvironment.org

Van Riper State Park
U.S. Highway 41
P.O. Box 88
Champion, MI 49814
(906) 339–4461

About the Author

Eric Hansen has hiked and backpacked extensively and now divides his time between the mountains and canyons of the West and the woods and waters of the northern Great Lakes. He has climbed most of the high peaks in Montana's Glacier National Park and completed twenty-one treks to the bottom of the Grand Canyon. After twenty years of exploring Michigan's Upper Peninsula, he hiked nearly 900 miles to research this guidebook. Eight hundred miles of hiking went into his earlier guidebook, *Hiking Wisconsin*.

He has written extensively for *Backpacker* magazine. His regional outdoor writing has appeared in *Milwaukee Magazine*, the *Milwaukee Journal-Sentinel*, *Shepherd Express*, *Silent Sports* magazine, and *Wisconsin Trails* magazine.

THE INSIDER'S SOURCE

With more than 120 Midwest-related titles, we have the area covered. Whether you're looking for the path less traveled, a favorite place to eat, family-friendly fun, a breathtaking hike, or enchanting local attractions, our pages are filled with ideas to get you from one state to the next.

For a complete listing of all our titles, please visit our Web site at www.GlobePequot.com. The Globe Pequot Press is the largest publisher of local travel books in the United States and is a leading source for outdoor recreation guides.

FOR BOOKS TO THE MIDWEST

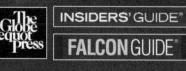 **INSIDERS' GUIDE®**

FALCON GUIDE®

Available wherever books are sold.
Orders can also be placed on the Web at www.GlobePequot.com,
by phone from 8:00 A.M. to 5:00 P.M. at 1-800-243-0495,
or by fax at 1-800-820-2329.